IMAGES
of America

LAKEWOOD

"LAKEWOOD WOULD BE VERY SOLVENT . . . A GOING CONCERN FROM THE BEGINNING . . . POSSIBLY THE LOWEST TAX RATE IN LOS ANGELES COUNTY."

☆

HERE ARE THE WORDS OF A NOTED MUNICIPAL ADVISOR:

"I HAVE NEVER SEEN A CITY AS WELL SITUATED FOR INCORPORATION AS LAKEWOOD."

Predictions. There were those in 1954 who predicted great things for the new city of Lakewood, but other commentators warned of disaster. Lakewood might be successful when new, but would its enviable neighborhood quality of life continue, they asked. Lakewood residents answered by their actions. They met the challenges of community building and found new ways to define Lakewood as a place of homes, parks, businesses, religious congregations, and hope. (Courtesy of the City of Lakewood.)

On the Cover: J.R. Eyerman's photograph for *Life* magazine is an iconic image of suburbanization. The moving vans dot Centralia Street, just west of Hayter Street in Lakewood, at the request of the Lakewood Park Corporation's publicity department. Eyerman stood on a precarious ladder in 1953 as homeowners reenacted their move-in day for his camera. (Time & Life Pictures, © Getty Images. Used by permission.)

IMAGES
of America

LAKEWOOD

City of Lakewood

ARCADIA
PUBLISHING

ISBN 978-0-7385-9990-8

Published by Arcadia Publishing
Charleston, South Carolina

Printed in the United States of America

Library of Congress Control Number: Applied For

For all general information, please contact Arcadia Publishing:
Telephone 843-853-2070
Fax 843-853-0044
E-mail sales@arcadiapublishing.com
For customer service and orders:
Toll-Free 1-888-313-2665

Visit us on the Internet at www.arcadiapublishing.com

Contents

ACKNOWLEDGMENTS

Lakewood's story was first told in photographs taken by the pioneering aerial photographer William A. Garnett. He flew repeatedly over the newly built tract houses of Lakewood between 1950 and 1953, documenting the transformation of empty fields into homes and neighborhoods. We gratefully acknowledge the significance of Garnett's work in dramatically recording the scope and suddenness of Lakewood's early development.

On the ground, the cameramen of Rothschild Studios photographed Lakewood houses for advertisements in local and national newspapers, showing domestic innovations like stainless steel kitchen countertops and garbage disposals. Photographers from *Time* and *Life* magazines also covered Lakewood's growth for stories that marveled at the number of homes being built and the speed at which they sold. We acknowledge their work in bringing Lakewood to national attention.

Lakewood's incorporation in 1954 made even more news, and photographers captured the excitement of the young men and women who won cityhood for Lakewood. Those "original incorporators" earnestly wished that the record of their achievement would be preserved for new generations of Lakewood residents.

In the years that followed, city staff members photographed the pageantry of Pan-American Association events, the opening day of park sports leagues, the building of the Lakewood Civic Center, and the celebratory milestones of a growing community. We acknowledge the efforts of Lakewood's City Clerk and Public Information Office to retain and catalog these images so that they could be included in this collection. Unless otherwise noted, all photographs were provided through the courtesy of the City of Lakewood.

The support and warm encouragement of the Lakewood City Council made this publication possible as part of the city's celebration of 60 years of incorporation in 2014. In gratitude, we dedicate this book to city council members Steve Croft, Diane DuBois, Ron Piazza, Todd Rogers, and Jeff Wood.

And we dedicate it to the generations of Lakewood families whose community spirit fills these images. Their hard work and deep commitment shine from these photographs as witness that Lakewood's early years were the beginning of a story that has grown to include all Lakewood residents.

INTRODUCTION

The City of Lakewood has grown and prospered since the days when its streets rumbled with the sound of moving vans bringing thousands of young husbands and wives to their new homes. As this collection of photographs from the city's archives will show, Lakewood has changed in some ways, but stayed the same in the ways that are most important.

We hope that you will see in these charming, nostalgic images from more than 60 years ago how the aspirations of a new community were realized in Lakewood's parks and playgrounds, in its places of worship, in its shops and offices, and in the homes of those who brought their hopes for a better tomorrow here.

As we begin to celebrate our 60th year of incorporation, we are reminded that their story is Lakewood's story.

In the beginning—always—is the land itself, a gentle plain created by the Los Angeles and San Gabriel Rivers and their sister streams. For tens of thousands of years, these streams carried the runoff from winter rains and channeled spring floods near the site of the future Lakewood City Hall.

This land was hospitable. It sheltered Native Americans who settled in small villages. It gave prosperity to the Spaniards who welled up from Mexico in 1781. And in 1784, it formed the vast rancho of Manuel Nieto, whose grant stretched from the sea to the distant foothills.

When Nieto died in 1804, his grant passed intact to his surviving children. They bickered over the property until 1833, when they petitioned Mexican governor José Figueroa to divide the grant among them.

The ranchos and their old ways continued without much change when California entered the Union in 1850. But in 1866, a killing drought ended the days when thousands of cattle and sheep roamed the ranchos' lands.

In 1881, after the land passed through the hands of several owners, John Bixby, a cousin of the Bixbys who controlled Rancho Los Cerritos, joined a group of speculators in buying Rancho Los Alamitos. Their investment skyrocketed in value in the years that followed.

When the Bixby Investment Company sold 6,979 acres to William A. Clark in 1897, the selling price was $348,950. Those 6,979 acres are now the city of Lakewood, the area of Long Beach called Lakewood Village, and north Long Beach.

William A. Clark's Montana Land Company raised sugar beets, hay, and alfalfa, but with the growth of nearby Long Beach, the company also envisioned residential development. Under Clark Bonner, manager of the company's holdings, a cluster of suburban estates was planned around the site of a championship golf course. The Great Depression ended those dreams just as Bonner began development in 1933.

The crash forced Bonner to adopt an alternate plan of more modest homes next to the new Long Beach Community College on Carson Street. Bonner called the development Lakewood Village, naming it after a fashionable resort town in New Jersey. By the mid-1930s, however, only a few lots had been sold, and even fewer houses had been built.

World War II began an era of profound change for Lakewood. The Douglas Aircraft Company completed a massive new defense plant in 1940, and homes for Douglas workers were begun in the Mayfair district north of Lakewood Village and the Lakewood City tract to the south. Even as defense workers moved in, the farmland between South Street and Carson Street remained empty—but not for long.

In 1949, most of the land comprising western Lakewood—some 3,500 acres—was purchased from the Montana Land Company for nearly $9 million by Louis Boyar, Ben Weingart, and Mark Taper. From their experience as homebuilders in Long Beach and Norwalk, they knew that the Lakewood area was ready to grow. The three men formed the Lakewood Park Corporation and with the financial assistance of the Prudential Insurance Company began building the first of 17,500 homes.

To speed construction, the three partners sought innovative ways to build what was to become the nation's largest postwar planned community. Using the efficient production methods that had helped win the war, crews of workers built Lakewood's houses on an "assembly line" basis to Federal Housing Administration specifications. During one unbelievable week of construction, 567 homes were begun.

Other design innovations included underground wiring for streetlights, landscaped parkway panels separating residential streets from major highways, and provision for neighborhood shopping centers, parks, places of worship, and schools within walking distance of every neighborhood.

Everything about the building of Lakewood was big: the 4,000 crewmen, mile-long lines of cement mixing trucks, the crowds of prospective buyers, and the number of homes sold each weekend.

Not everyone thought that a huge new suburb could be successful. Don Rochlen, who had been hired to promote the Lakewood Park development, went before the Long Beach City Council with an update on the project. The Long Beach council members scoffed, saying that there would be no one to buy all those houses except the gophers.

It was soon clear that Lakewood's thousands of new houses would have new owners, none of them gophers. Most of the new buyers were veterans taking advantage of the GI Bill of Rights. No down payment for veterans was required, and payments on the mortgage could be spread over 30 years. A two-bedroom home was $47 a month (excluding taxes and insurance) and a three-bedroom home was $54 a month.

To attract prospective buyers, the company built a 100-foot tower next to its sales office at the corner of Lakewood Boulevard and Candlewood Street. Lighted at night, it could be seen for miles.

Lakewood's innovative design also included a massive retail complex, larger than any in the nation and with acres of free parking. The idea of a regional shopping center was new then, and it took the vision of the St. Louis-based May Company department stores to make Lakewood Center possible in 1950. Under the leadership of the May Company and with additional financing from Prudential Insurance, national retailers were able to open dozens of modern shops by 1954.

During this period of tremendous growth, the unincorporated areas known as Lakewood and Lakewood Village, Mayfair, and Lakewood Gardens were administered by the Los Angeles County Board of Supervisors—five men who were 25 miles away from Lakewood's new neighborhoods.

Lakewood residents faced a complex series of decisions: Lakewood could remain unincorporated county territory and continue to be served by county agencies without becoming a city, Lakewood could annex to Long Beach and become a district within that city, or Lakewood residents could take on the burdens of cityhood and make their new community an independent municipality.

Each solution had its proponents. But a growing number of Lakewood residents began to see the value of local control and were willing to take on the responsibility of creating a new city. The push for incorporation received added momentum when the city of Long Beach, in a series of divisive political moves, attempted to annex all the unincorporated neighborhoods of Lakewood.

John Wentz, administrative assistant to the city manager of Long Beach, had prepared a report on the future of Lakewood in 1951. In his report, Wentz asked if Lakewood should remain unincorporated. Could it incorporate? Or should it be annexed to Long Beach? Wentz's answer was annexation. He proposed dividing Lakewood into small sections to make it easier to achieve a sympathetic majority for annexation in each. Under the Wentz plan, annexation elections would be held on an almost daily basis. With local opposition divided, annexation would be a certainty, Wentz concluded.

The battle over annexation began to take shape in 1953 with the creation of the Lakewood Civic Council. Organized to serve as the leader of the anti-annexation fight, the LCC included in its membership Gene Nebeker, Don Rochlen, Guy Halferty, Francis Veeder, Jackie Rynerson, Bill Burns, Ed Walker, and Jim Knox, among others. John Todd, another LCC member who later became city attorney, recommended a novel strategy: protest petitions could be circulated among the property owners in the neighborhoods targeted for annexation. According to state law, if a majority of owners in a neighborhood protested the annexation vote, an election could not be legally called.

Todd's stalling tactic worked while the proponents of incorporation made a case for cityhood to their Lakewood neighbors. Eventually, most of the annexation attempts were defeated, some by vote and others by protest. But the threat of annexation remained. Incorporation was the only logical alternative.

To unite Lakewood residents, the backers of incorporation highlighted the concept of retaining the county services that residents already had. And by showing how contracting for these services could keep taxes low, the pro-incorporation forces persuaded many who had favored remaining unincorporated.

An incorporation committee was formed under cochairmen Joe Covas and Clarence Smickel. Committee members Bob Baker and Bill Burns were charged with the task of preparing and circulating incorporation petitions. They organized 600 neighborhood volunteers to collect incorporation signatures. In only 10 days, incorporation advocates collected twice as many signatures as needed to call for a vote of Lakewood residents.

On March 9, 1954, Lakewood voters, by a 3 to 2 margin, approved incorporation. A new city was born. On April 16, 1954, Lakewood officially became the 16th-largest city in the state—larger than Santa Barbara or San Bernardino—and the first city in Los Angeles County to incorporate since 1939.

The voters also decided which of 39 candidates would be the city's first five council members. The voters chose Robert W. Baker, William J. Burns, Angelo M. Iacoboni, (who was selected by the city council to serve as mayor), Gene Nebeker (who was chosen vice mayor), and George Nye Jr.

The election results came as a surprise to those who doubted that Lakewood's young husbands and wives had the courage to take up the many responsibilities of managing their future. The least surprised were the hundreds of volunteers who had worked so hard to see their dream of "Tomorrow's City" come true.

The first Lakewood City Hall was located in a storefront in the former Faculty Shops in Lakewood Center. A desk and a typewriter were placed in the front part of the room and a table and folding chairs set up in the back. That was the Lakewood City Council Chambers.

The first job of the city council was to find a means to preserve the benefits of living in Lakewood without burdening the residents with higher taxes. With the help of city attorney John Todd and with the cooperation of the Los Angeles County Board of Supervisors, the city council members created a unique plan for providing city services.

Called the Contract City Plan and later renamed the Lakewood Plan, this system involves contracting with county agencies and private firms for public services. For the new city, contracting promised to maintain a high level of service at a significantly reduced cost. The Lakewood Plan was soon copied in a wave of incorporation movements in Los Angeles County in the 1950s. Today, the contract plan that Lakewood pioneered shapes the future of more than 140 California cities and dozens of cities in all parts of the nation and even in other countries.

In the years after 1954, as the needs of Lakewood residents grew, so did the scope of local government. In 1957, Lakewood took over the independent Park, Recreation, and Parkway District and created a city department to provide recreation programs. Also in 1957, the city acquired the privately owned Lakewood Water and Power Company and began to provide water to most of the western portion of the city.

In the following decade, an unincorporated portion of the county east of the San Gabriel River was brought into the city in a series of annexation votes.

Since the 1980s, Lakewood has asked residents to share their hopes and concerns in community surveys. Their response over the years has been amazingly consistent, even as Lakewood's demographic profile has changed greatly.

Lakewood residents value safe neighborhoods. They value high-quality services. They want trash collected and streets swept. They want local government to be responsive, accessible, and frugal. They value the traditions of Lakewood—particularly the city's emphasis on family recreation—and they want park programs to be there for their children and grandchildren.

City officials understand the permanence of these values. Beginning in the 1990s, the city increased its investment in local street repairs, improved parks, expanded recreational programs, and brought down the rate of serious crime with innovative crime prevention and enforcement programs. The city upgraded its water system and toughened it against possible disaster. The city also put new technology into every phase of its day-to-day operations—from law enforcement to customer service to recreation program registration.

When Lakewood residents look back on their city's past, it is obvious to them that times have changed. Yet in the midst of change, there remain timeless values that Lakewood residents have handed down from one generation to the next. The greatest is the value of Lakewood's neighborhood quality of life.

Lakewood has always had a generous measure of the things that make living in Southern California a pleasure. But the residents of Lakewood have something more. They continue to enjoy the intangibles for a good life—a caring community, a history of volunteer involvement, a respect for tradition, and a lot of old-fashioned neighborliness.

As hundreds of volunteers began walking petitions for cityhood in Lakewood neighborhoods in early 1954, Los Angeles County Supervisor Herbert Legg remarked, "Let's give them this chance to govern themselves, and one of these days they'll be showing us a thing or two . . . ."

That's exactly what they did—and what Lakewood still does.

One

Before Lakewood

Lakewood was born from the pastoral lands of the Rancho Los Cerritos in the 19th century, the sugar beet fields of the Montana Land Company at the turn of the century, and the truck farms of Japanese American tenants before December 1941. Not far from their fields were the homes of faculty members who taught at Long Beach Junior College (later Long Beach City College) and military families connected to the Long Beach Naval Station. Into their semirural neighborhood, the threat of world war brought the Douglas Aircraft Company.

In 1940, the Montana Land Company turned over vacant land next to the Long Beach Airport for the construction of Douglas's massive bomber assembly plant, one of the nation's first fully air-conditioned manufacturing facilities. Tens of thousands of war workers were recruited to work there between 1941 and 1945. Most of them were like Rosie the Riveter—the young wives of service men who took their place on assembly lines to build the weapons that helped win World War II.

When war work ended in early 1946, Lakewood was still partly farmland and partly suburb, with an uncertain future. Many of the workers at Douglas and other war industries were laid off. The region faced an economic slump.

But new economic forces were already shaping the region's future. Southern California was becoming a center for aerospace manufacturing, electronics, and high-tech innovation. When the Cold War required a new arsenal for defense, Southern California became its workshop. When consumer demand expanded passenger aircraft production, Douglas had the facilities to build a new generation of faster, larger airliners.

Thousands of homes were needed for these workers, and they were needed all at once. The land was at hand. Only imagination was needed to turn fields into neighborhoods.

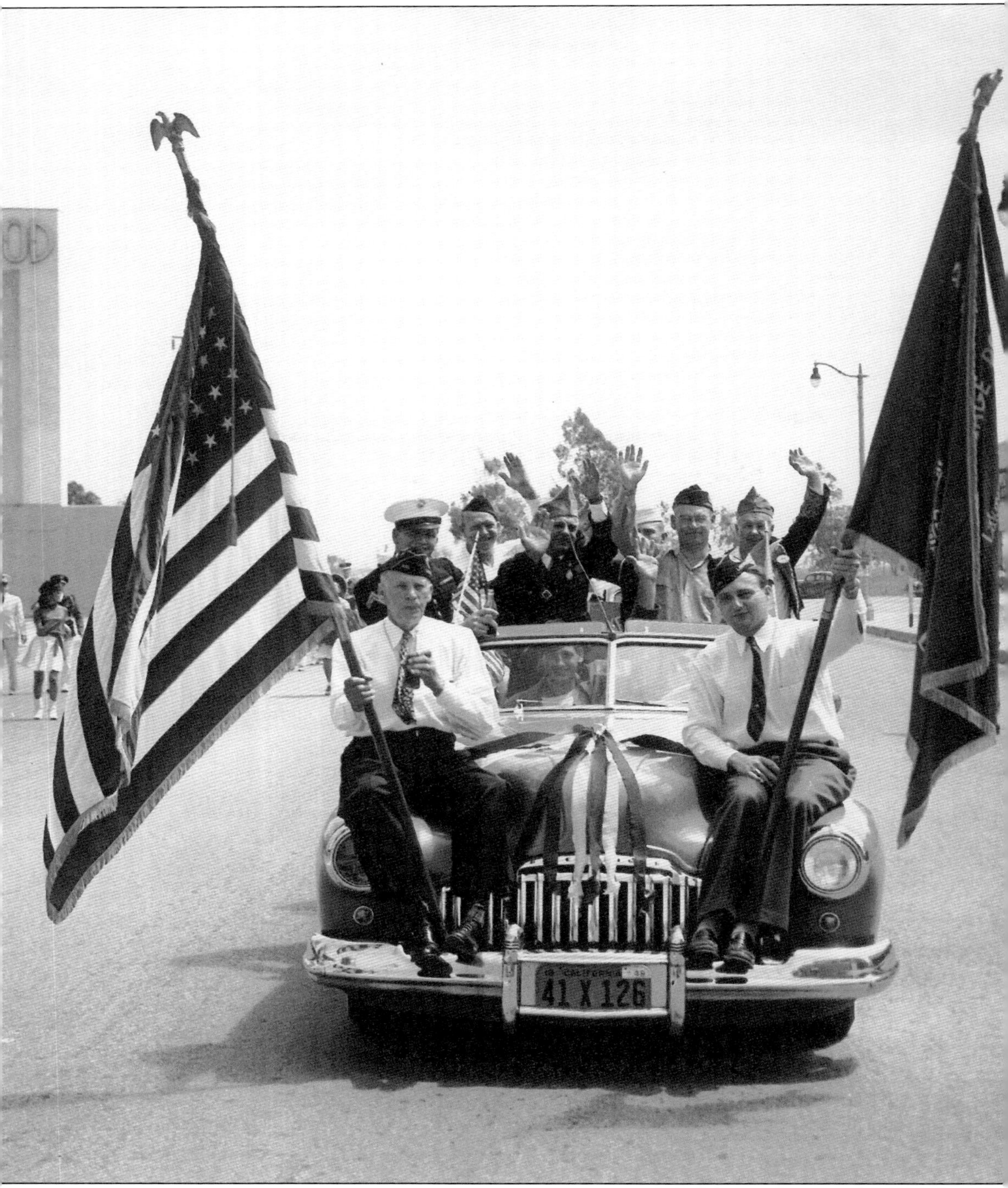

LAKEWOOD VETERANS CELEBRATE. Veterans of World War II celebrate Memorial Day on Norse Way in Lakewood Village in 1949. Veterans who had spent some of their service years in Southern California moved in increasing numbers to suburban Long Beach. It was to house them and their families that Lakewood would be built.

Selling Lakewood Village, 1933. The Montana Land Company advertised "semi-sustaining" house lots to lure buyers during the Great Depression. The lots in Lakewood Village were large enough, said the sales brochure, to grow a kitchen garden, raise fruit trees for canning, and even keep chickens for eggs. But the lots sold slowly.

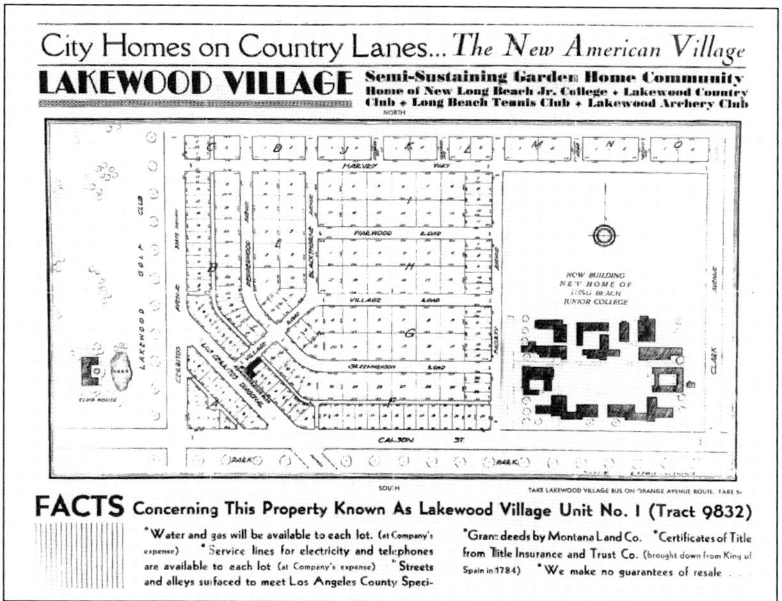

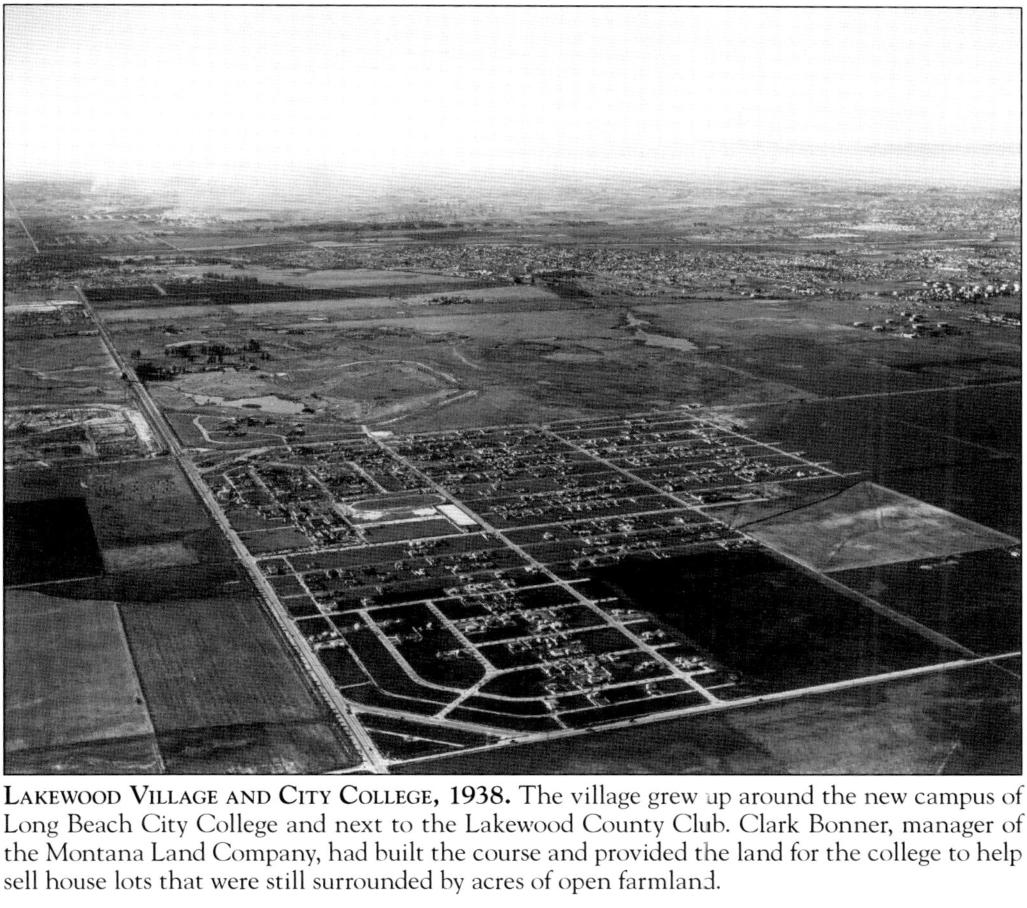

Lakewood Village and City College, 1938. The village grew up around the new campus of Long Beach City College and next to the Lakewood County Club. Clark Bonner, manager of the Montana Land Company, had built the course and provided the land for the college to help sell house lots that were still surrounded by acres of open farmland.

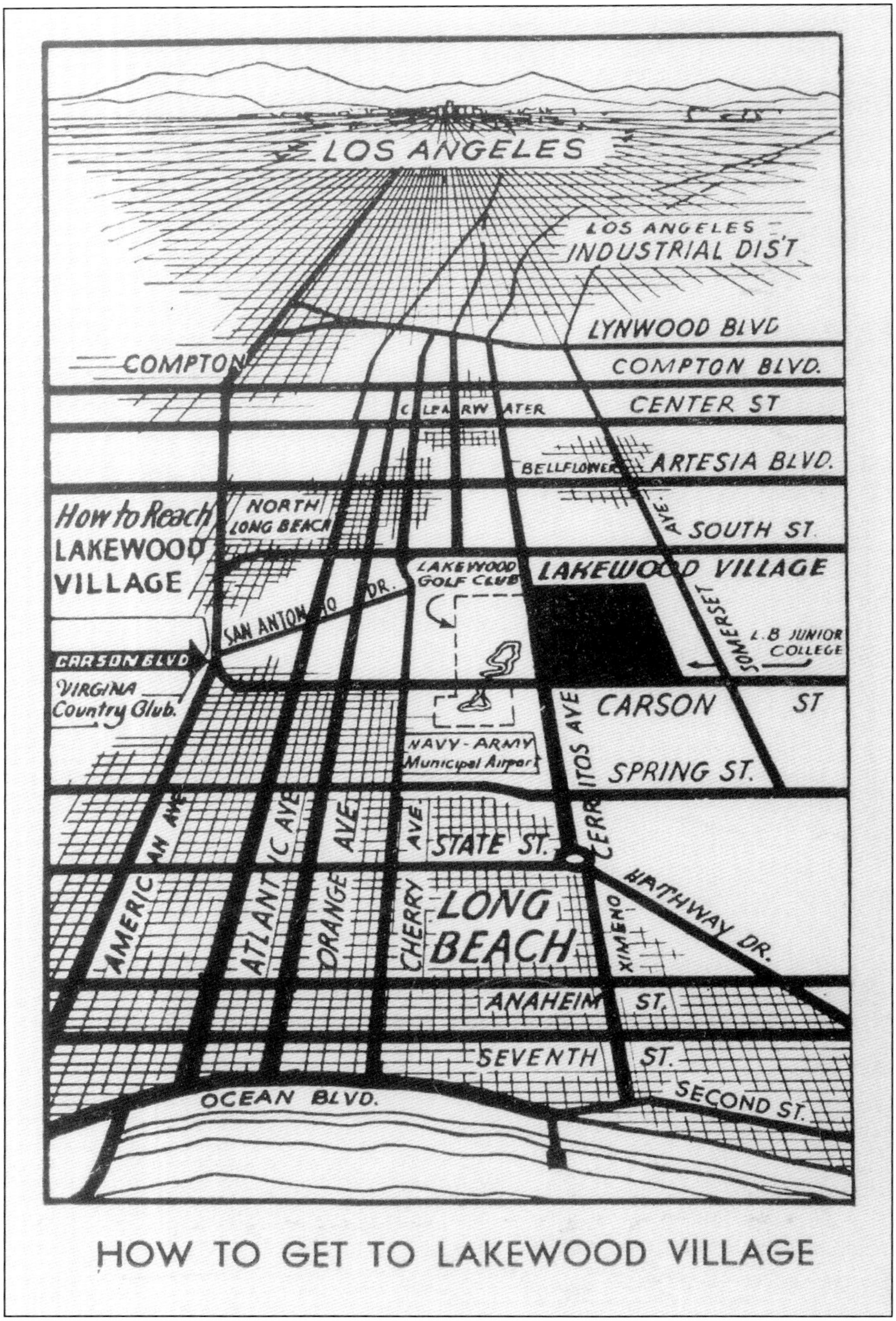

Mapping a New Suburban Frontier. In an era before freeways, the marketers of Lakewood Village positioned their suburban tract between the older community of Long Beach and the industries of southeast Los Angeles County. This sales map also shows Clearwater (now part of Paramount), State Street (now Pacific Coast Highway) and American Avenue (now Long Beach Boulevard). Long Beach Airport is listed as Navy-Army Municipal Airport.

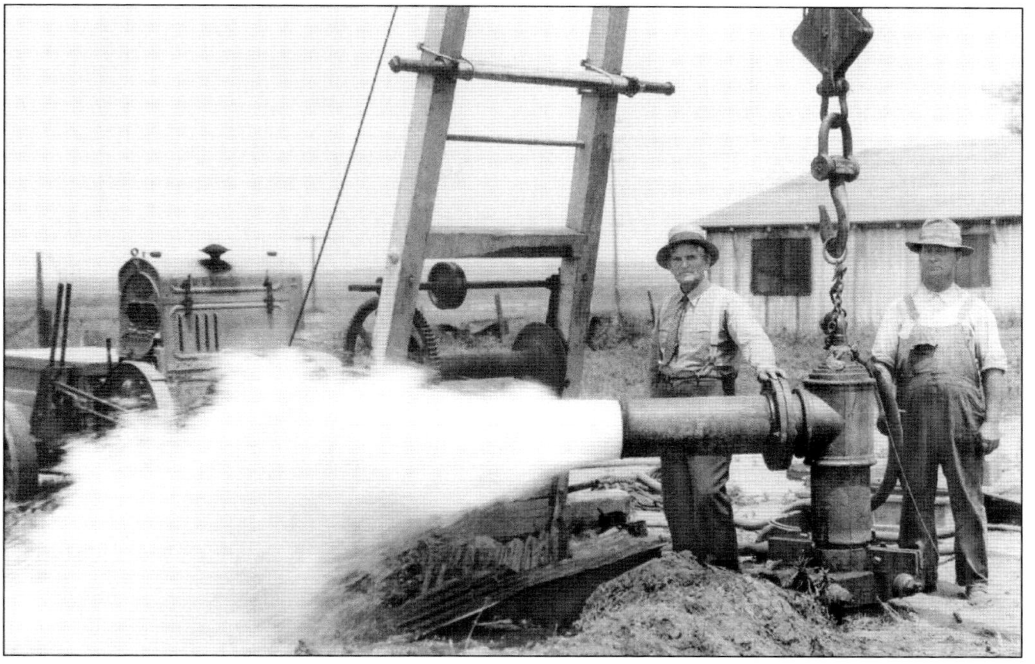

Oil and Water Mix in Lakewood. Edward Bouton's original artesian well, located near today's Lakewood Golf Course, supplied all of Long Beach's water needs until the well ran dry. Other wells, shown above, watered the fields of the Montana Land Company until the end of the 1940s. Oil gushed from nearby Signal Hill in the early 1920s, shown below, crowding the southern horizon with hundreds of wood derricks. Lakewood Village was originally conceived as a suburban retreat from the noise and smells of the oil boom.

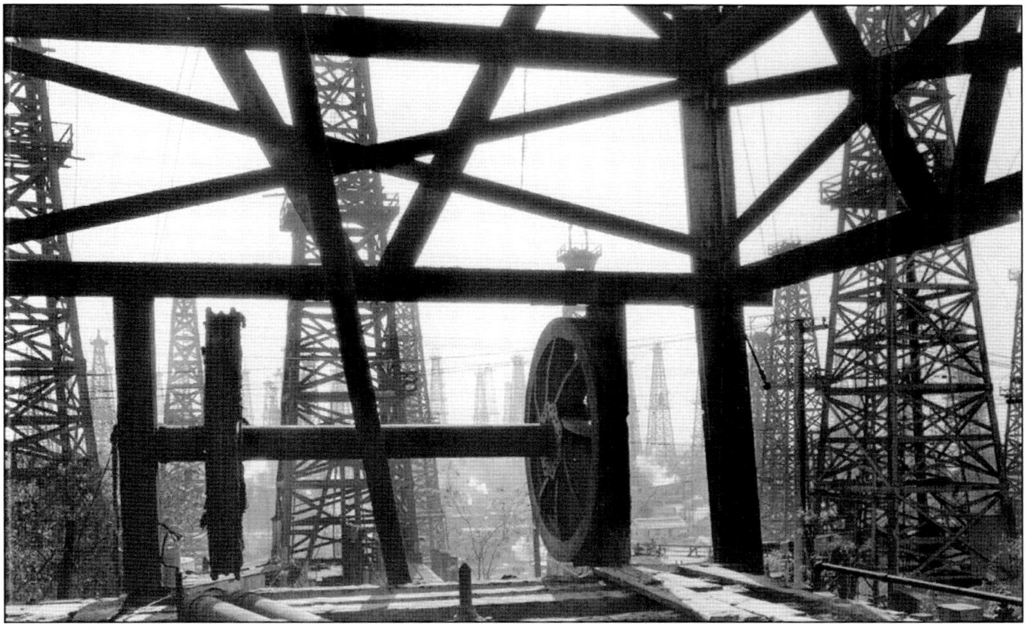

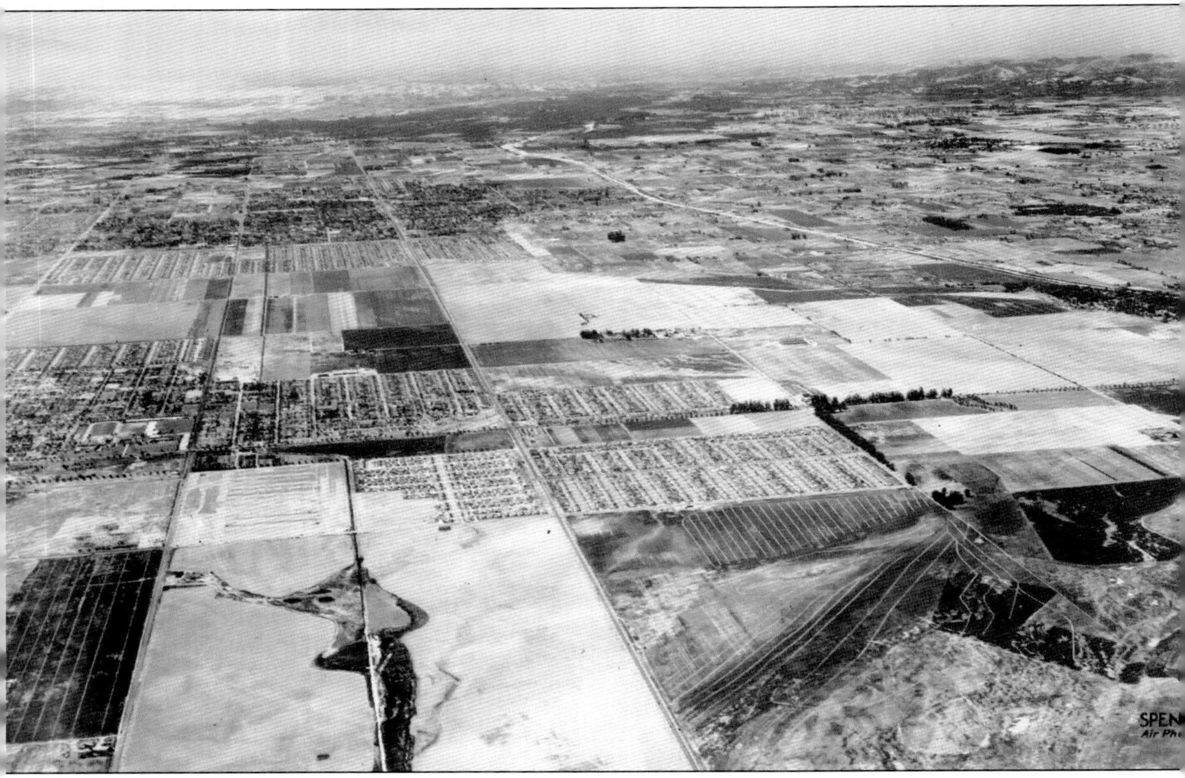

Lakewood from the Air, 1940. The future Lakewood was still largely agricultural in 1940, although the Lakewood Village, Lakewood City, and Mayfair housing tracts had begun to fill the fields north of the Long Beach municipal airport. Work on the Douglas Aircraft plant, seen on the bottom left, had just begun in 1940. Tall eucalyptus trees, center, surround the farm offices of the Montana Land Company on what is now Arbor Road and the site of Lakewood's Water Resources Department. The San Gabriel River, right, meanders through dairy farms and feedlots in what would one day be the city of Cerritos. The distant Whittier hills and downtown Los Angeles are lost in the haze that would grow worse during the war years, making smog an unwanted part of life in the Los Angeles Basin. (Courtesy of Spence Air Photo.)

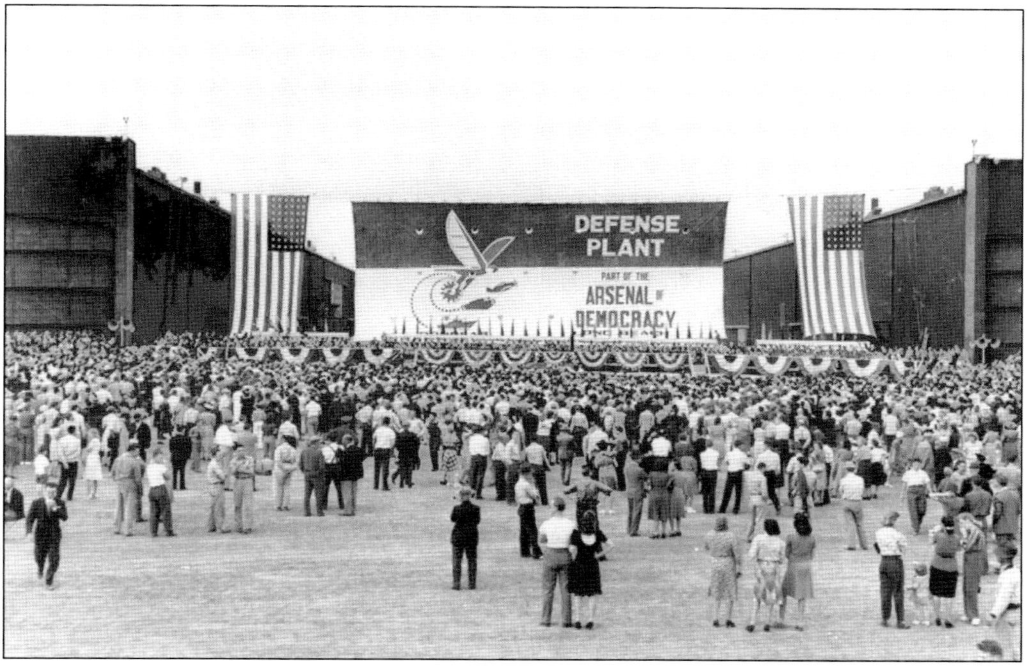

LAKEWOOD GOES TO WAR. The opening of the Douglas Aircraft plant in 1941 made Lakewood a hub of war production. The around-the-clock workforce, shown above, grew to more than 45,000. Many of them were the wives and daughters of the men who had gone to war, their efforts made famous by the fictional character Rosie the Riveter. Douglas workers built more than 4,000 of the company's famous C-47 transport planes, 3,000 B-17 bombers, shown below, and more than 2,000 Douglas light bombers. At the end of the war, General Eisenhower credited the C-47 as one of the reasons for the Allies' victory over the Axis powers.

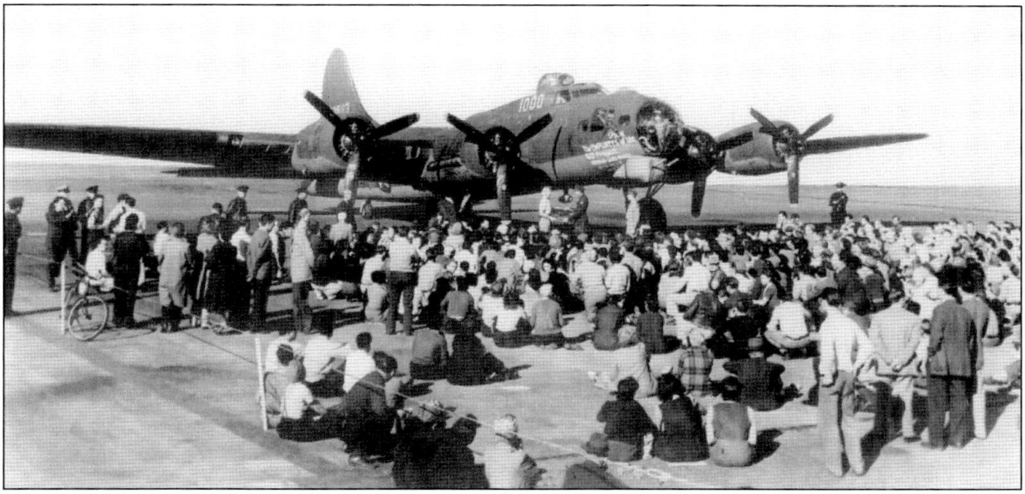

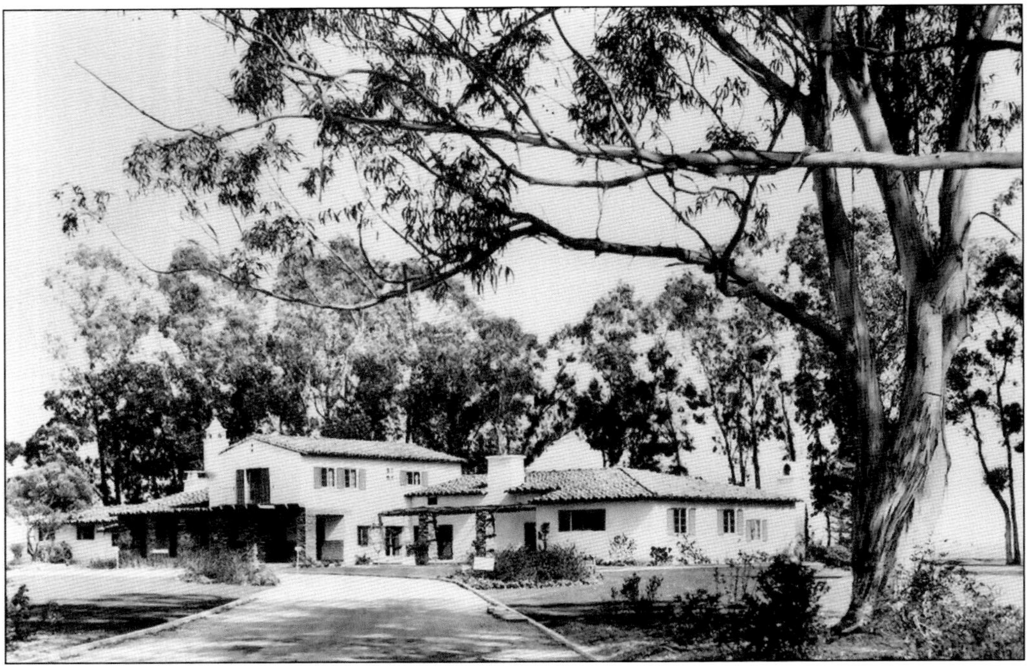

Lakewood County Club. The social hub of Clark Bonner's Country Club Estates in 1933 was the golf course and clubhouse, shown above, that Bonner built to promote his new Lakewood development. Dances, recitals, weddings, and community meetings filled the clubhouse as nearby Lakewood Village grew. The golf course, below, was laid out by noted designer William Park Bell. It soon became the site of major tournaments. Bouton Lake—the course water hazard—is actually an artificial reservoir that is now part of a reclaimed water irrigation system. The original Bouton Lake was created from the overflow of the artesian well drilled by Edward Bouton in 1895.

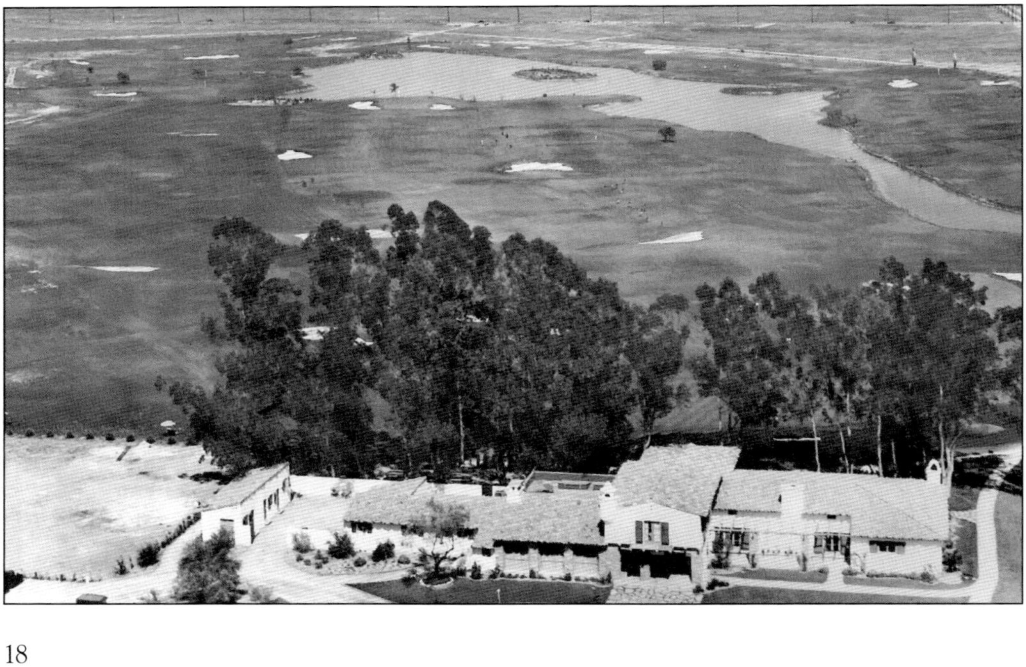

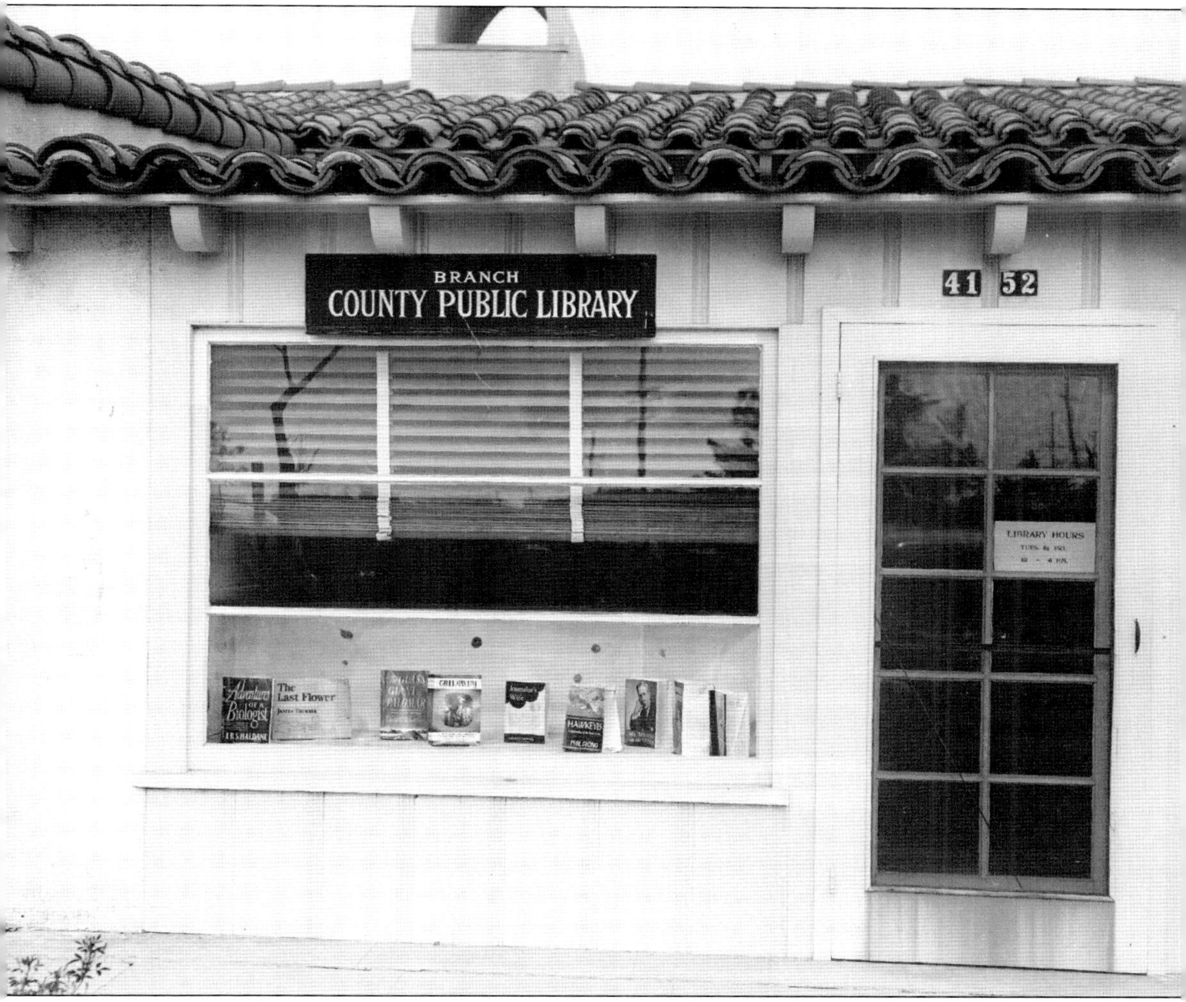

Lakewood's First Library. Library service in unincorporated Lakewood began in January 1938, with the opening of the Lakewood Village branch of the Los Angeles County Public Library. The small library was housed in 650 square feet of leased storefront on Norse Way. The library contained 1,218 books when it opened, with Jayne C. Hathcock as its first librarian. She served not only the residents of Lakewood Village but also the students who were attending Long Beach Junior College (later Long Beach City College). An addition to the building greatly enlarged the library in 1945. By 1953, it was clear that even expanded hours and a bookmobile were not enough to serve the thousands of new residents of Lakewood. (Courtesy of County of Los Angeles Public Library.)

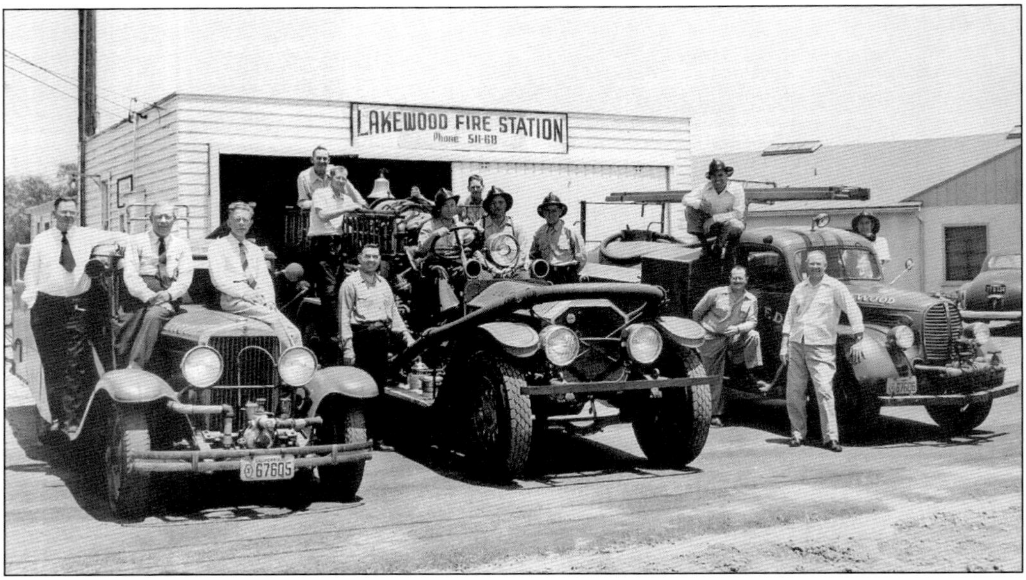

LAKEWOOD'S FIRST FIRE STATION. The members of the Lakewood Volunteer Fire Department are, from left to right, (first truck) William F. Bly, Bill Mott, and Paul E. Portier; (second truck) H.E. Jones, G.E. Rusk, Sterling Parr, C. Walter Pipps (assistant chief), Earl Bollschweiler (fire chief), C.O. Bursell, and J.J. Marshall; (third truck) Ford Coole, Jess Salter, John E. Junior, and Ralph Sundstrom. Organized in 1937, the Lakewood volunteers built their own firehouse at 4412 Greenmeadow Road, seen above. The volunteers disbanded in 1945, when the county fire department extended service to unincorporated Lakewood. County Fire Station 45, shown below, was located on Arbor Road in what is now part of Lakewood Village in Long Beach.

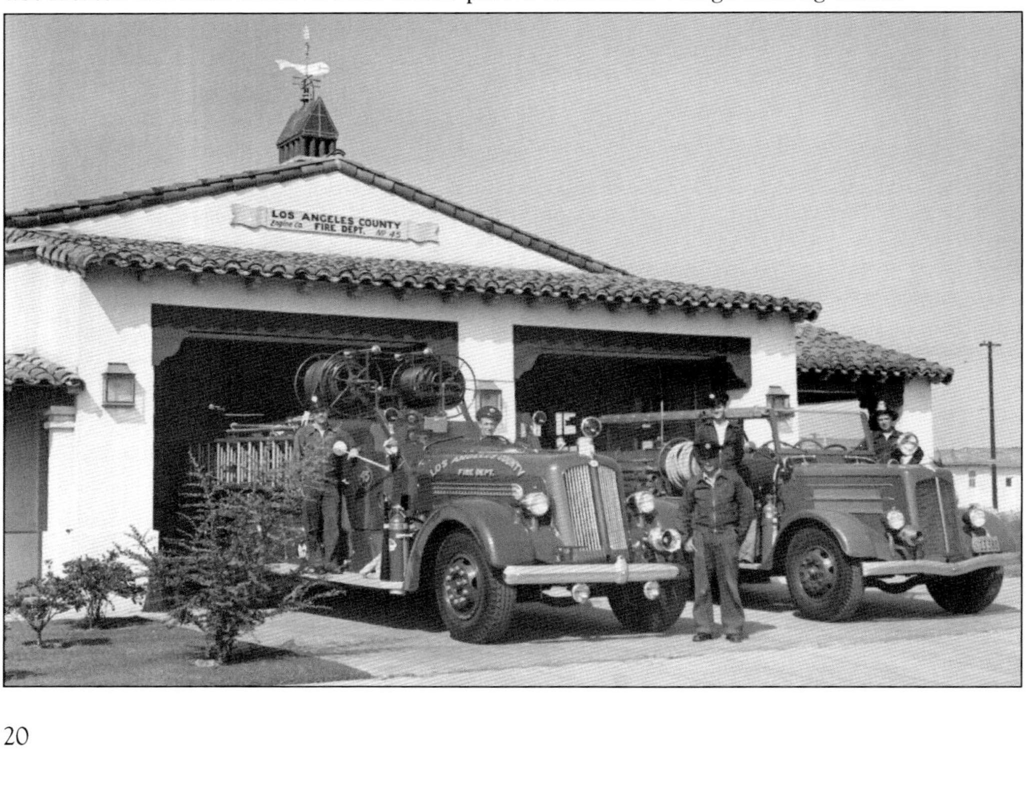

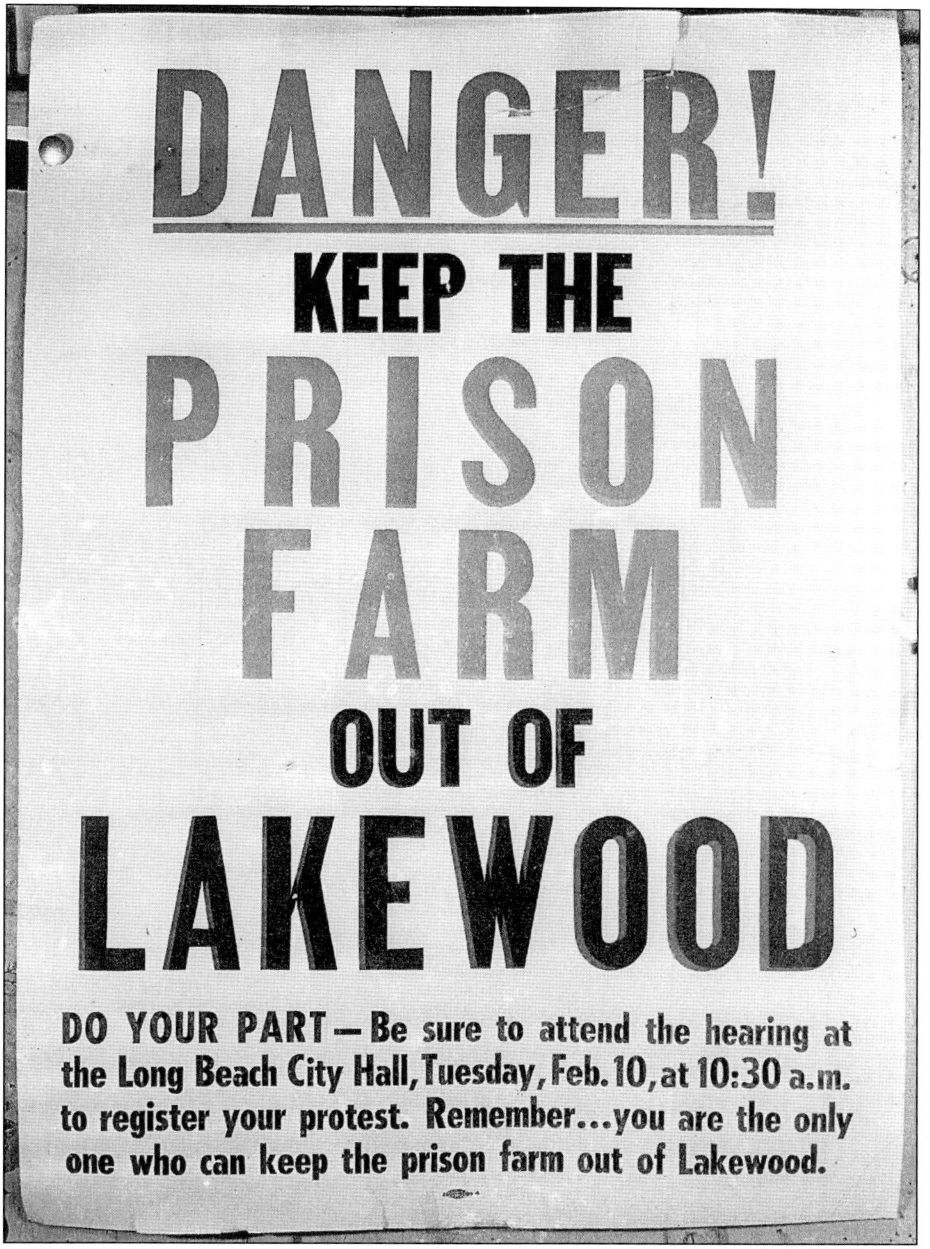

Lakewood Residents Object. Lakewood residents mounted a campaign in 1953 against Long Beach's proposal to build an "honor farm" near Carson Street. An army of 700 Lakewood mothers and their children picketed outside Long Beach City Hall with signs reading "Our kids don't want to grow up with a jail!" and staged a sit-down demonstration. Despite the protests, the honor farm was built. The honor farm was not the only issue that raised community concerns. Parents saw the open and unfenced drainage ditches as a danger to children. Local community leader John Sanford Todd brought the parents' protests to the board of supervisors, who eventually had the ditches cleared, lined in concrete, and fenced. The experience taught Todd and other residents the value of local control over Lakewood's future.

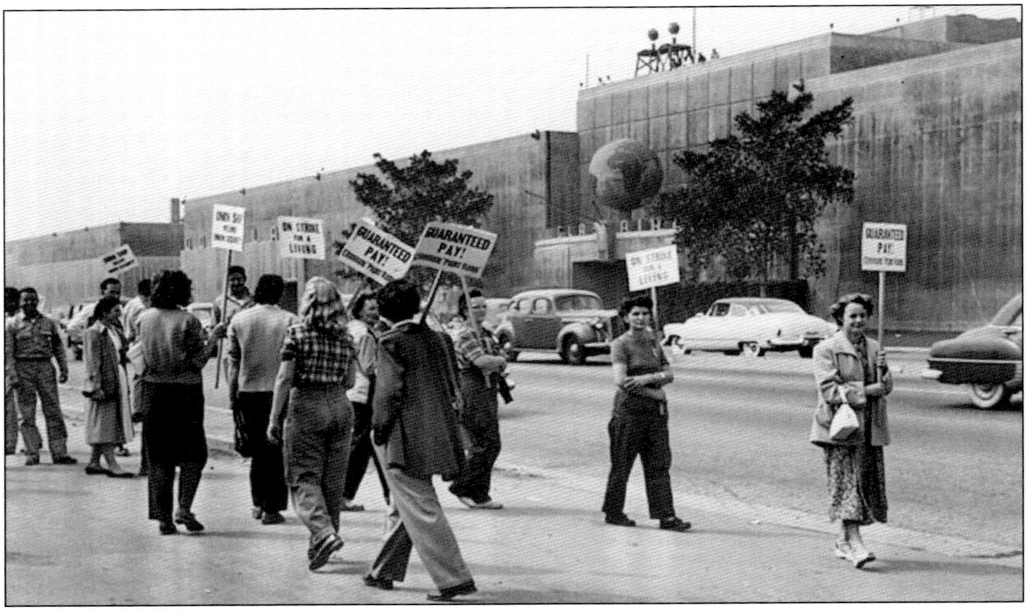

WORKERS STRIKE AT DOUGLAS. When World War II ended in 1945, layoffs at the Douglas Aircraft plant on Lakewood Boulevard rocked the local economy. Defense spending ultimately picked up and new passenger aircraft were ordered, restoring many of the lost jobs. Demands for better wages and working conditions sent Douglas employees to the picket lines in a series of strikes beginning in the early 1950s. (Courtesy of USC Digital Library.)

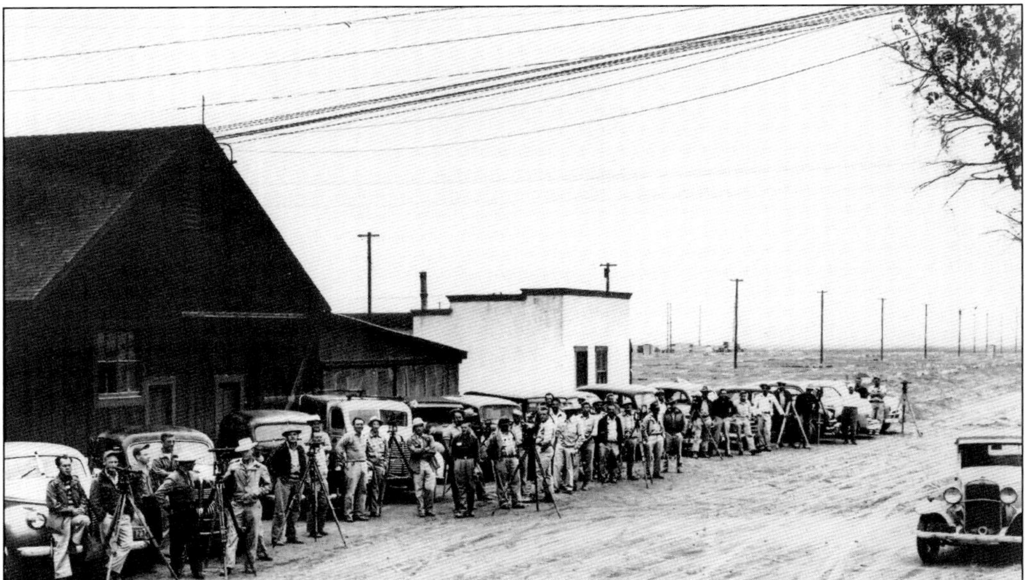

SURVEY CREWS, 1949. When the war ended, Clark Bonner made plans to expand his Lakewood development. Those plans were cut short in late 1947, when Bonner, still in his 50s, died suddenly. In 1949, Violet Bonner, his widow, sold the company's remaining 3,500 acres to the Lakewood Park Corporation for nearly $9 million. Teams of the company's surveyors went to work at once to lay out the largest suburban development of its time.

Two

The City Builders

Lakewood was the dream of three remarkable men—Ben Weingart, S. Mark Taper, and Louis Boyar. They acquired the remaining land of the Montana Land Company, including the Lakewood Golf Course, in 1949, following the sudden death of Clark J. Bonner, the land company's manager.

As the Lakewood Park Corporation, the three developers envisioned a complete city of homes, commercial centers, places of worship, schools, parks, and community facilities. Using the best available designs and planning models, the Lakewood Park Corporation laid out a residential development that would cover nearly seven square miles.

Lakewood would be larger than the better known Levittown development on Long Island and be distinguished by innovative design features that became a model for new suburbs throughout Southern California. Electric disposals in every kitchen sink made Lakewood "the city without garbage" according to newspaper advertisements. Landscaped parkway panels along Lakewood's major boulevards kept residential streets safe from traffic. Parks and elementary schools planted in the midst of each neighborhood made it possible for kids to walk to school and play. Clustering neighborhood retail centers at major intersections made getting to the market easier for housewives. Streetlights, sidewalks, and other neighborhood infrastructure were in place and paid for without special assessments.

Eager buyers lined up by the thousands on weekends in the spring of 1950 to see "Tomorrow's City." The mortgage terms were easy and down payments—particularly for veterans—were low. The residents of Lakewood found themselves in a new kind of neighborhood and among all-new neighbors. Nothing like this—a complete city almost overnight—had ever been built before. The new residents faced a big challenge—turning Lakewood into their hometown.

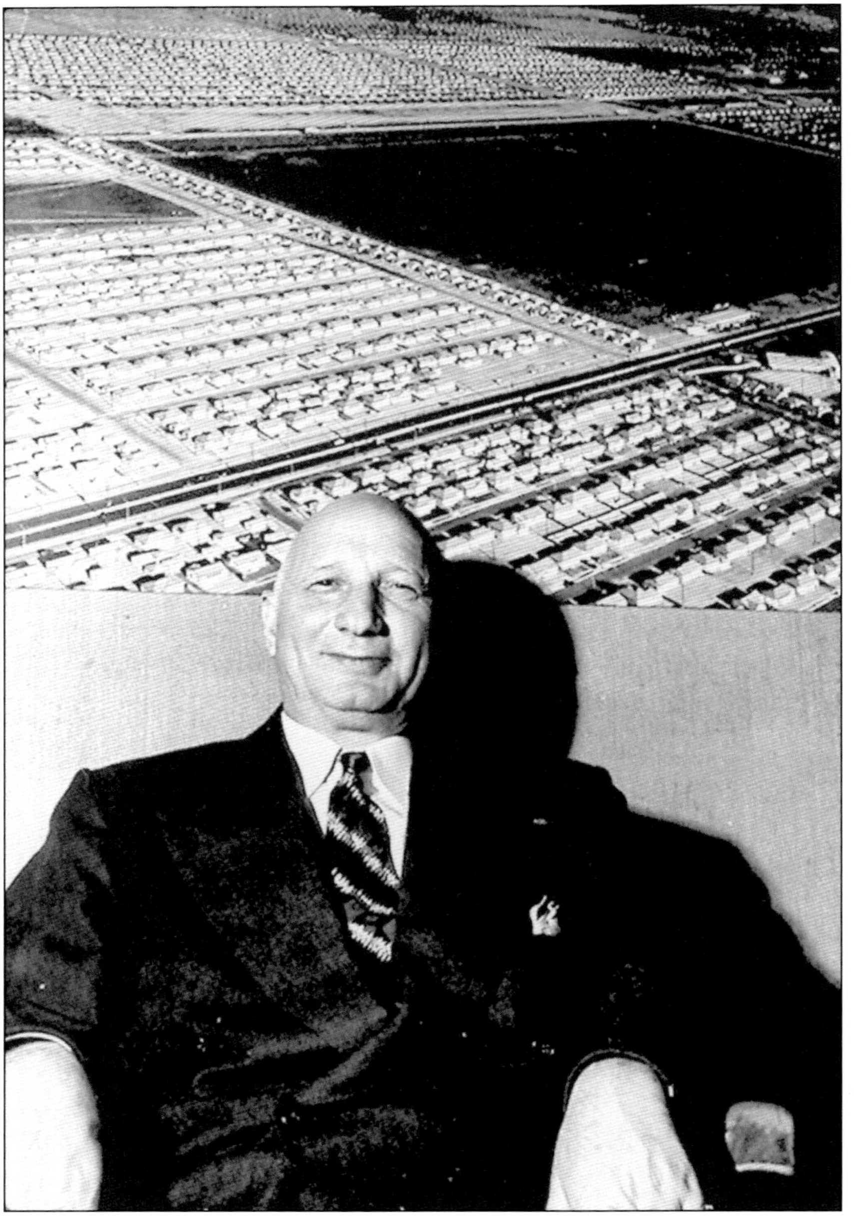

Ben Weingart. One of the three partners in the Lakewood Park Corporation, Weingart was born in 1888 in Atlanta, Georgia, and orphaned at age five. He dropped out of school in the third grade and worked a series of odd jobs. Hopping freight trains as the advance man for a quack eyeglass doctor, he eventually made his way to Los Angeles, where he found work as a laundry deliveryman servicing hotels downtown. An entrepreneur since childhood, when he had sold candy to his schoolmates, Weingart purchased the hotels he serviced when the properties faced foreclosure during the Depression. When he died in 1980, at age 92, his obituary described him as "one of the least-known and most influential members of the Los Angeles financial community for half a century," noting he had been Los Angeles County's largest property taxpayer as owner of 42,000 apartment units and the Fed-Mart chain of discount stores.

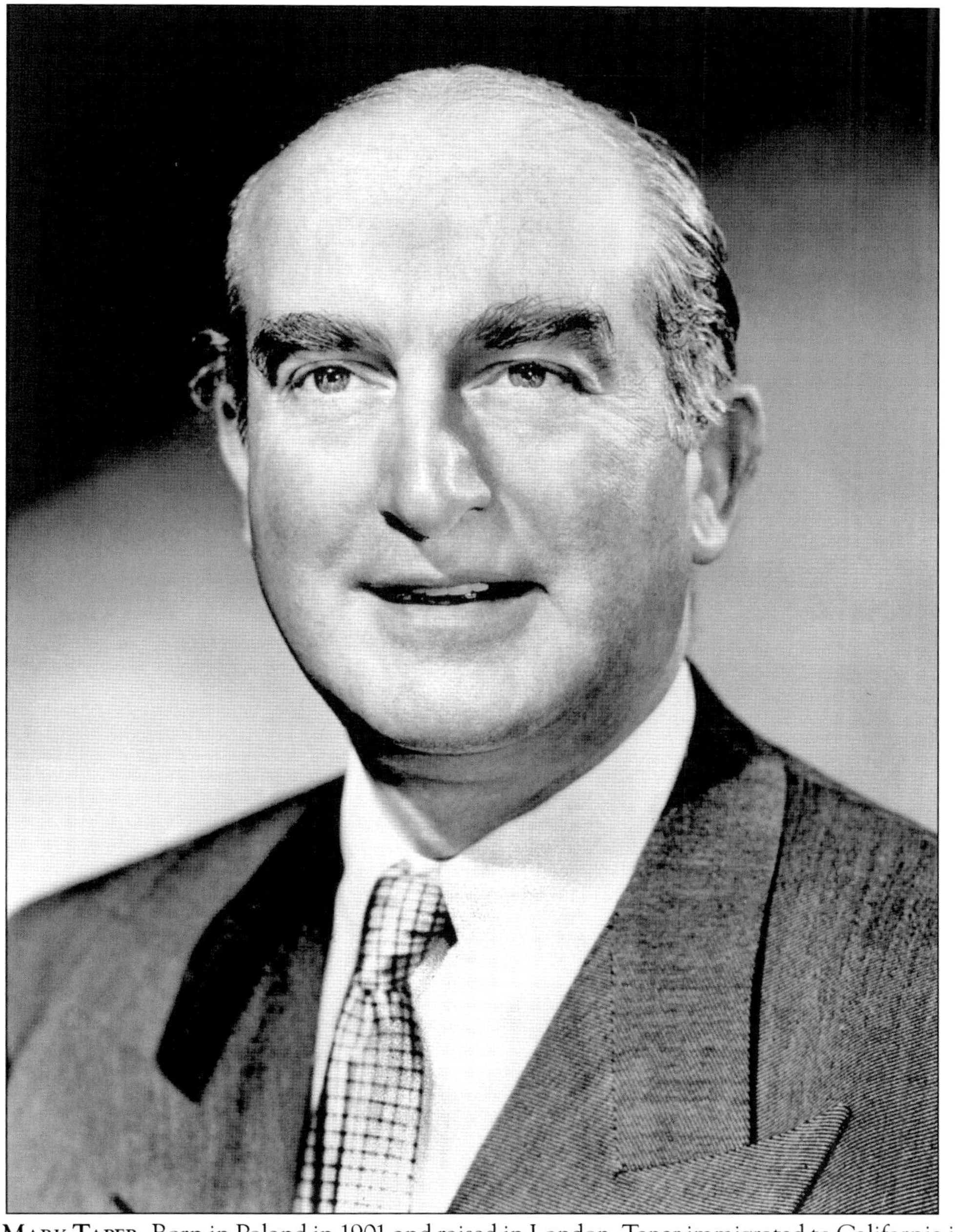

S. MARK TAPER. Born in Poland in 1901 and raised in London, Taper immigrated to California in 1939. In his early years in Britain, the precocious Taper had pursued a number of careers: a grade school teacher at age 13 when older teachers left to fight in World War I, manager at age 16 of his father's factory that manufactured uniforms, a shoe store owner at age 19, and eventually the owner of a chain of five shoe stores at age 25. After his first "retirement," he launched a successful career selling and later developing government-subsidized housing in Britain. He had intended to retire again when he came to Los Angeles, but Taper was tempted by the opportunities for home construction. Taper's Biltmore Homes built 35,000 houses in Norwalk, Long Beach, Compton, and Seal Beach before joining Ben Weingart and Louis Boyar in building Lakewood.

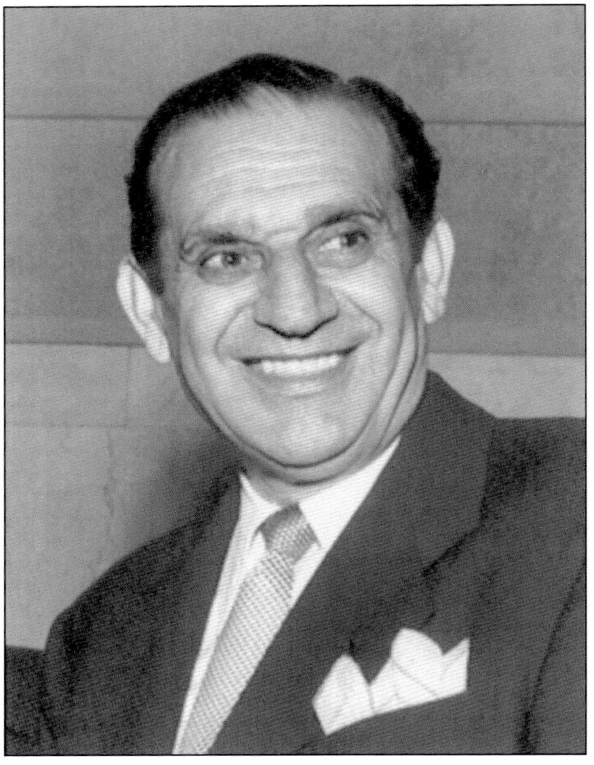

Louis H. Boyar. Louis H. Boyar, the least well-known of the three Lakewood Park Corporation partners, had been working on his plans for a "dream community" since 1939, when he leveraged a $700 loan to begin his own construction company. Born in San Francisco in 1898, Boyar went on to build new communities in the San Fernando Valley and Ventura County after the amazing success of Lakewood.

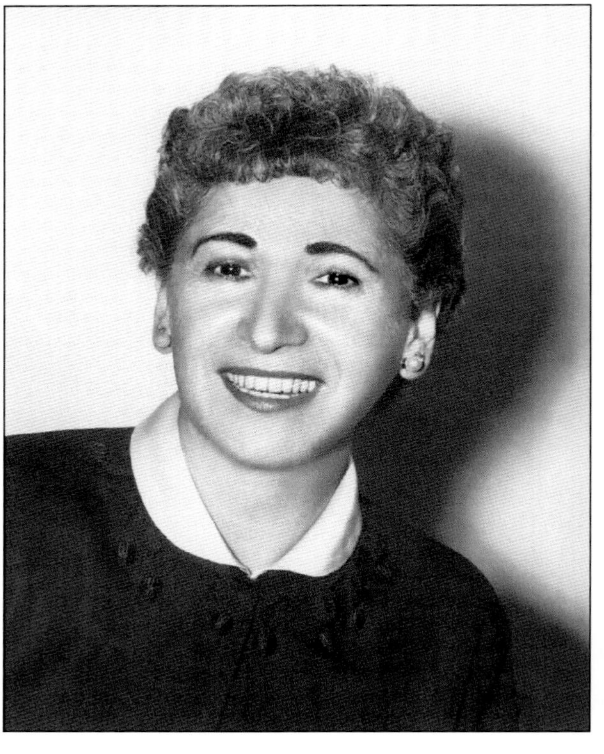

Mae Boyar. Louis Boyar's wife is credited with one of Lakewood's most distinctive features—the landscaped parkway panels that separate residential streets from Lakewood's major highways. Mae Boyar is said to have told her husband that children like to play in the street but that traffic is dangerous. She reasoned that the parkway panels would keep residential streets quiet enough for kids to play.

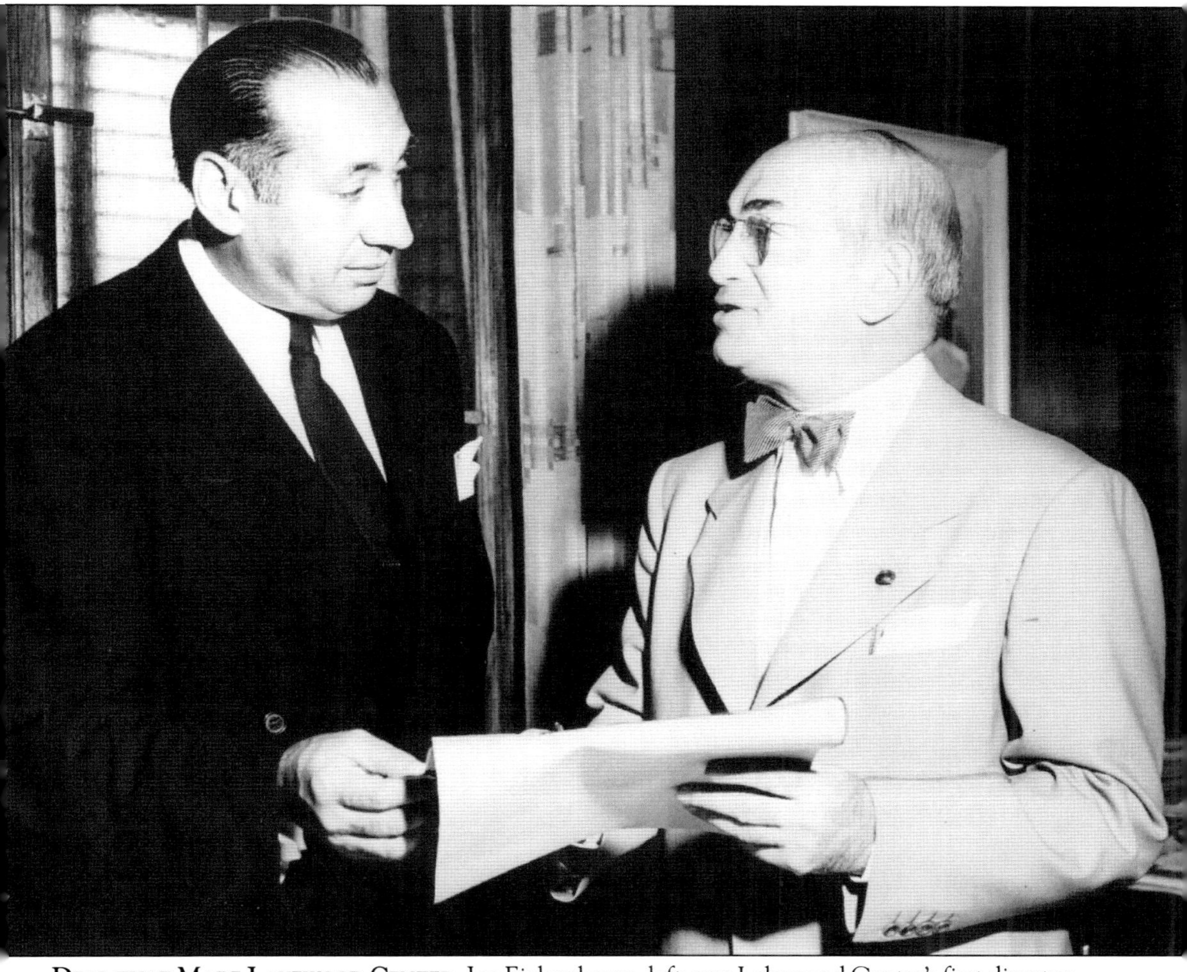

Deal that Made Lakewood Center. Joe Eichenbaum, left, was Lakewood Center's first director and leasing agent. The center was built in phases because its developers initially did not have tenants to rent the store spaces. Eichenbaum recalled later that the concept of a suburban shopping center was so new that many retailers did not want to invest in it: "This kind of planning was unheard of. Retailers feared tougher competition in a mall. No one wanted to come in first because it was so new." Eichenbaum scored a major success in 1951 when Tom May, right, of the May Company signed a $3.5 million lease. The *Los Angeles Mirror* newspaper noted that May's gamble was "considered one of the most daring steps ever taken in branch retailing." Many more chain stores would follow May's lead, establishing their first suburban branches in Lakewood Center.

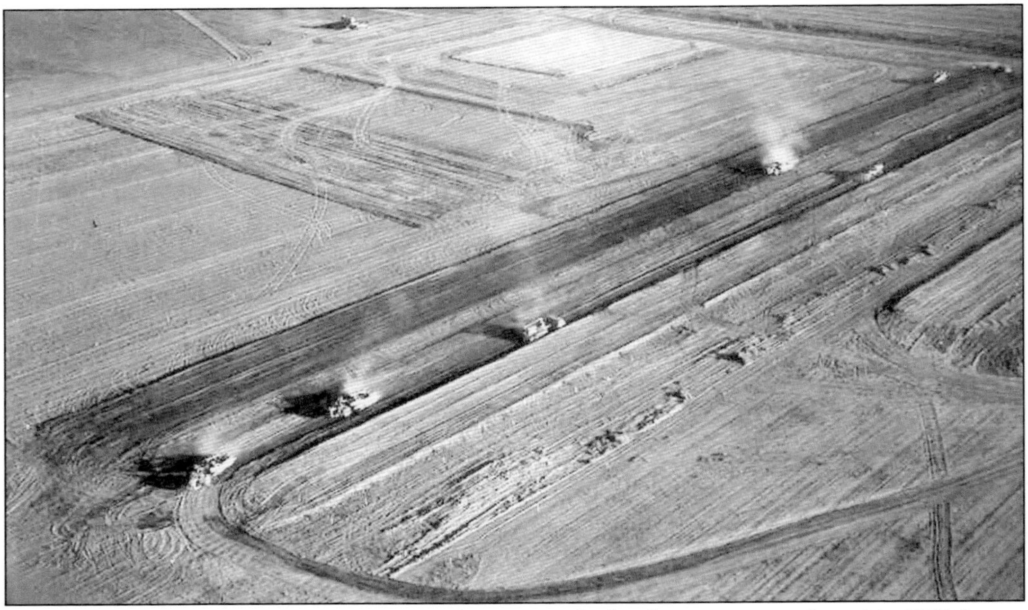

Graders Turn Fields into House Lots. As soon as the last harvest was gathered in 1949, heavy equipment began preparing what newspapers called "The $250 Million Planned Community." Lakewood developers planned sites for schools, parks, and churches, and 16 neighborhood shopping centers in addition to 17,500 houses and the massive Lakewood Center retail complex. (Courtesy of William A. Garnett.)

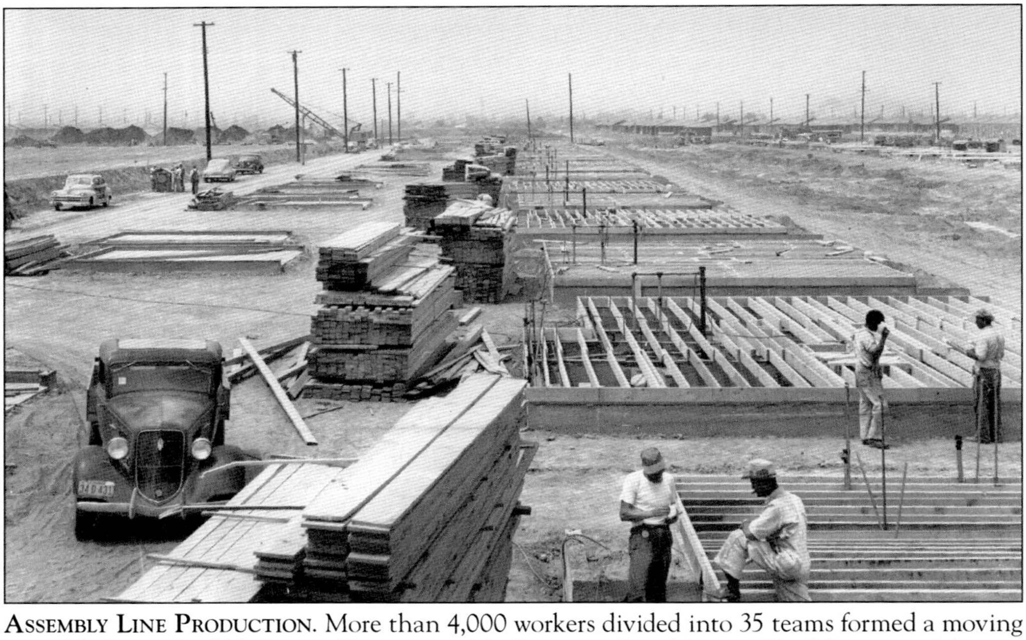

Assembly Line Production. More than 4,000 workers divided into 35 teams formed a moving assembly line to build Lakewood houses quickly. Precut and prefabricated building materials were delivered in exact amounts. Workers used power tools, including electric saws and pneumatic hammers. Expediters directed the project using two-way radios, and the foremen barked orders over a loudspeaker system. (Courtesy of Rothschild Photo.)

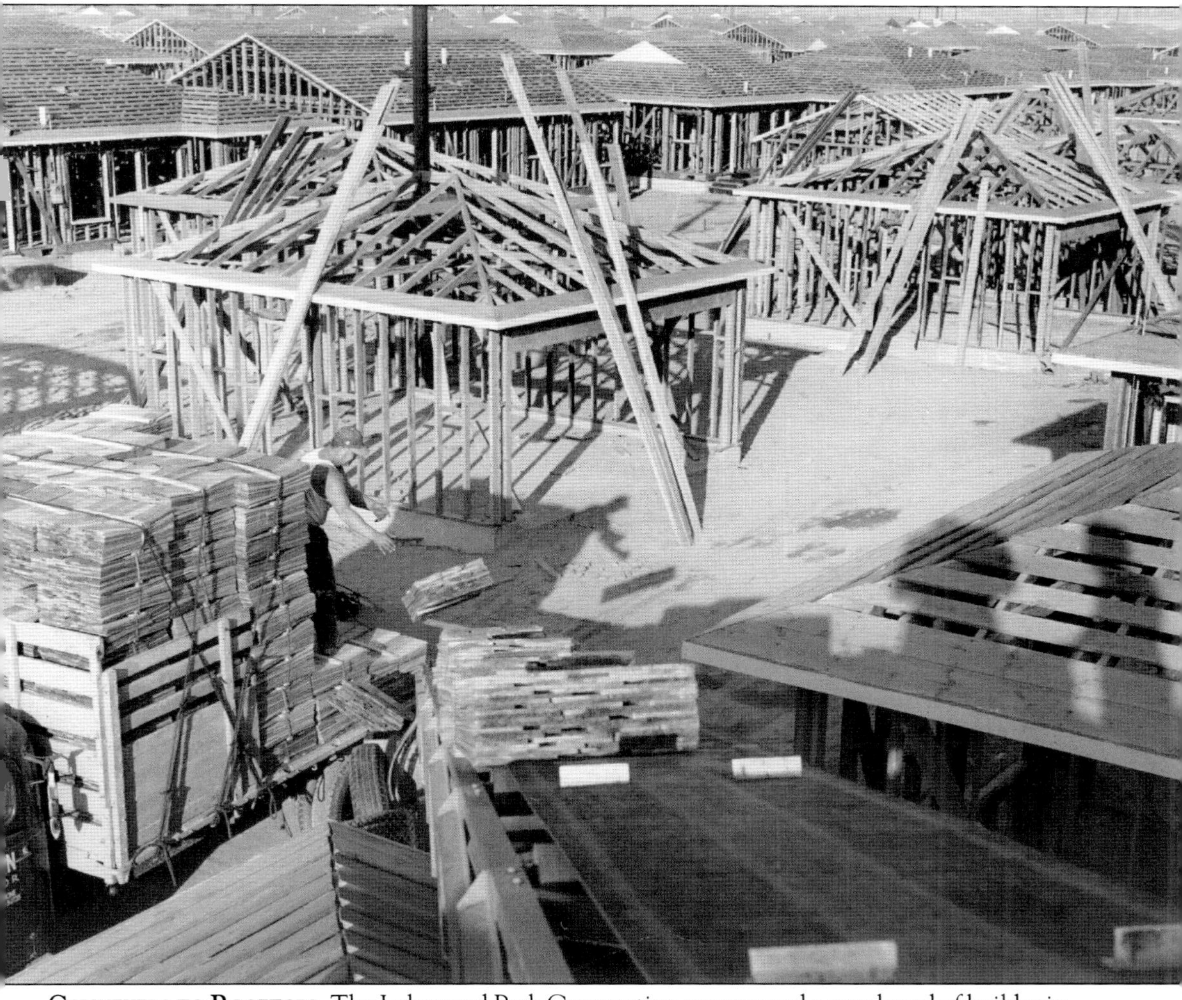

Conveyers to Rooftops. The Lakewood Park Corporation represented a new breed of builder in the post–World War II period who built complete communities, not just houses, using economies of scale and the latest in construction technologies to mass-produce homes in assembly-line fashion. Among the innovations that sped the construction of Lakewood's homes was a fleet of specially designed trucks equipped with a conveyer belt to lift bundles of wood shingles to the workmen waiting above. So efficient was Lakewood's construction process that it was said for every 10 new foundations poured, enough concrete was saved to finish the 11th. Despite the emphasis on speed, Lakewood homes were built to strict Federal Housing Administration standards. (Courtesy of Rothschild Photo.)

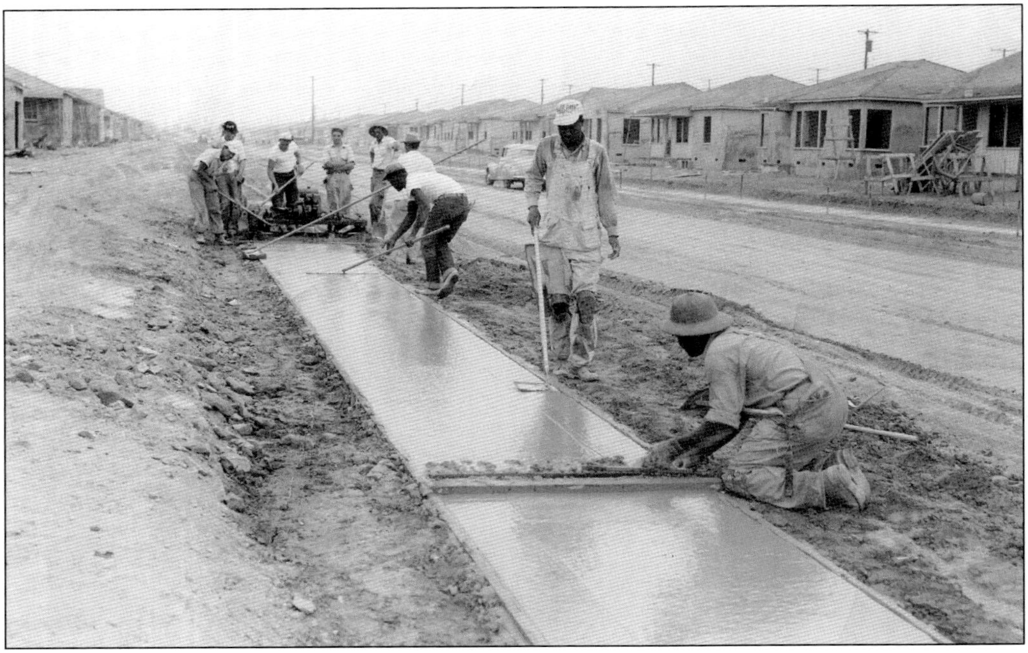

BUILDING TOMORROW'S CITY. Louis Boyar's plans for the Lakewood Park development were approved by the Los Angeles County Planning Commission in 1949. The plans included sidewalks, shown above, underground wiring for streetlights, parks adjacent to neighborhood schools, and abundant shopping facilities within walking distance. Construction plans called for the contractors to begin no fewer than 50 homes per day. During one unbelievable week, 567 homes were started. Special teams of carpenters, shown below, did the framing. Other construction teams framed windows and doors, stuccoed exterior walls, and installed wiring and plumbing. (Both, courtesy of Rothschild Photo.)

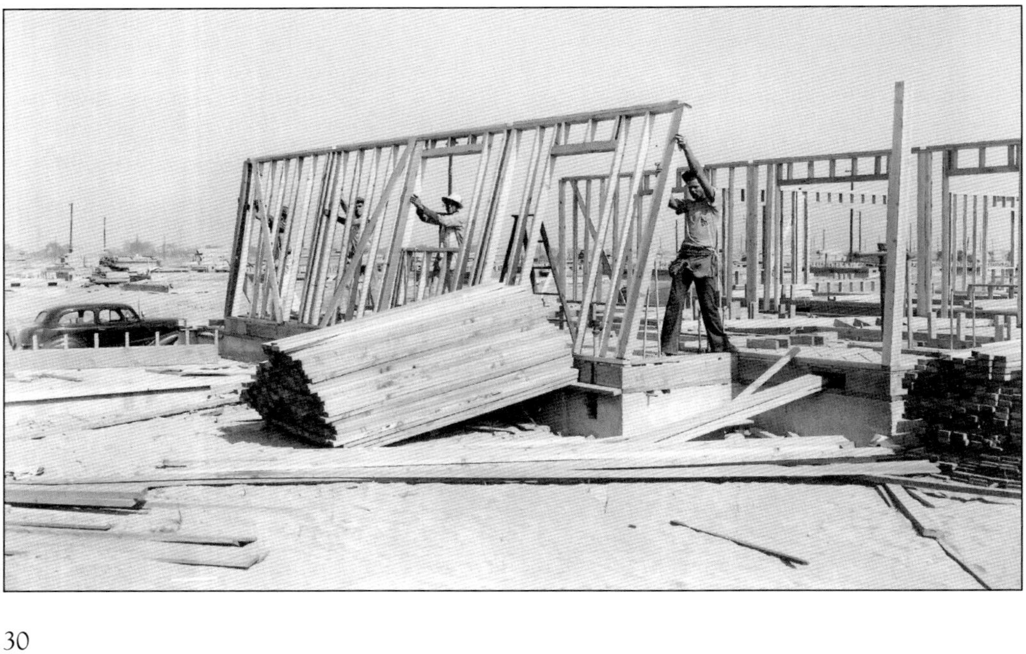

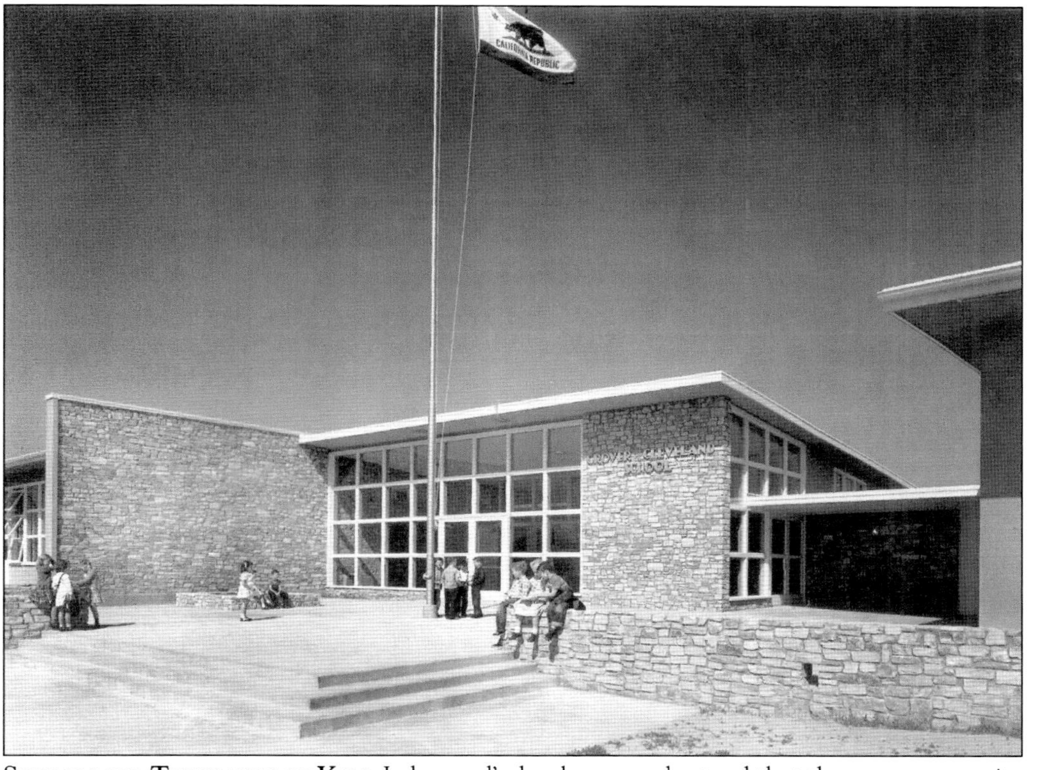

SCHOOLS FOR THOUSANDS OF KIDS. Lakewood's developers understood that the new community they were building would almost instantly become home to thousands of school-age youth. In conjunction with the boards of the Long Beach and Bellflower school districts, the developers set aside sites in Lakewood's new neighborhoods for up-to-date elementary schools, like the Grover Cleveland School on Hackett Avenue. (Courtesy of Rothschild Photo.)

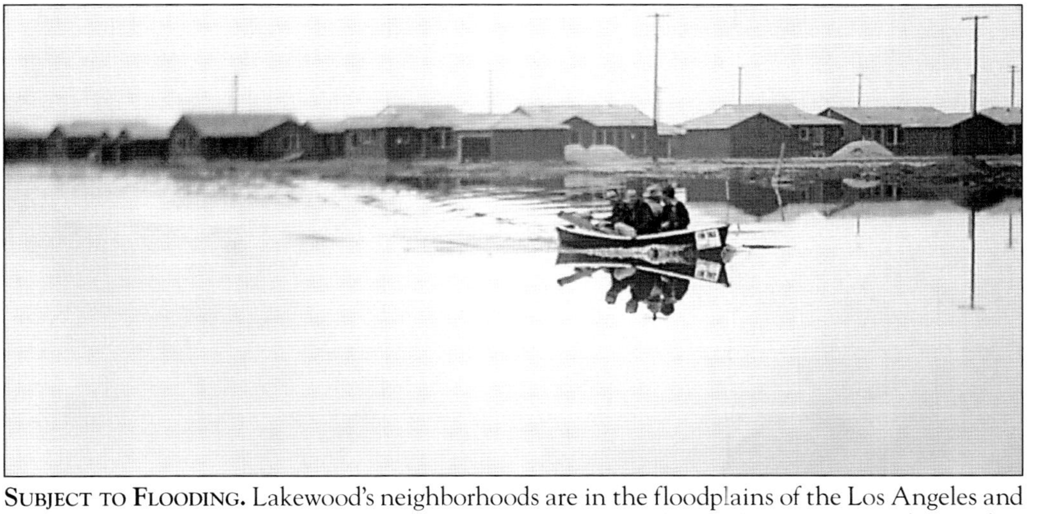

SUBJECT TO FLOODING. Lakewood's neighborhoods are in the floodplains of the Los Angeles and San Gabriel Rivers, both notorious for seasonal flooding. Lakewood's streets were designed to channel moderate runoff during storms, but severe flooding was a threat until the Army Corps of Engineers completed the flood control system in the 1960s.

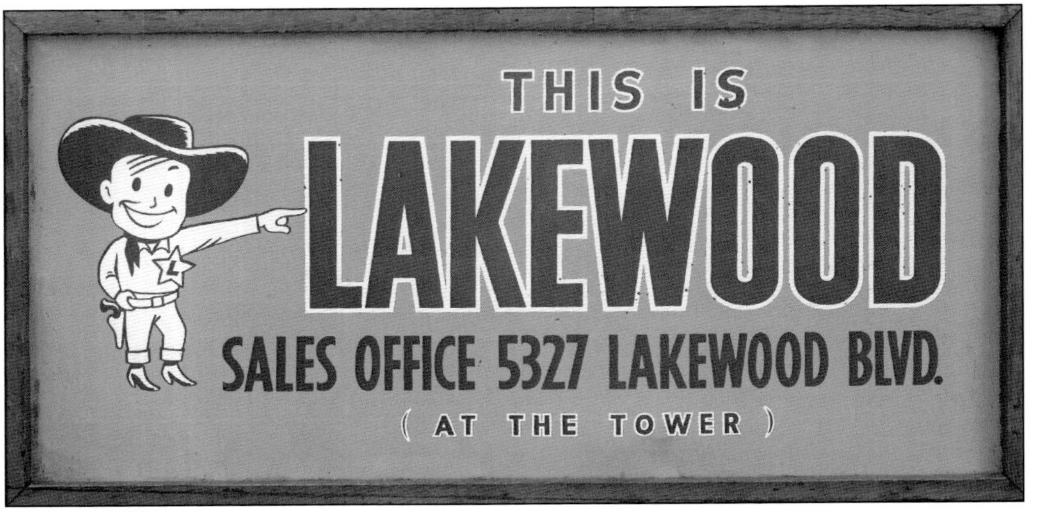

This is Lakewood! "Dreaming of the Good Life?" beckoned one Lakewood Park advertisement. Homeownership was a dream come true for Lakewood's original homebuyers, most of whom had never before owned a house. Home prices ranged from $7,575 for a two-bedroom, 825-square-foot house, to $8,525 for a three-bedroom, 1,050-square-foot house. With a federally guaranteed mortgage (at four-percent interest for 30 years), monthly payments ranged from $47 to $54 a month, with a down payment as low as $595 for a two-bedroom home. Veterans required no down payment. Although the prices were low, it was still a struggle for many Lakewood families to afford a new home.

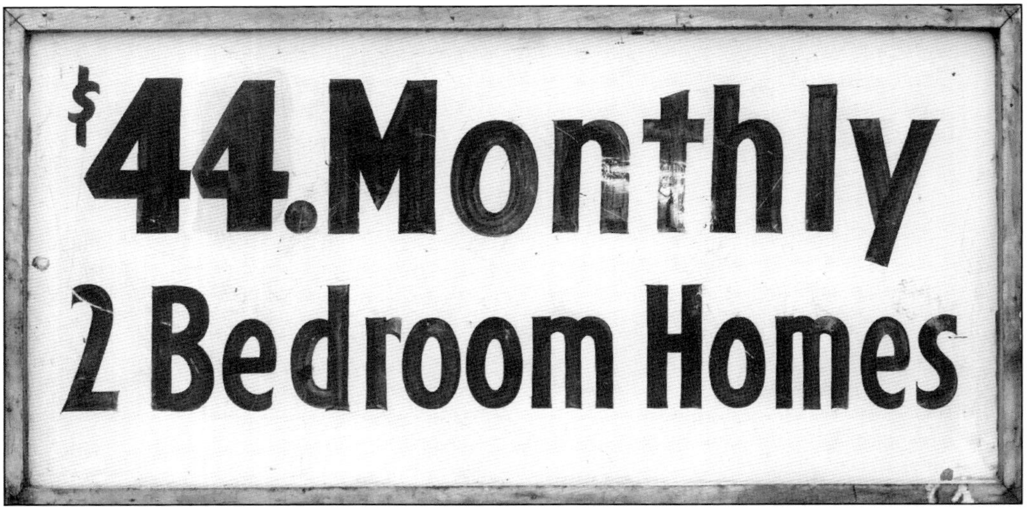

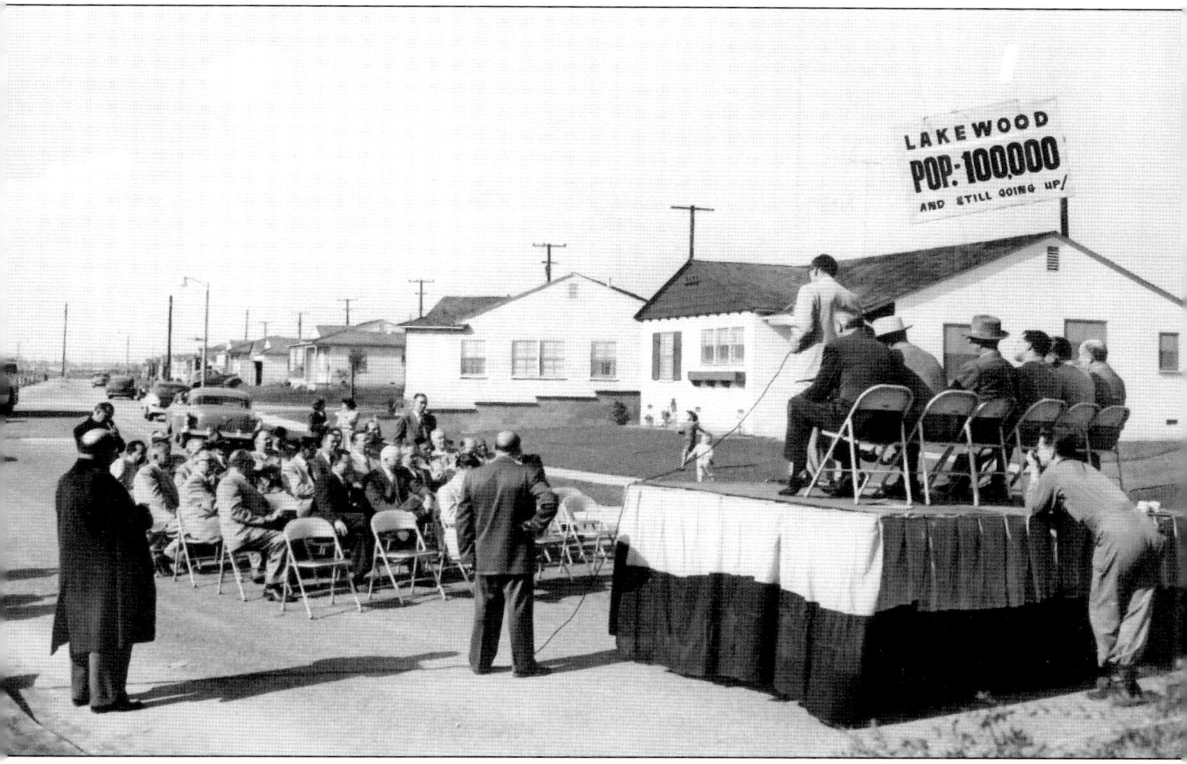

FEDERAL HOUSING ADMINISTRATION CELEBRATES COMPLETION OF LAKEWOOD MUTUAL HOMES, 1952. Lakewood's development never stopped, although the start of the Korean War slowed the financing of new construction. Lakewood's developers responded to the credit crunch with a novel application of an existing federal law that allowed homeowner cooperatives to buy land in common and receive federally guaranteed loans to build. The Lakewood Park Corporation set up paper cooperatives of company employees who applied for a federally backed loan to buy land from the company. The cooperative then contracted with the company to build the houses. Homebuyers were told that they became members of the cooperative with their down payments. The cooperative then sold the houses to its new members and dissolved. Although this unusual process had been approved by Federal Housing Administration officials in Los Angeles, Lakewood's developers were later grilled by a Senate banking subcommittee. (Courtesy of Rothschild Photo.)

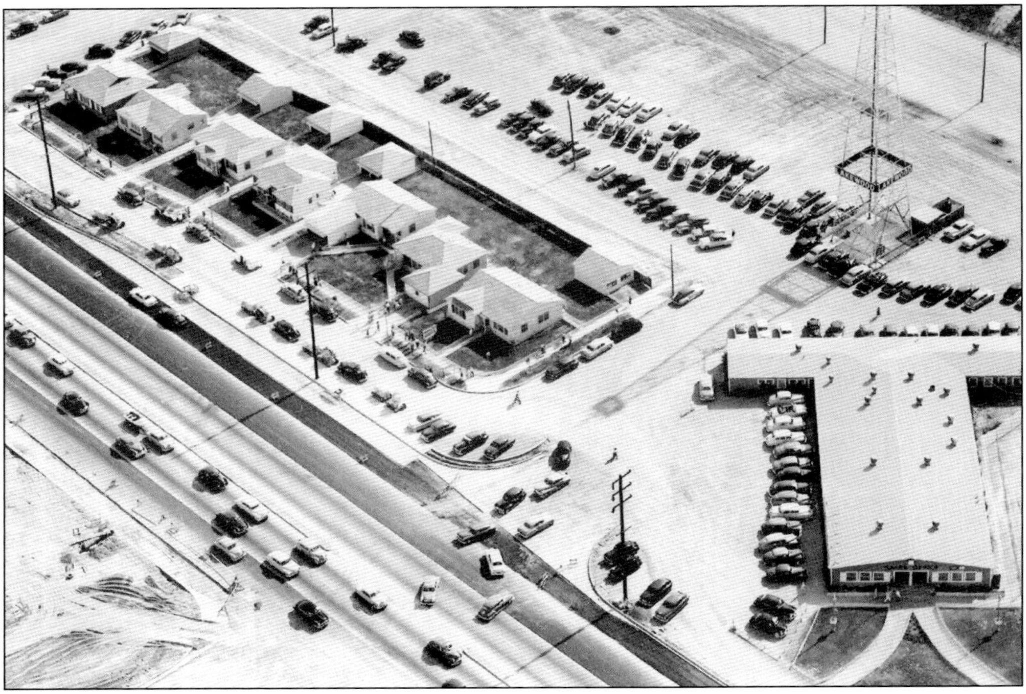

THOUSANDS COME TO LAKEWOOD. Lakewood attracted buyers with a street of completely furnished and landscaped model homes, shown above. On the first day of sales in 1950, some 25,000 people lined up to have a look. At the end of the first month, more than 200,000 people had flocked to the sales office, and more than 1,000 families had purchased homes. As many as 50 houses a day were sold, with a record 107 sold in one hour. At the end of the first 10 months, 7,200 had been sold. Home seekers waited in long lines, as shown below, to talk to one of the 35 salesmen who staffed the office from 9:00 a.m. to 10:00 p.m. on weekends. (Below, courtesy of Rothschild Photo.)

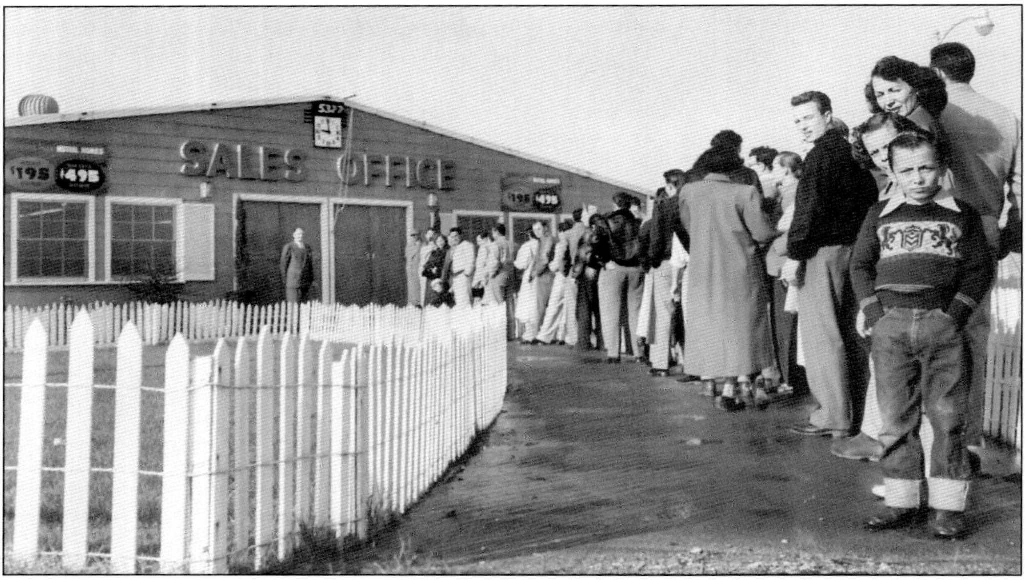

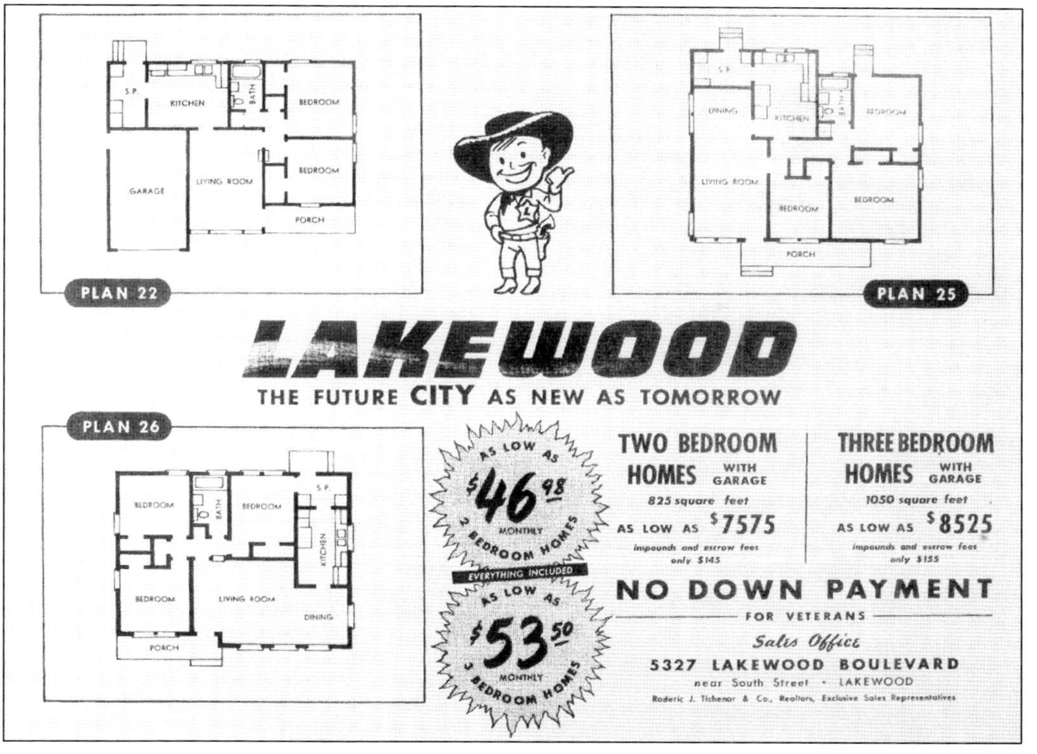

Options to Choose From. Lakewood's developers provided considerable variation in floor plans, exterior treatment, and orientation on Lakewood's 50-by-100 house lots—"Not a Bit Like the Usual 'Tract' House We've Seen," one advertisement proclaimed. There were 13 basic plans in the first phase, with four variations of each, offering homebuyers a total of 52 different exteriors for which there were 39 different color combinations. Prospective buyers were also attracted by the "luxury features" available for their home, including a cedar shingle roof, hardwood floors, trellised porches, and landscaped front and side lawns complete with a tree planted in the parkway.

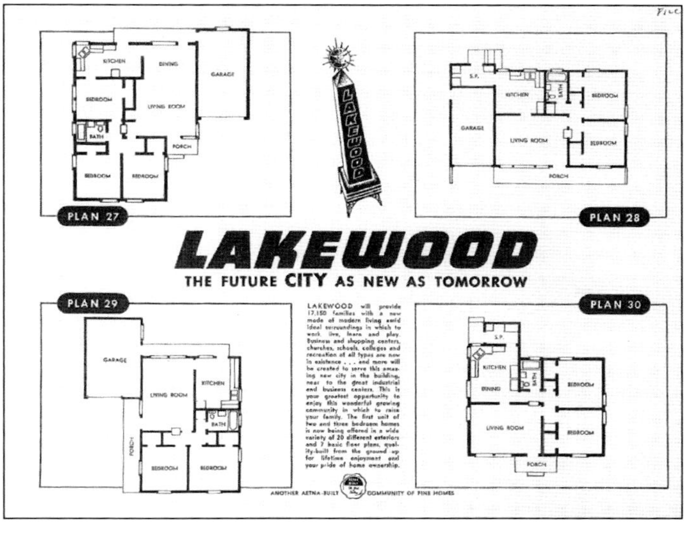

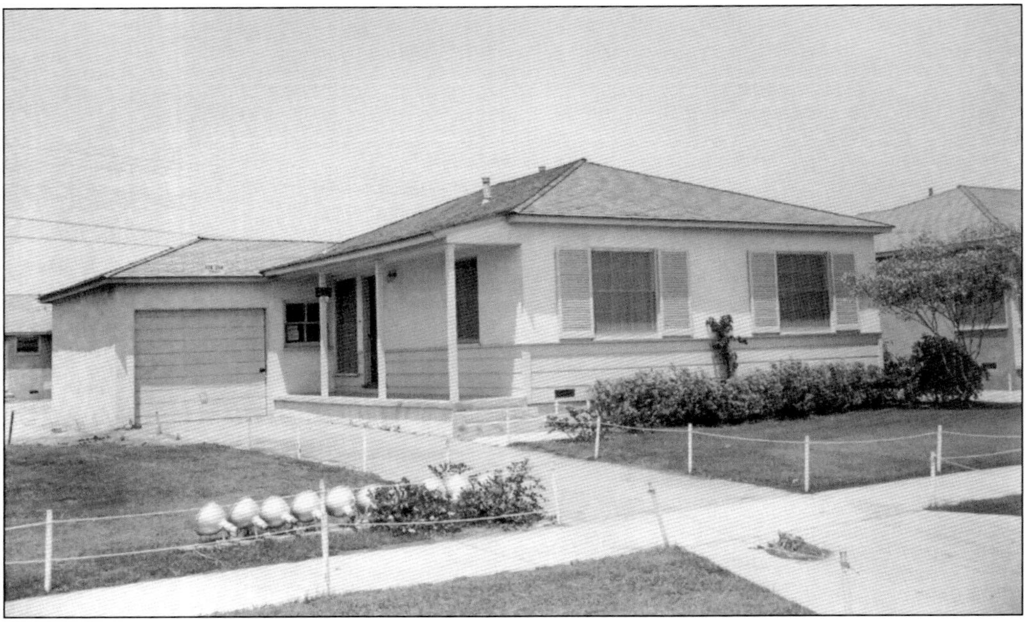

Homes for Young Families. Lakewood homes were designed for new families with modest incomes. Some models had an attached, one-car garage while others had a detached, two-car garage. Service porches had room for a washer and a sink. Although small, the houses had a generously-sized backyard for rambunctious youngsters.

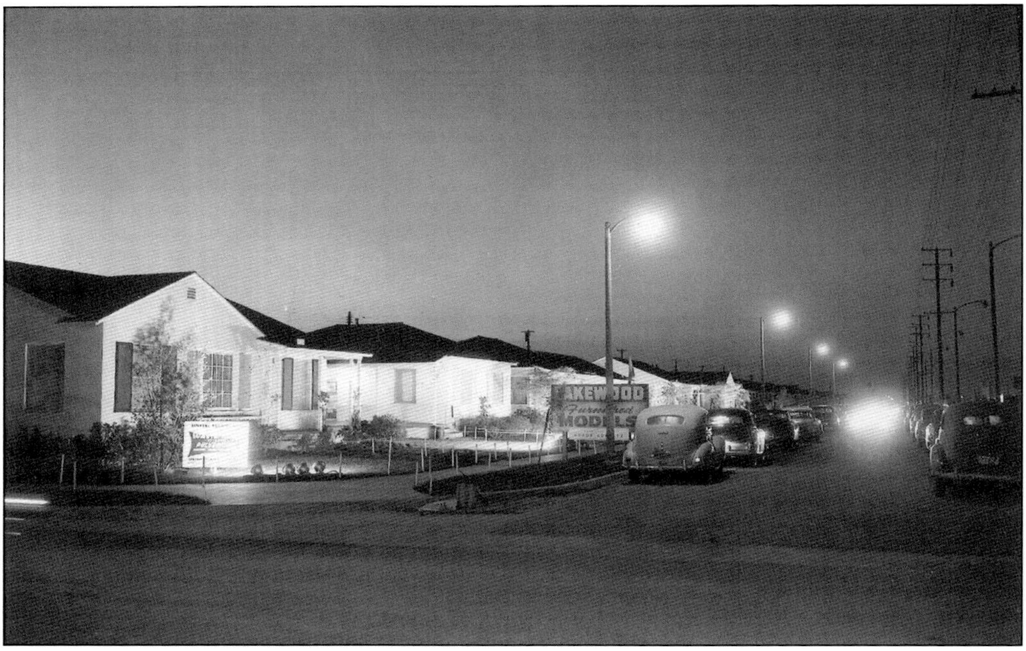

Nighttime Sales for Working Buyers. Lakewood's street of model homes stayed open late for shift workers and their wives, who appreciated the opportunity to include a Norge refrigerator, an O'Keefe & Merritt gas range, and a Bendix Economat washer as part of their monthly mortgage payments. (Courtesy of Rothschild Photo.)

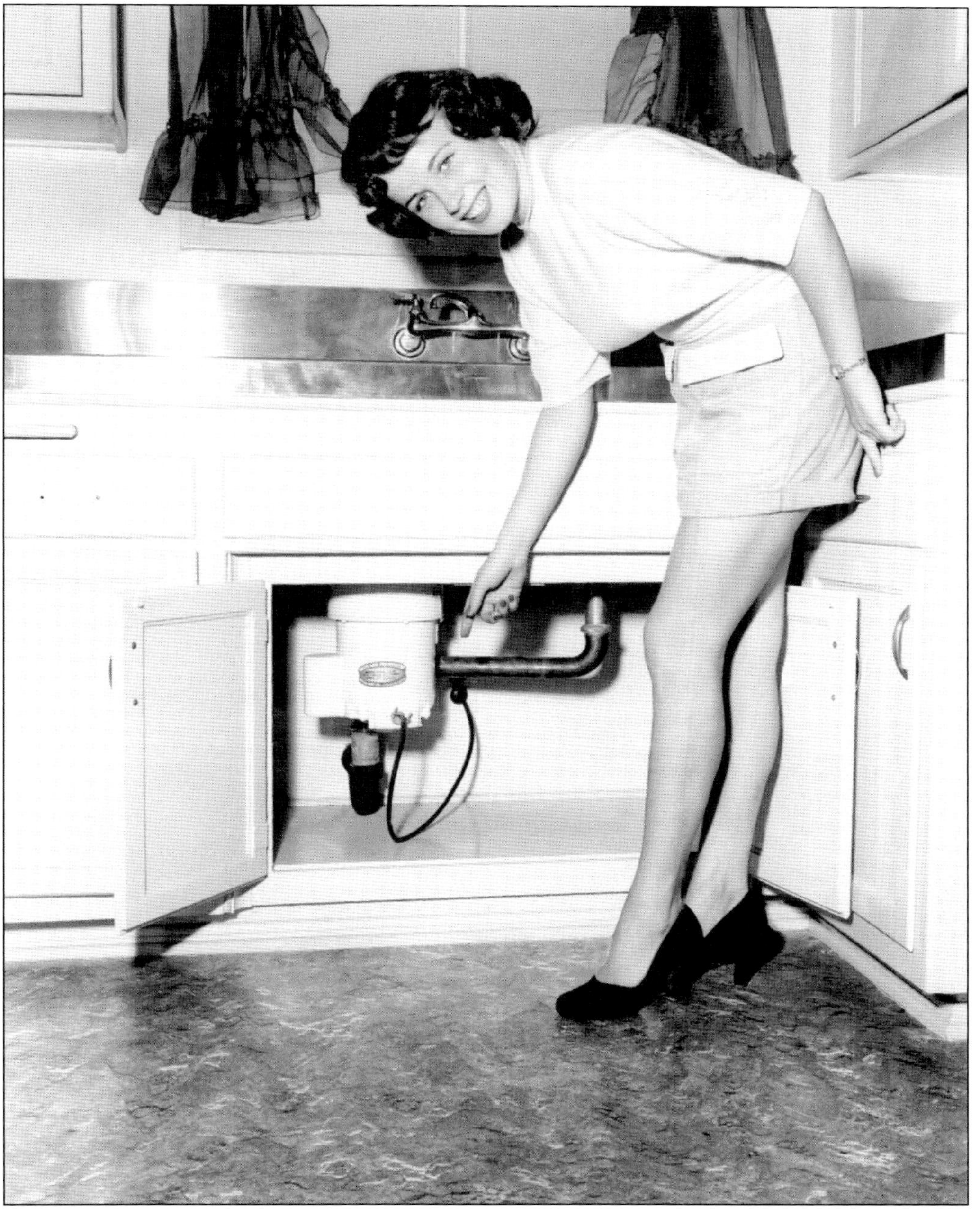

No More Garbage. The kitchens in Lakewood houses featured double sinks with a Waste King Pulverator, making Lakewood "the largest planned garbage-free community in America." The convenience of a modern kitchen was only one selling point. Longtime resident Ruth Houston later recalled her excitement as a child when her family moved into their three-bedroom Lakewood home. It was a huge improvement over their previous home in rural Illinois, where a family of eight had crowded into a two-bedroom house with no indoor plumbing. Their new home was roomy and bright, with a patio window, a kitchen outfitted with lots of cabinets, and a "nice white, pretty bathtub and shower." (Courtesy of Rothschild Photo.)

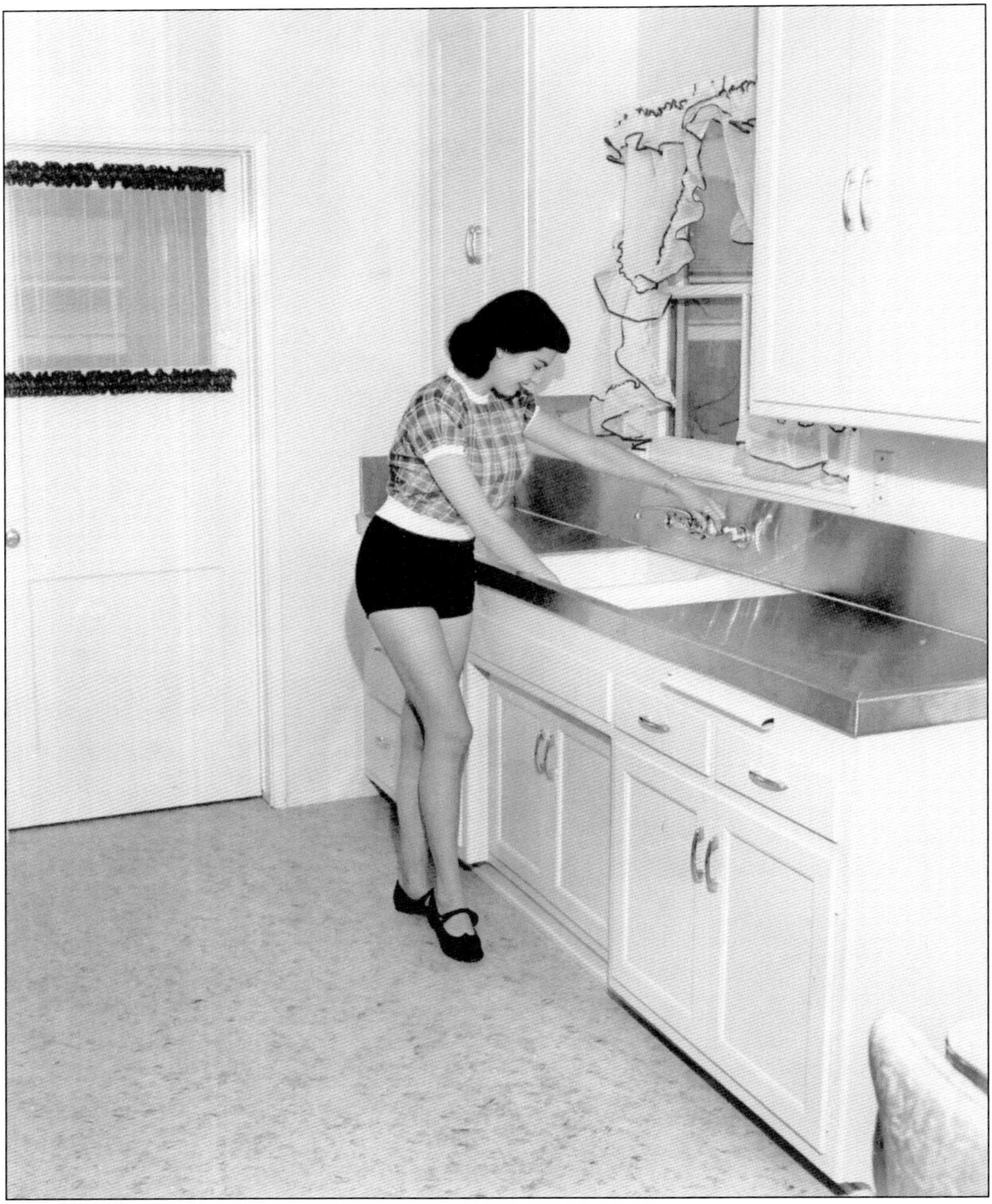

Stainless Steel Counter Tops. The marketing campaign for Lakewood Park in 1950 emphasized the modern details of the homes' "scientifically planned" kitchens. Stainless steel—the metal of the jet age in the 1950s— countertops were highlighted in nearly every advertisement. Aluminum window screens—another standard feature—were included among the benefits of buying a Lakewood home. Everything about Lakewood was new, and the first buyers found themselves unexpected pioneers. "We were all young couples," early resident Gwen Travis remembered, "and only the third family on the block. The closest grocery store was McCoy's Market at South and Bellflower. Having only one car, which my husband used to go back and forth to work, I always walked to get groceries." (Courtesy of Rothschild Photo.)

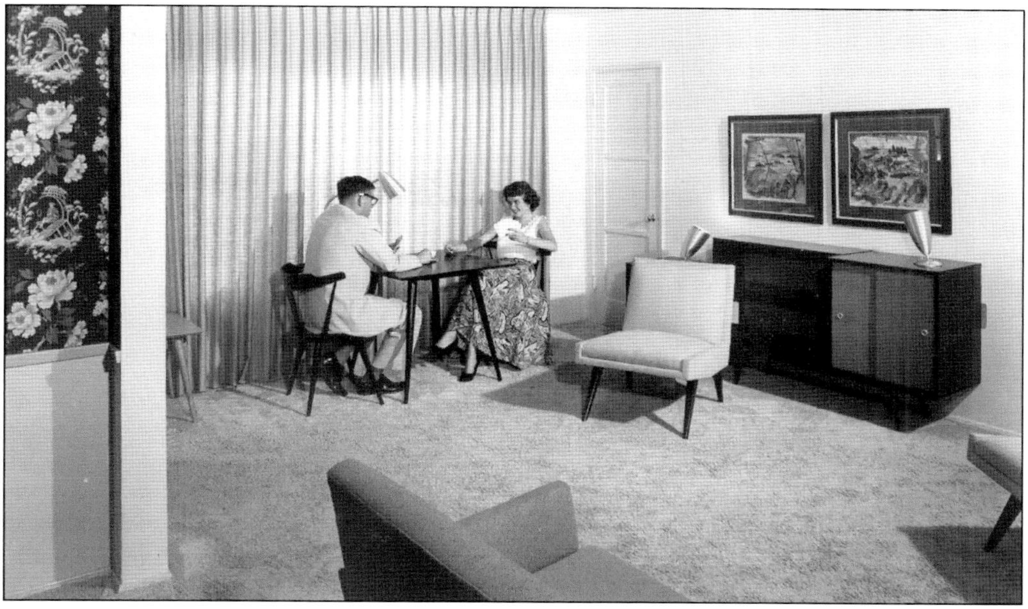

Gracious Living. Prospective homebuyers could see the advantages of buying by touring Lakewood Park's model homes. They were guided by a corps of Long Beach City College fraternity members and athletes. The model homes were furnished and decorated by the May Company and the Aaron Schultz furniture store in styles that included Maple, Traditional, Modern, and Provincial. Buyers were attracted to Lakewood for many reasons, such as the dream of year-round outdoor living, the many family-oriented amenities that the community offered, and Lakewood's location near Douglas Aircraft and other industries. (Both, courtesy of Rothschild Photo.)

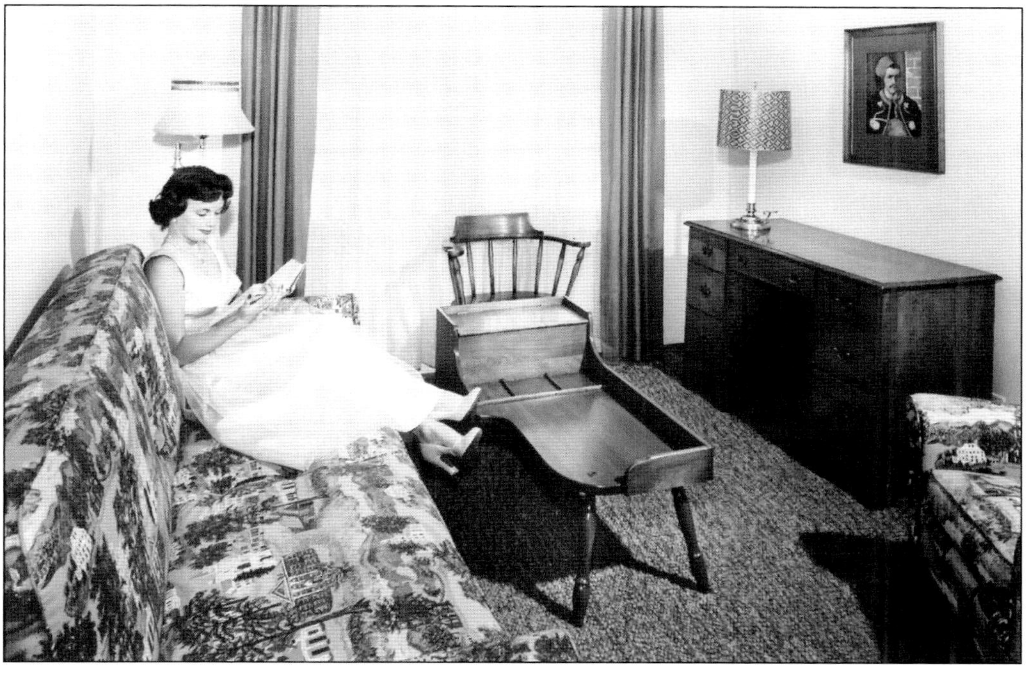

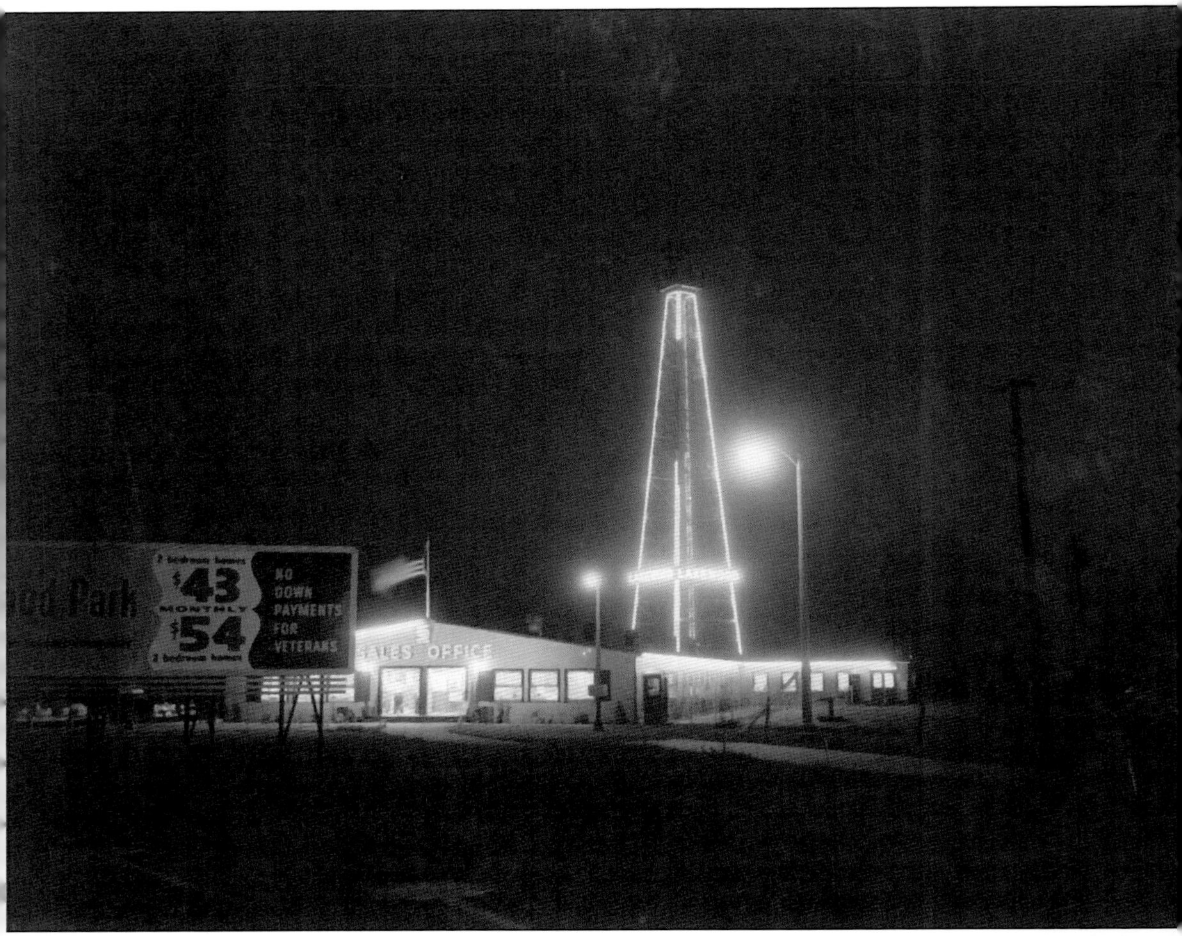

Look for the Tower. In addition to advertisements promising a dream home, Lakewood's developers attracted buyers by erecting "the tower," a 100-foot-tall steel derrick strung with bright electrical lights. It stood behind the Lakewood Park sales office on Lakewood Boulevard, beckoning buyers to come in, look at the colorful sales brochures, and talk with one of the salesmen on duty. Inside the barnlike sales office, there were 40 rooms available for processing escrow and sales applications. The salesmen made only a modest commission—about $35—for each sale. (Courtesy of Rothschild Photo.)

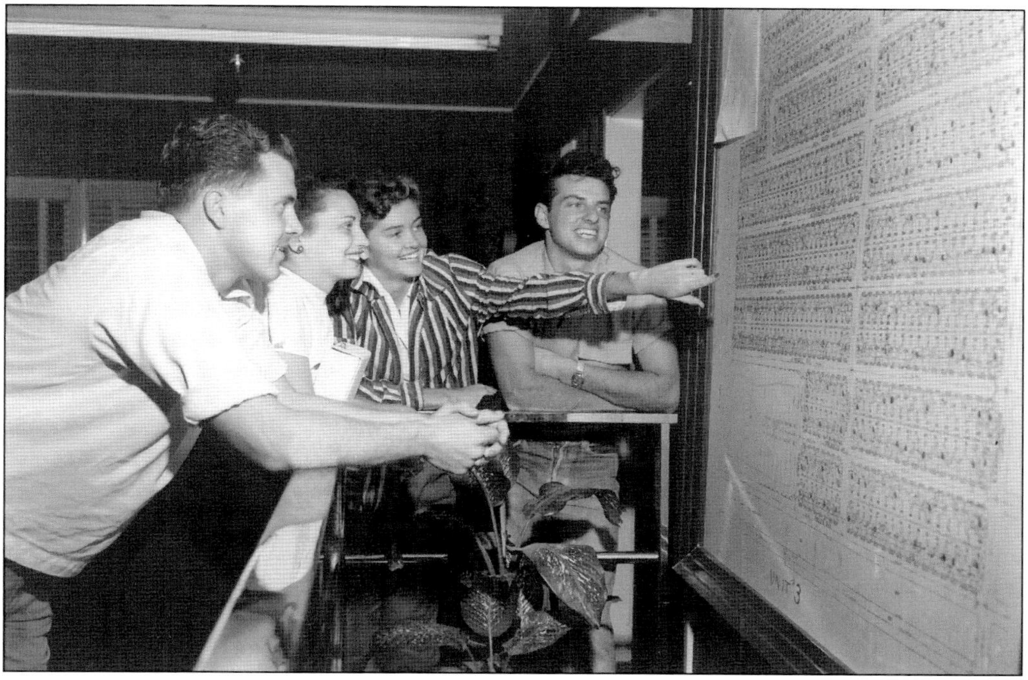

Buying a Lakewood Home. Buyers crowded into the Lakewood Park and Lakewood Mutual Homes sales offices every weekend from 1950 to 1953. Mostly, the buyers were young, with jobs in the region's booming economy. New residents were moving in at the rate of 60 families a day. Not all buyers were welcome, however. The salesmen were instructed to discourage nonwhite buyers, but Lakewood's developers were not alone in this practice. Despite a 1948 Supreme Court decision making racially restrictive covenants illegal, most developers believed that racially mixed communities would not be profitable. (Both, courtesy of Rothschild Photo.)

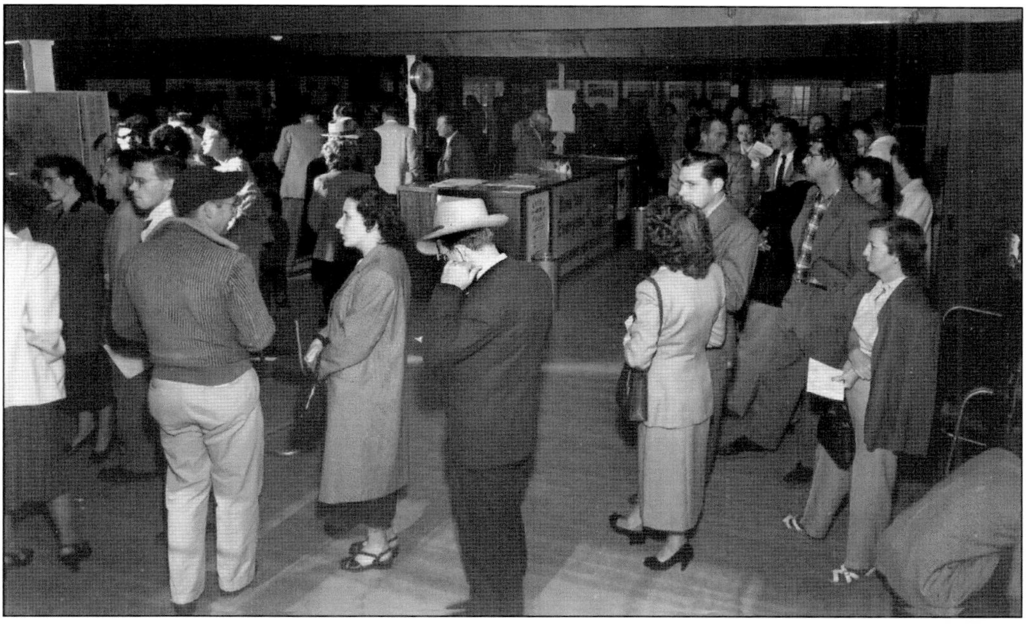

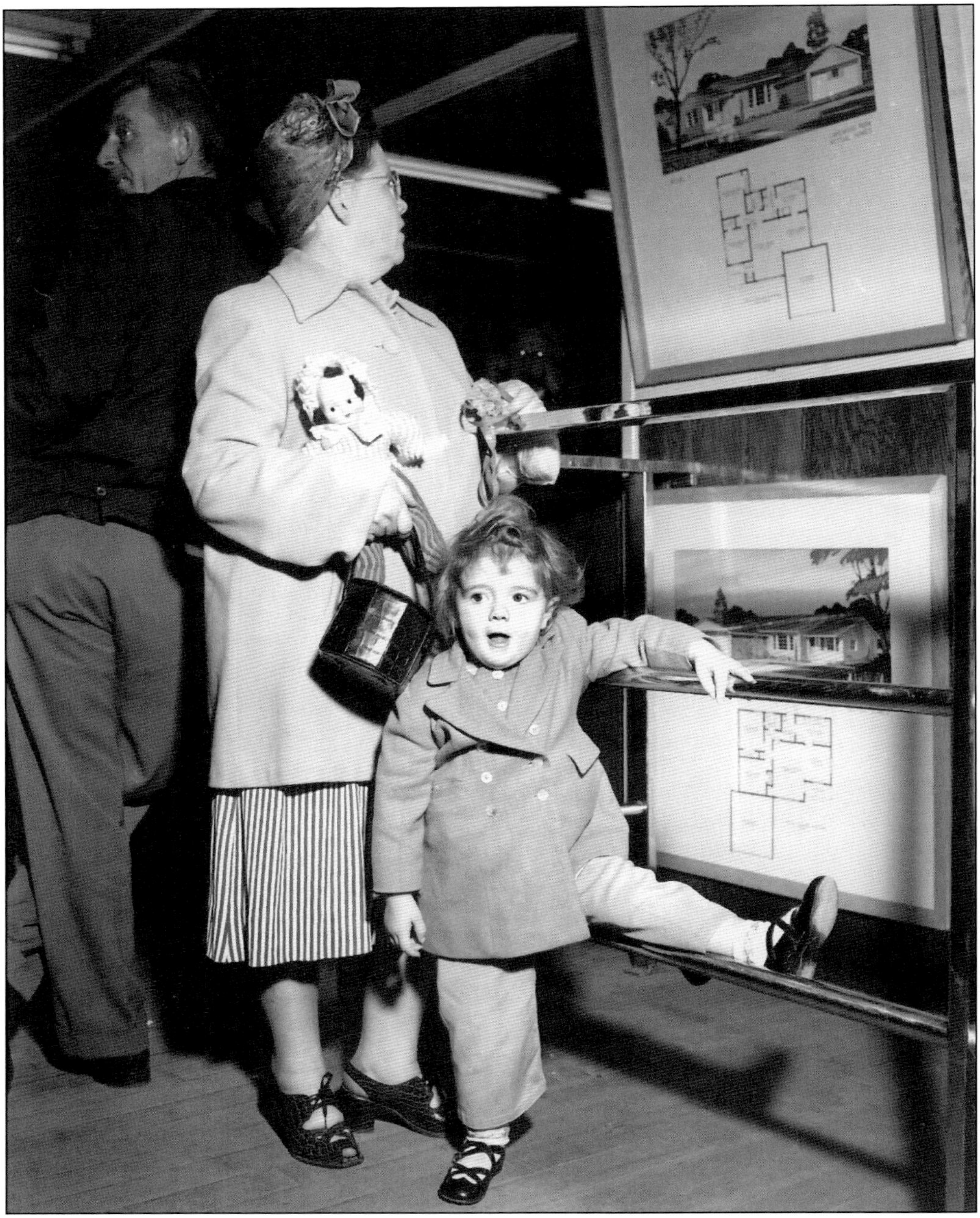

Looking for a Home. Most Lakewood homebuyers were buying their first houses. Most families had at least one child, with another on the way. "Everybody was in the same boat, looking for a new house and not having a great deal of money to spend," recalled Janet MacHale in 2004. "We were all struggling to get the house and furnishings together." Although the down payment was relatively low, some buyers had to borrow from their parents before they could sign the sales agreement and begin escrow. Many new residents turned to their neighbors for help putting up fences, installing TV antennas, and getting their lawns mowed. (Courtesy of Rothschild Photo.)

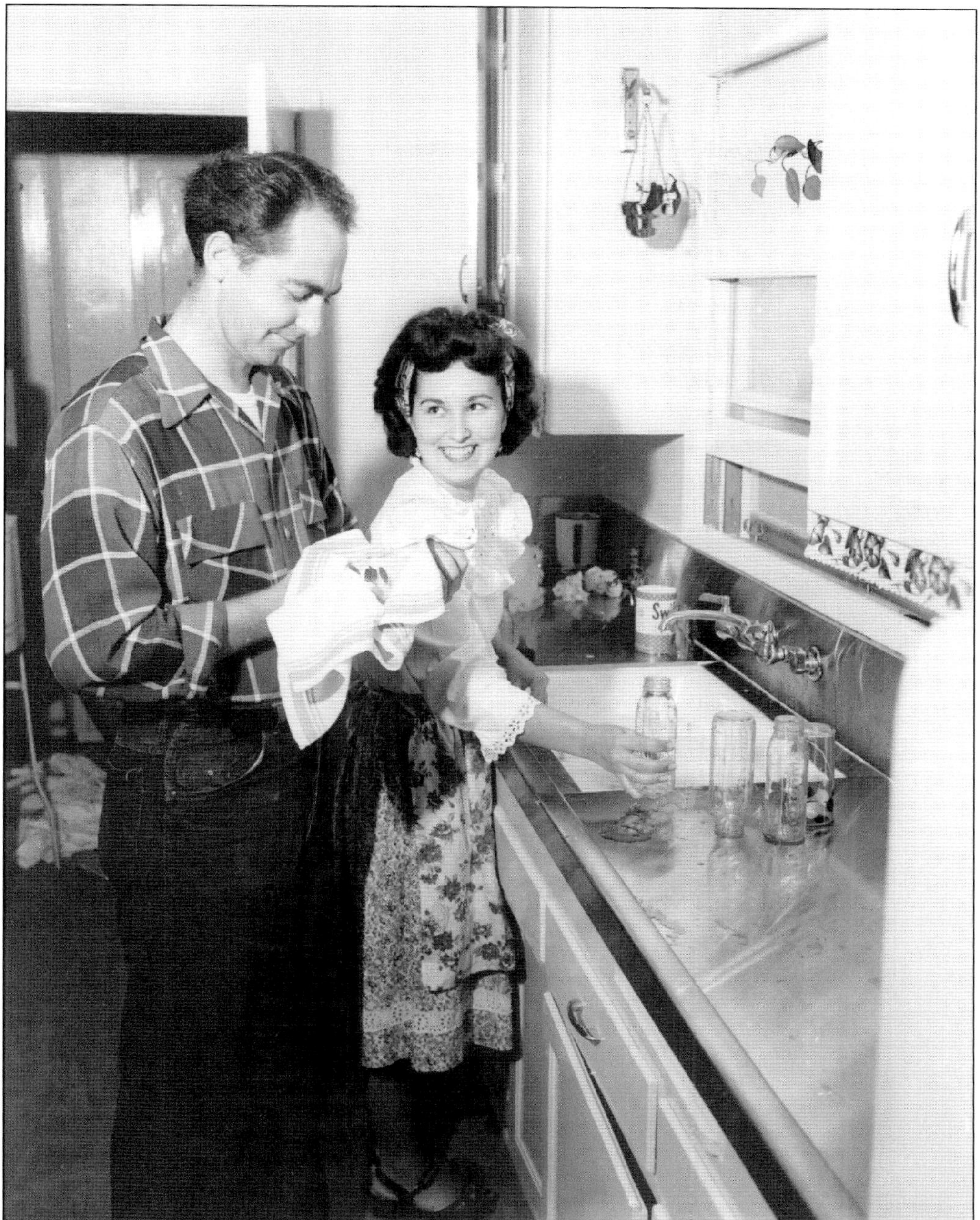

New Families Move In. The average age of new Lakewood homeowners in 1950 was 32 for men and 26 for women. The families that moved into Lakewood averaged 4.2 persons, higher than the national average of 3.2. Most families made between $4,000 and $7,000 a year. The average income was $5,100. That was $2,000 higher than the national average in 1950. A new resident on Hayter Avenue, interviewed by the local paper, reported that he earned $4,400 a year. Including property taxes and insurance, he paid $70 a month for his three-bedroom house. He paid $19 a month on his new television set and $48 a month for his new furniture.

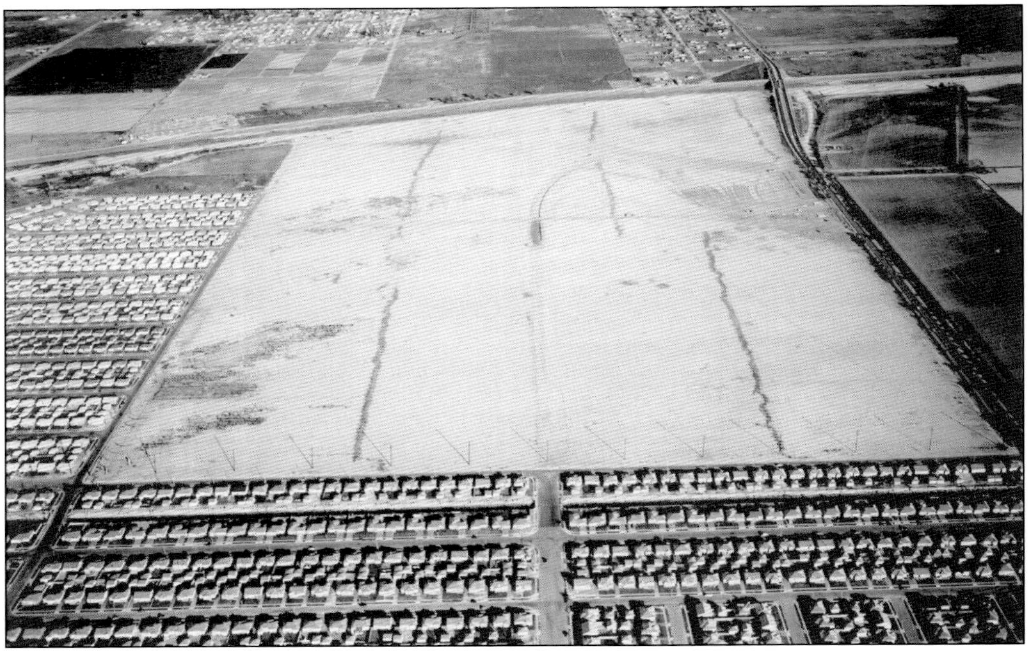

BUILT IN JUST 10 MONTHS. This portion of central Lakewood, seen in these views looking west, went from an empty field in February 1952, shown above, to rows of new houses in December, below. The 17,500 houses of Lakewood Park, Lakewood Mutual Homes, and Carson Park were all built within 33 months. *Time* magazine said that it was the biggest housing development in the world. It was also 105 acres of concrete sidewalks and 133 miles of paved streets lined with 5,000 concrete light poles, all paid for by the developers. (Both, courtesy of William A. Garnett.)

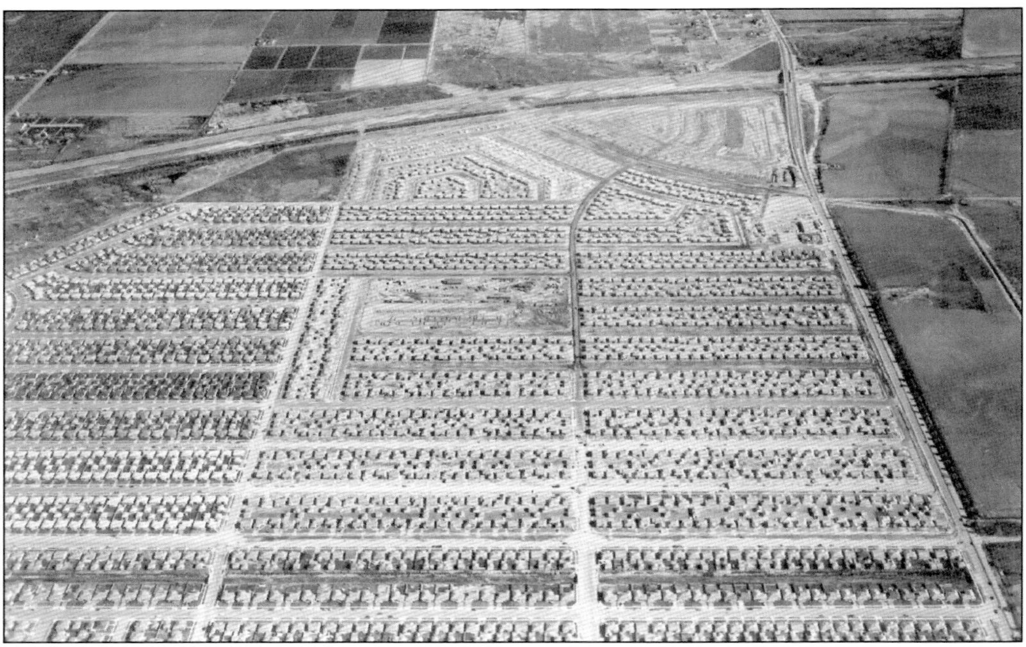

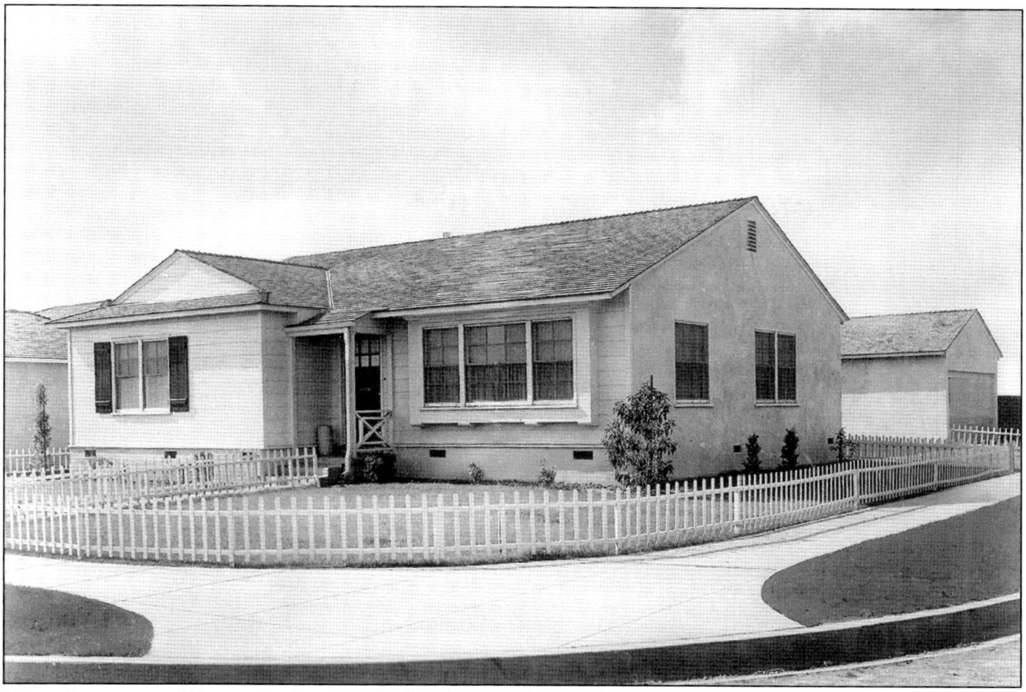

New Image of Home. Lakewood's developers focused on providing housing for the tens of thousands flocking to Long Beach for its many good-paying jobs, its favorable climate, and the greater opportunities that life in the West offered. Some critics complained that the new homes of Lakewood were plain and small, and wondered if their new buyers would be able to build a genuine community in such a place. (Both, courtesy of Rothschild Photo.)

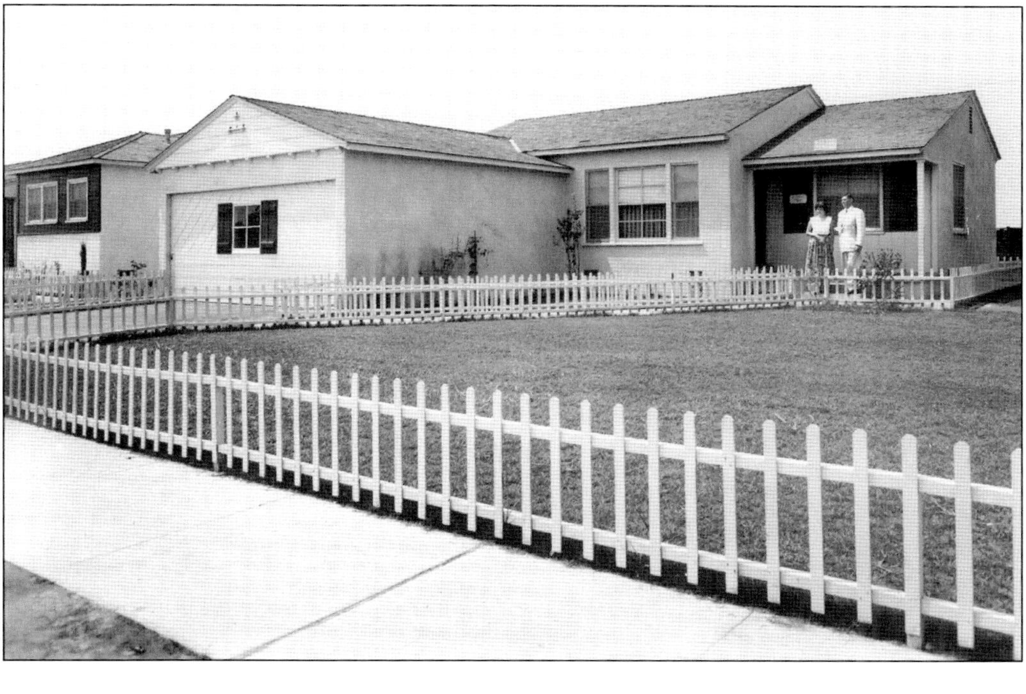

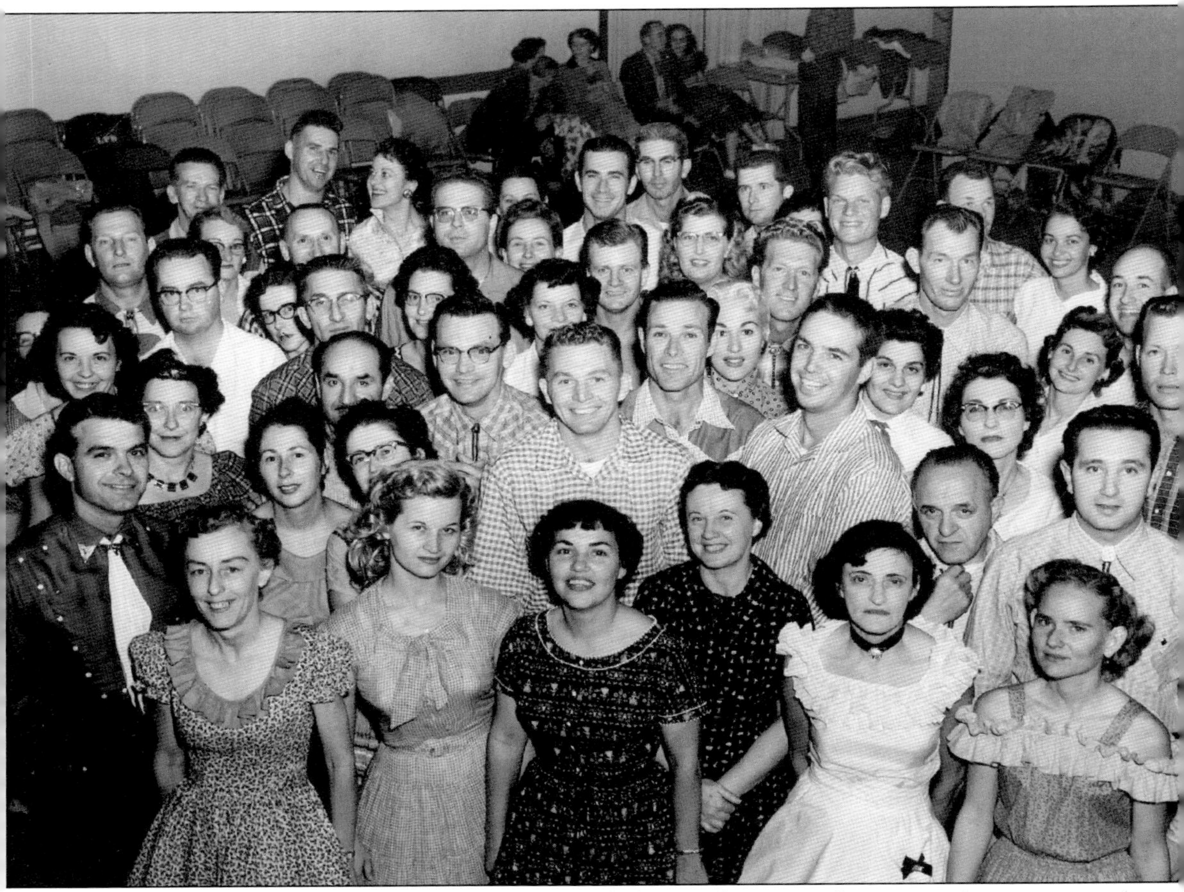

Square Dancers at Mayfair Park. Lakewood's first residents were thrown together in an entirely new kind of community—one without traditions, a settled social structure, or long-standing institutions. They were Lakewood's original "do it yourself" generation, forming social clubs and veterans' associations, joining new civic groups like the Lakewood Taxpayers Association and the Lakewood Civic Council, and having fun even while they created new traditions. Lakewood's residents came from big cities in the Midwest and the East and from rural crossroads in the Southwest. They came from diverse cultures and backgrounds. Their accents and politics and habits were different, and all of that required getting used to. They shared common aspirations, however; they wanted Lakewood to be their children's new hometown.

Three

Shop at Lakewood Center

Lakewood was big, very big. And at Lakewood's heart was planned the biggest shopping center in California.

Lakewood Center was one of the first regional shopping centers in the nation and a new kind of "downtown" for the suburbs. Lakewood Center would bring together shopping, entertainment, law enforcement, social services, and community activities. But would the concept work?

Lakewood Center was a risky decision; nothing like it had been built in Southern California. Major retailers were skeptical that shoppers would want to drive to the center and walk its open-air mall. They feared that mall shopping was too radical for shoppers used to a traditional downtown.

The May Company and Prudential Insurance accepted the risks. The May Company agreed to build a 345,000-square-foot store, the company's largest suburban store. Prudential agreed to underwrite some of the enormous development costs. The distinguished architectural firm of Albert C. Martin and Associates was given the commission to design the May Company building and lay out the shops, markets, and offices that would line a half-mile-long pedestrian mall.

Reassured, chain retailers lined up in 1951 to lease the shops being built between the May Company and the smaller Butler Brothers store. In successive phases, Lakewood Center expanded north and south of its principal anchor, adding supermarkets, gas stations, a bowling alley, a garden center, a medical office building, and the offices of county agencies.

Lakewood Center expanded again in the 1970s and 1980s, becoming an enclosed mall with even more sales area. New shops and Lakewood's popular restaurant row on Candlewood Street added to the center's continuing popularity.

Today, Lakewood Center is still one of the largest shopping centers in Southern California, and one of the busiest. More than 60 years after the center's first stores opened, "Shop Lakewood" is still the best advice for value, quality, and convenience.

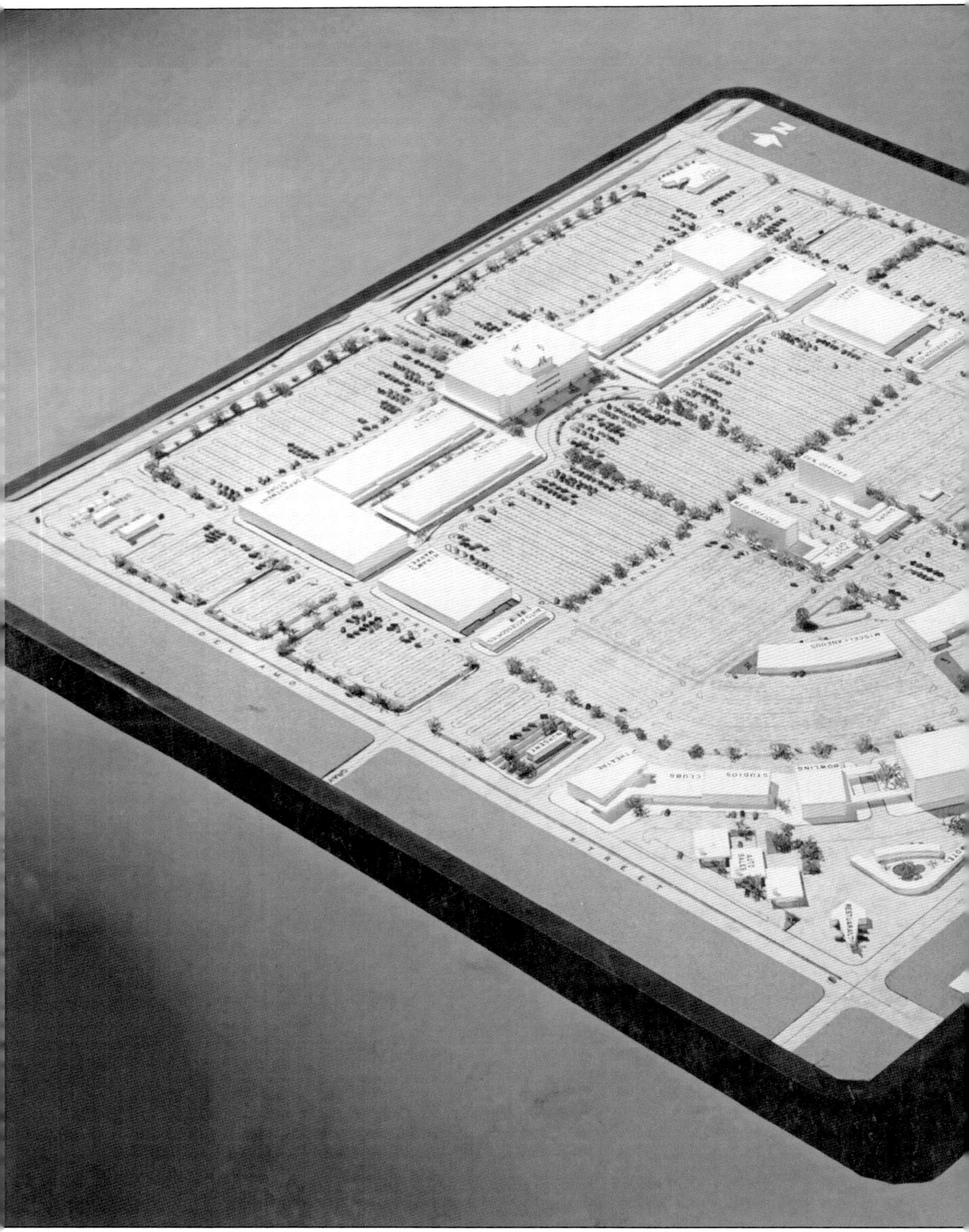
DEL AMO
STREET
THEATRE
CLUBS
STUDIOS
BOWLING
MISCELLANEOUS
AUTO SALES
RESTAURANT
NURSERY

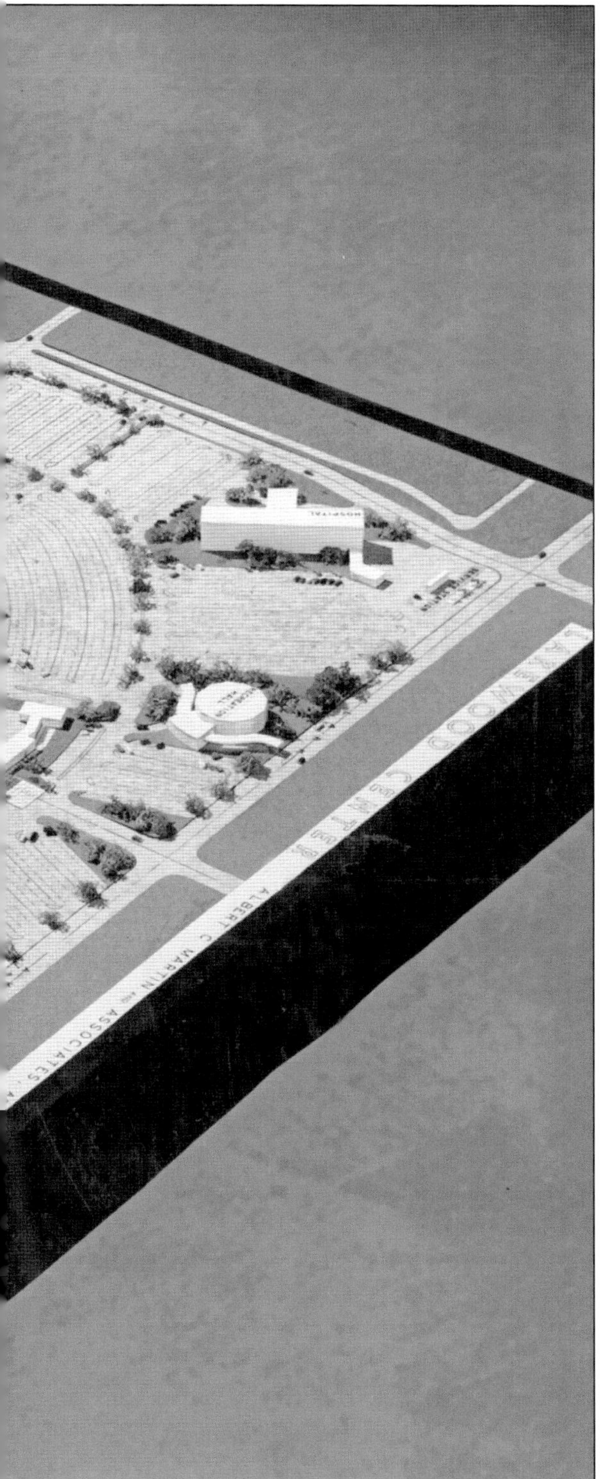

Imagining Lakewood Center. Lakewood Center might have looked like this architectural model had all the developers' plans been realized. Designed by the noted architectural firm of Albert C. Martin and Associates, the concept for Lakewood Center included the May Company department store as the mall's centerpiece, flanked by two wings of specialty shops. Hiram's Market is on the left of the model and Boys Market is on the right along with the Butler Brothers department store. Gas stations, a garden center, and Hody's Family Restaurant also were built during the center's early phases of development. Meeting and club rooms, and a recreation hall and community pool were planned but never built, although a post office and an office building were eventually constructed. The entire center was to be surrounded by more than 10,000 parking spaces, making Lakewood Center one of the first fully auto-centered shopping districts in the nation.

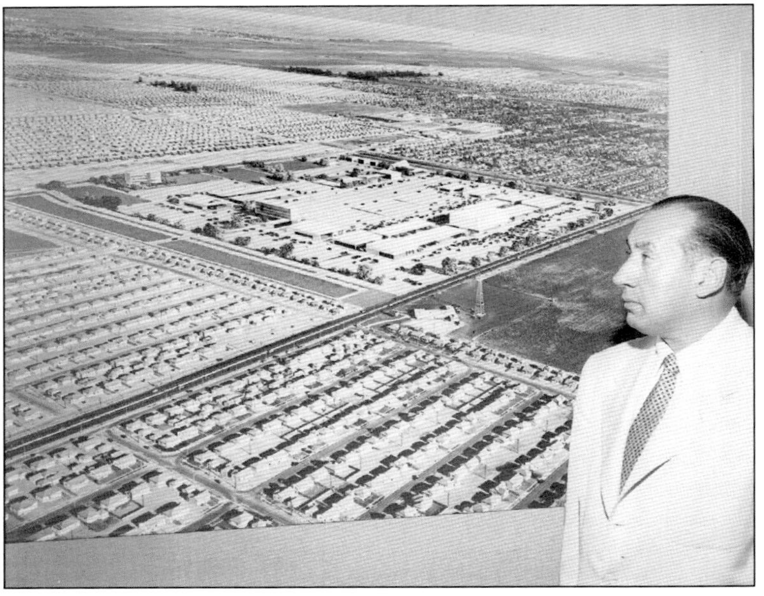

A DOWNTOWN FOR LAKEWOOD. Joe Eichenbaum, mall manager in 1950, stands before a photograph mural inset with Lakewood Center's initial concept. The developers of Lakewood made Lakewood Center the new community's "downtown," a novel idea in 1950.

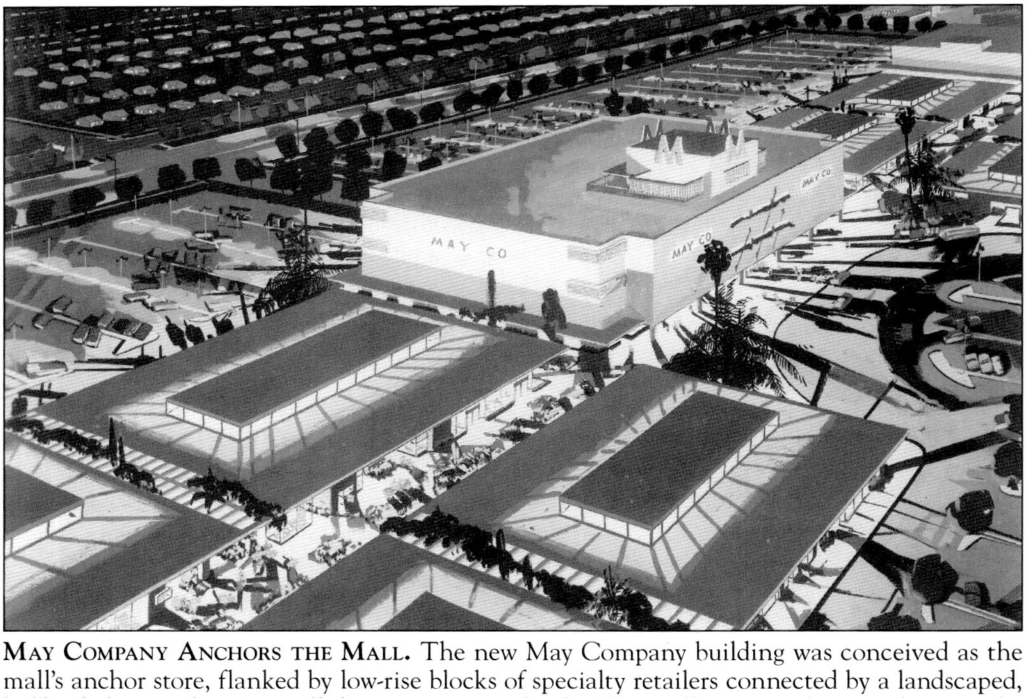

MAY COMPANY ANCHORS THE MALL. The new May Company building was conceived as the mall's anchor store, flanked by low-rise blocks of specialty retailers connected by a landscaped, half-mile-long pedestrian mall that was open to the sky. The mall's master plan was drawn up by Albert C. Martin and Associates.

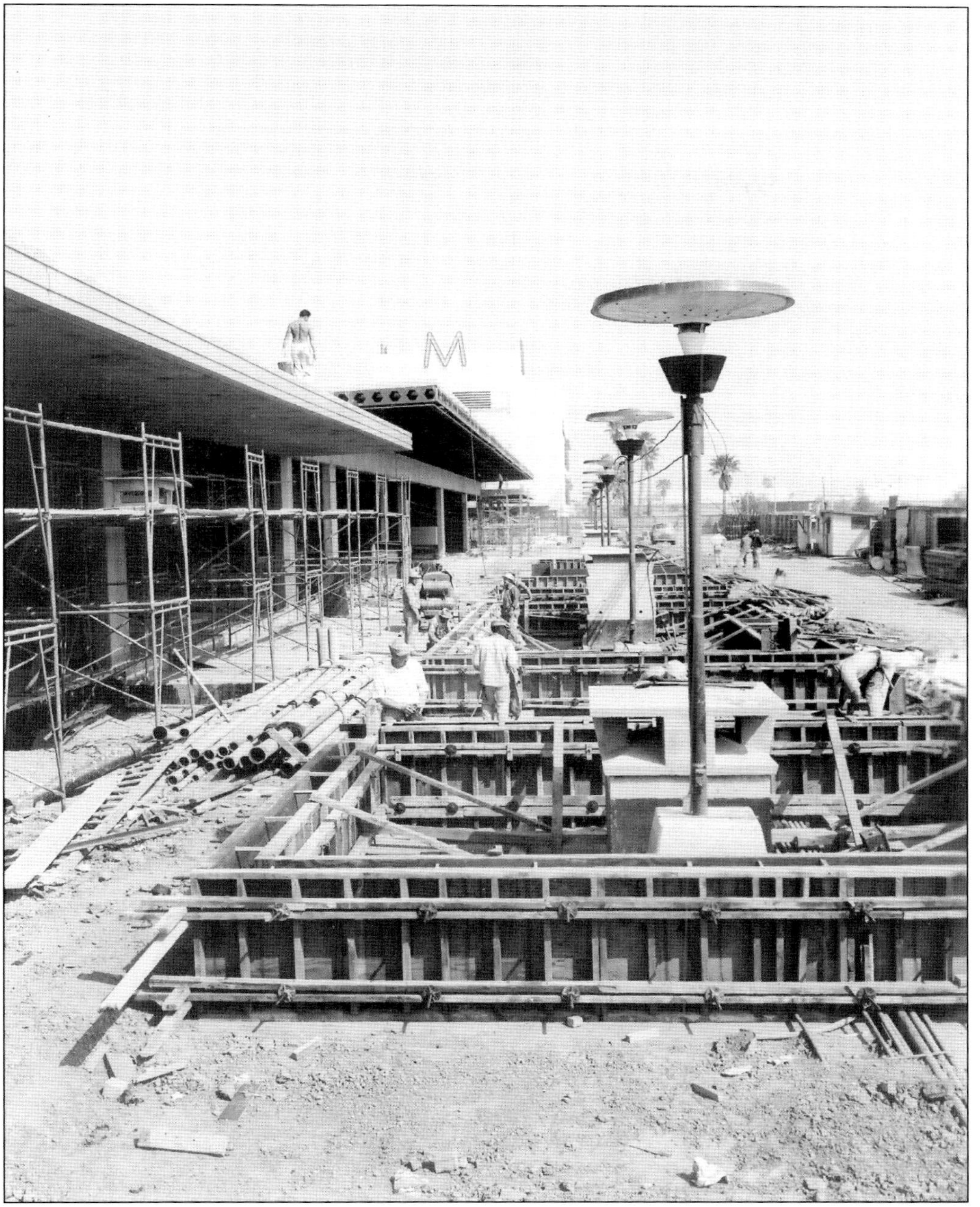

Lakewood Center Takes Shape, 1951. Surveys showed that nearly 25 percent of prospective consumers in Los Angeles County were located within a 30-minute driving radius from Lakewood. As the West's largest shopping center, promoted as "the 154-acre 'shopping heart' of Lakewood" (260 acres if the parking lot acreage was included), Lakewood Center was a city in itself, or, as Joe Eichenbaum called it, a "shopping city." Although Lakewood Center was planned with the automobile in mind, it was specifically designed to cater to pedestrian shoppers. The mall through Lakewood Center was built in phases. The unit north of the May Company opened in 1951. The second unit opened in November 1952.

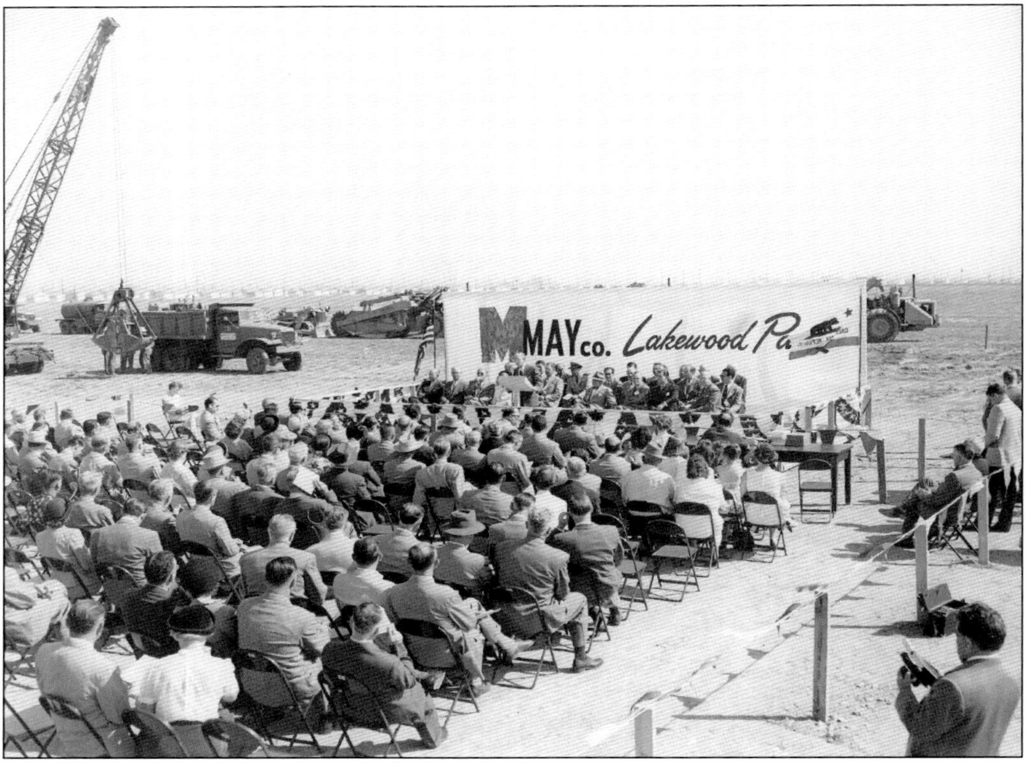

345,000-Square-Foot May Company Store. Ground broke for the May Company on October 14, 1950, shown above, and the partially completed Lakewood Center officially opened on February 18, 1952, with the grand opening of the May Company department store. The May Company's agreement to build a massive new store, seen below, was the key to the future development of Lakewood Center. The agreement allowed Lakewood's developers to secure more than $8 million in financing from the Prudential Insurance Company. The Lakewood May Company was the largest suburban department store in the country at 345,000 square feet.

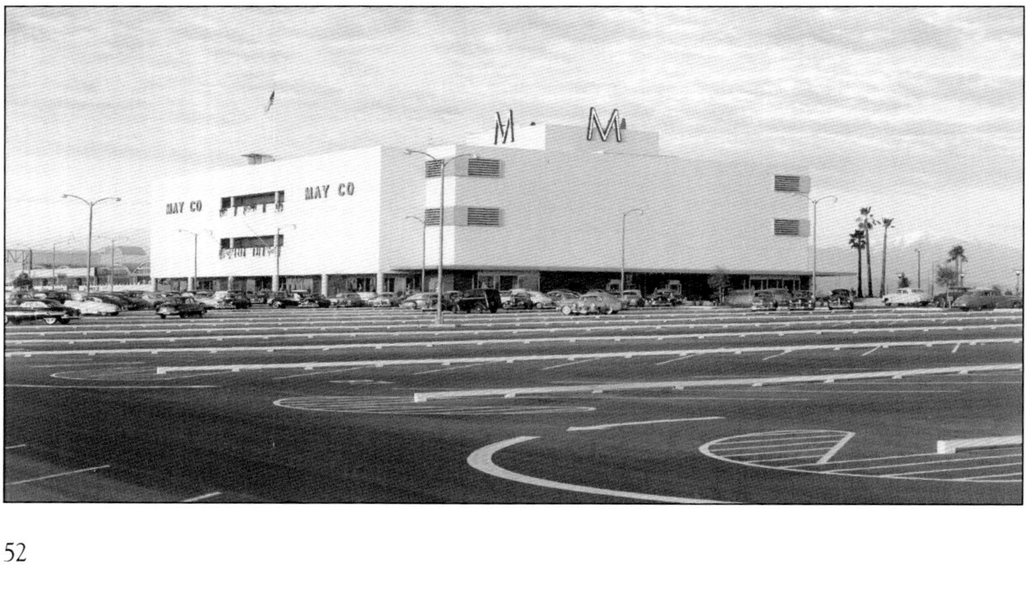

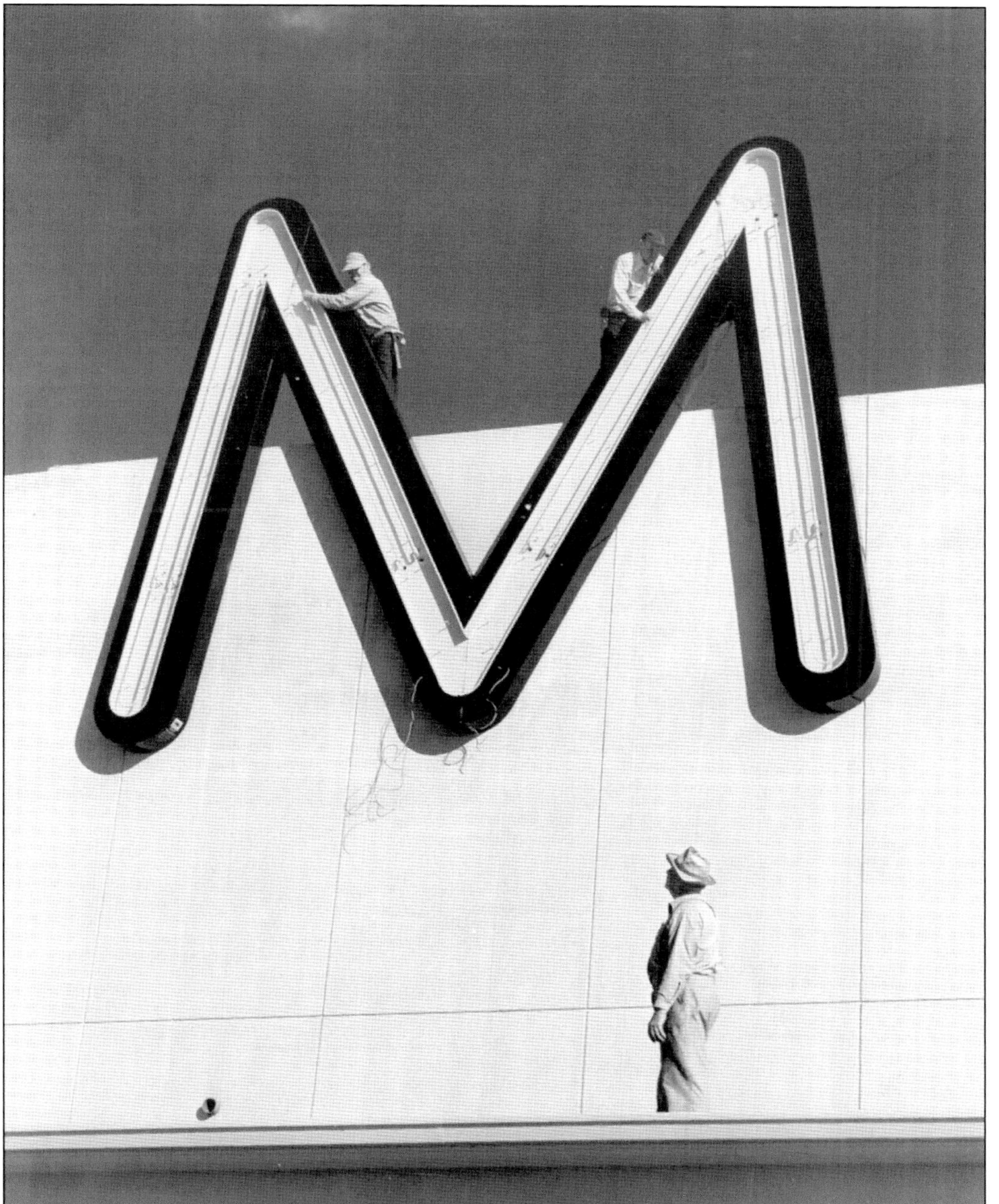

The Big Ms Go Up, 1952. The May Company store was a white, windowless, rectangular concrete box built in the International Style and topped with four giant Ms, each 16 feet high and brilliantly lit at night with bright yellow neon tubes. Each M faced one of the cardinal directions. They could be seen for miles above the roofs of Lakewood, until the trees along the city's streets grew above the rows of rooftops. "I remember that when we would go to San Pedro to visit the relatives, we could see the big Ms for miles around," remembered Linda Kay Gahan. "That was really a big thing, because you could say, 'Well, I live near the big M for May Company.' It was very, very impressive."

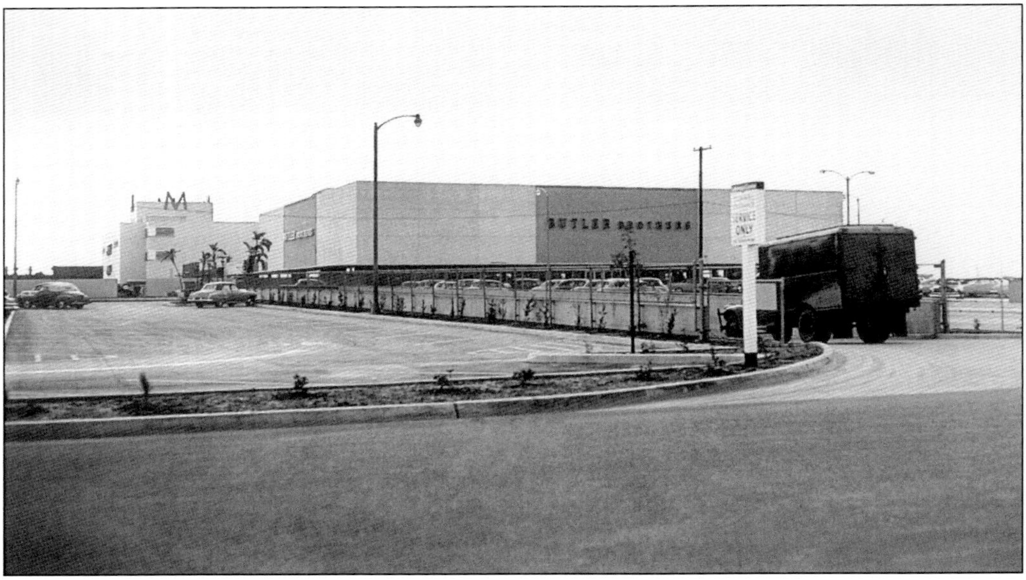

Tunnel Under the Mall. Lakewood Center also featured a delivery-truck tunnel. The half-mile long tunnel allowed trucks to make deliveries directly to the center's basement area, freeing ground floors for sales and displays and separating truck traffic from automobile traffic. The delivery tunnel, with its three-foot-thick concrete walls reinforced with 805 tons of steel, was designated a Civil Defense fallout shelter capable of holding 6,000 people in the event of a nuclear attack. Lakewood's residents also prepared for an atomic attack in civil defense training courses in which mothers would learn how to protect their children.

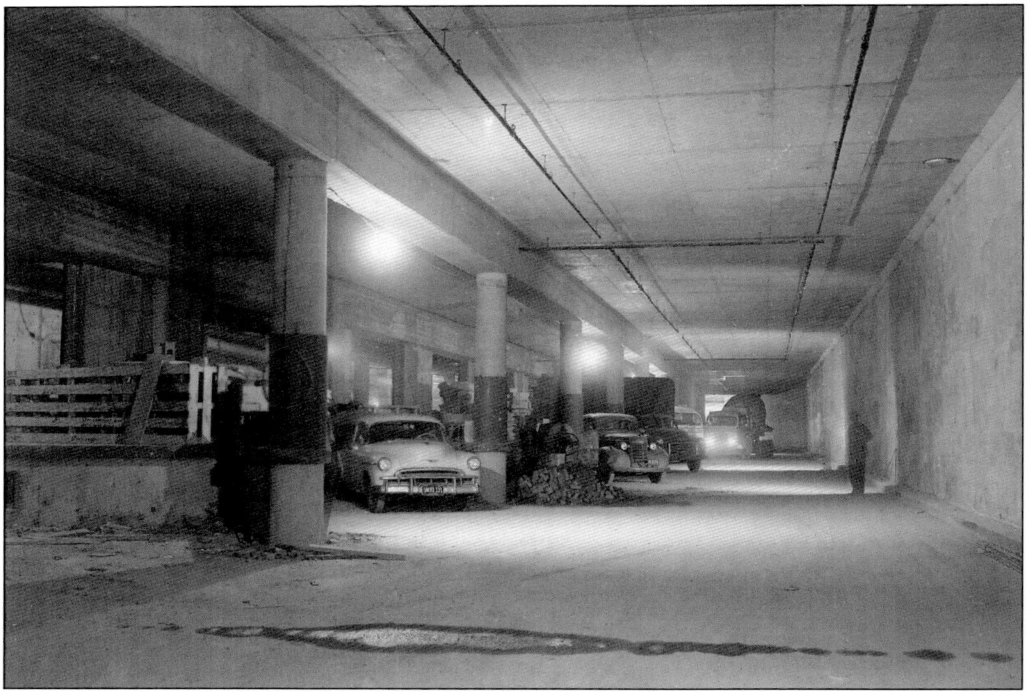

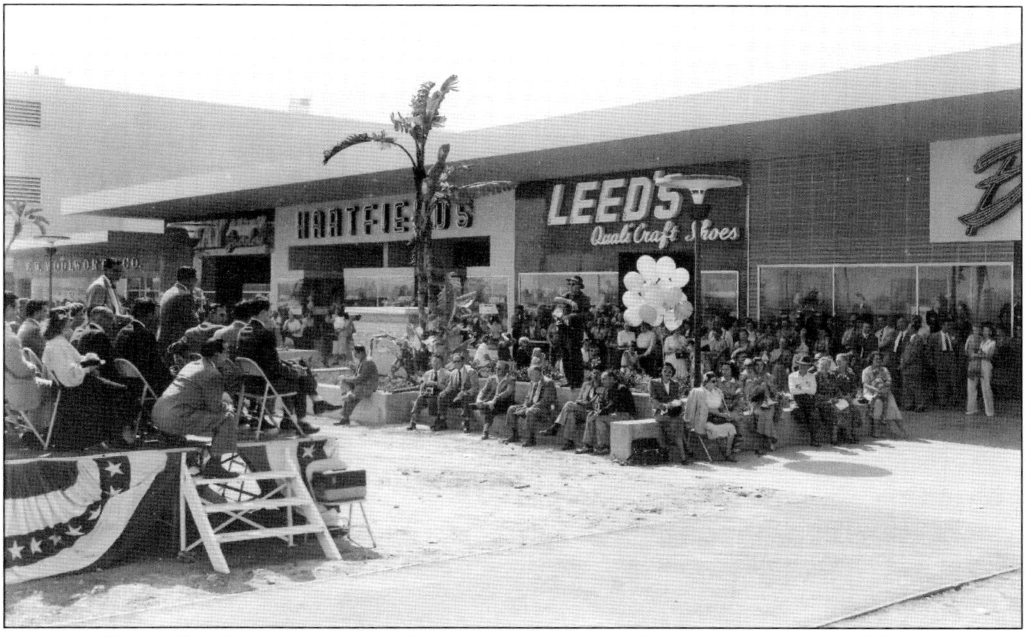

OPENING DAY. The first unit of specialty stores between Butler Brothers and the May Company opened on October 3, 1952. Shoppers thronged the 17 new stores that included Bond Clothes, Lee's Department Store, Leed's shoes, Heartfields Jewelers, a Woolworth's, Sav-On Drugs, and Kay Jewelers.

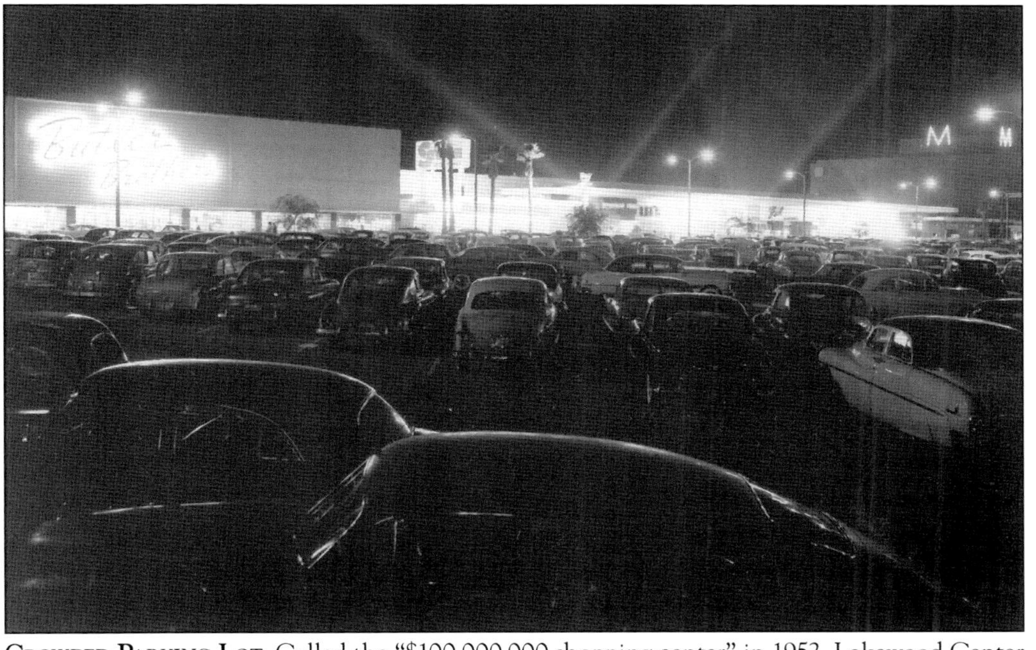

CROWDED PARKING LOT. Called the "$100,000,000 shopping center" in 1952, Lakewood Center was busy day and night. The center's parking lots were originally laid out with 7,632 nine-foot-wide parking spaces and with enough unpaved area to permit the parking of up to 10,000 cars. On some busy evenings before the holidays in 1952, nearly all the center's parking spaces were filled.

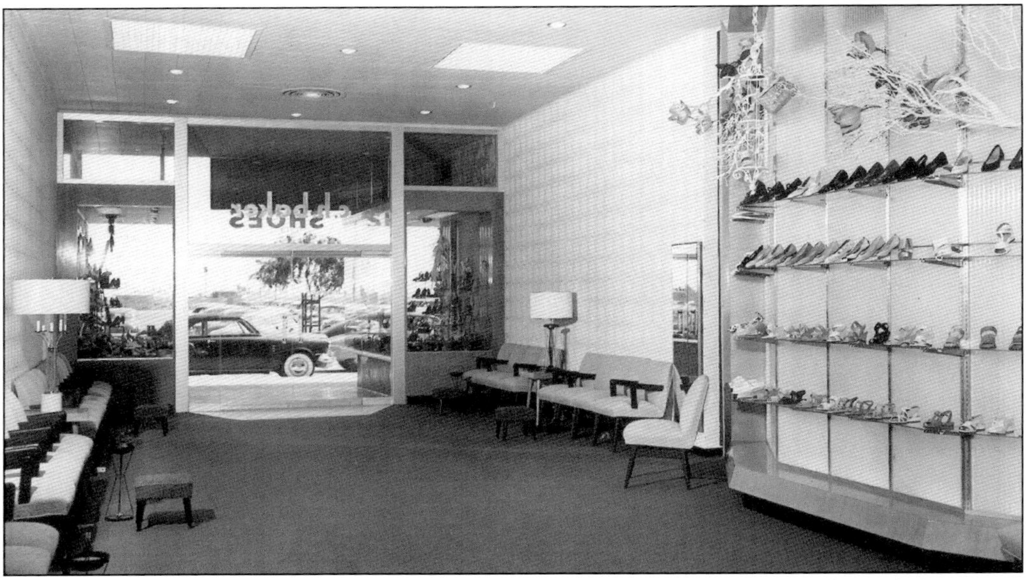

Chain Stores Make the Mall. C. H. Baker shoes, above, and Comars shoes, below, were among the new shops that lined the mall in 1951 and 1952. Stylish in their appointments, the shoe stores were also a mark of Lakewood Center's success. National chains were initially reluctant to open a new store so far from the traditional downtown streets. Lakewood Center's instant popularity help change the face of retailing throughout California and the West. (Both, courtesy of Rothschild Photo.)

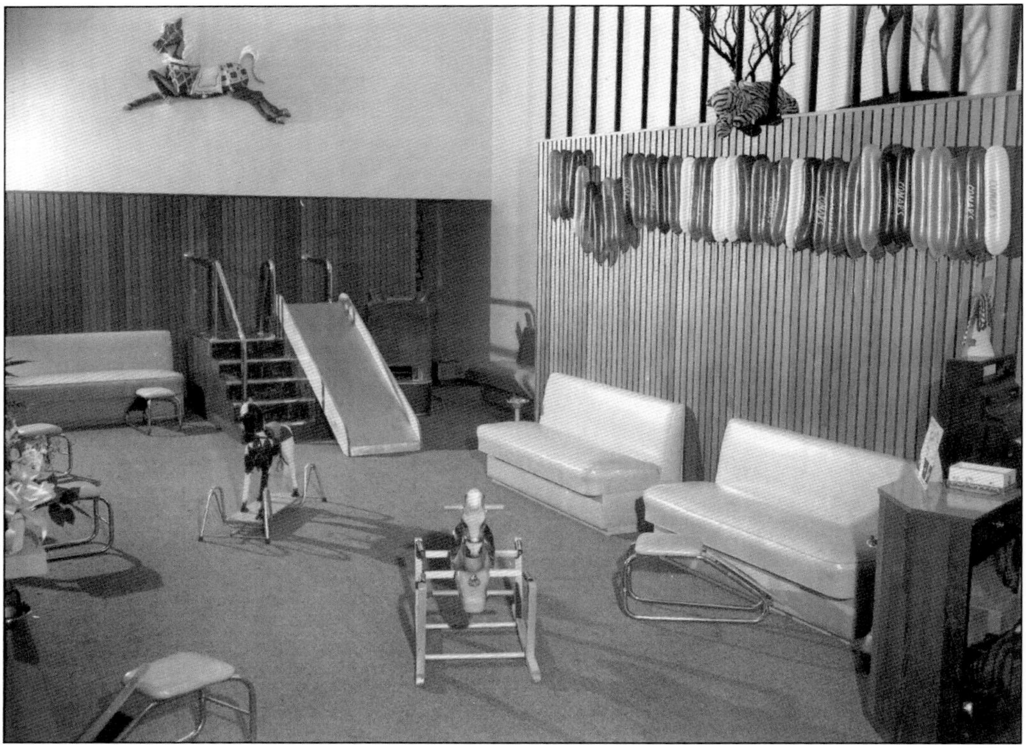

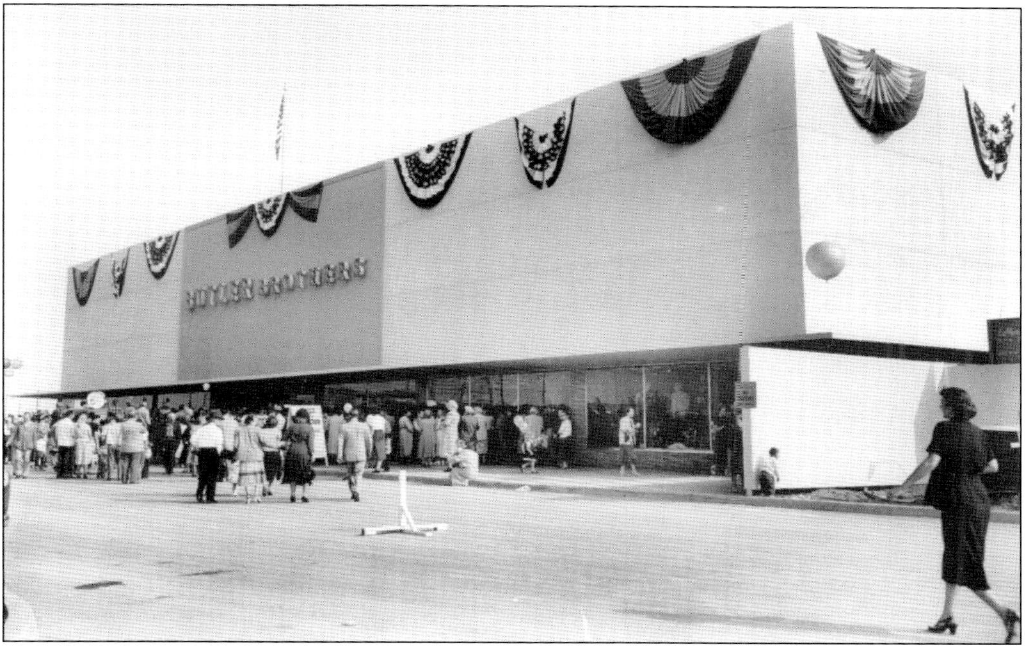

Lakewood Center's First. The first store to open in the shopping center was Butler Brothers department store, shown above, in October 1951. That same month, Hiram's Supermarket, seen below, a car wash, and an 18-pump service station opened, followed by an Armstrong Garden Center. By the end of the 1950s, two smaller department stores anchored the north and south ends of the mall, with the May Company in the center. The two junior department stores were Butler Brothers and W.T. Grant.

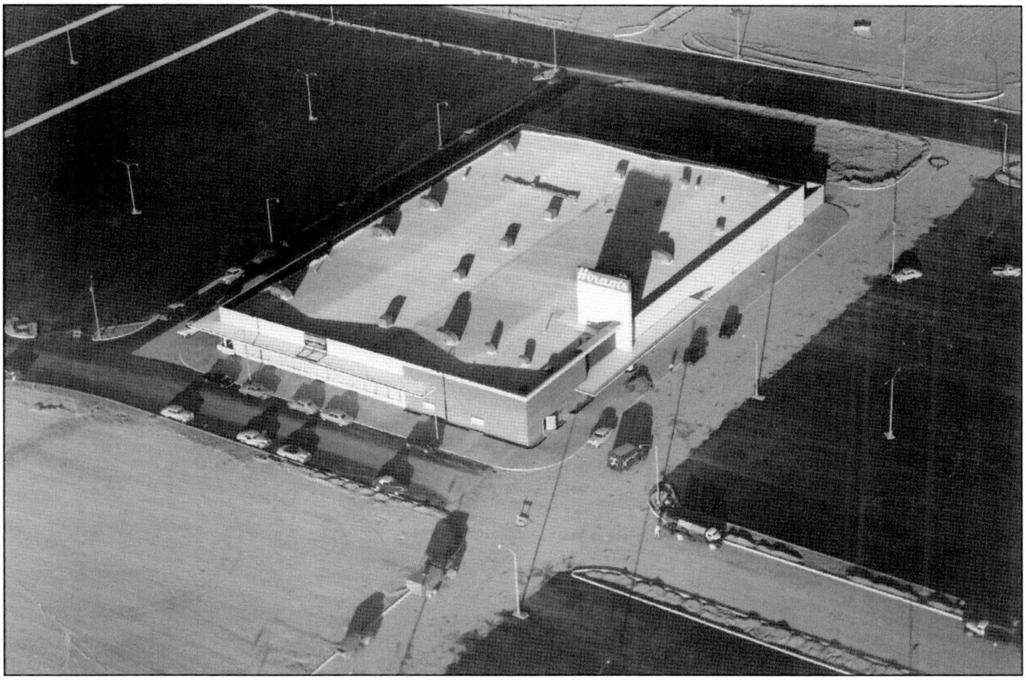

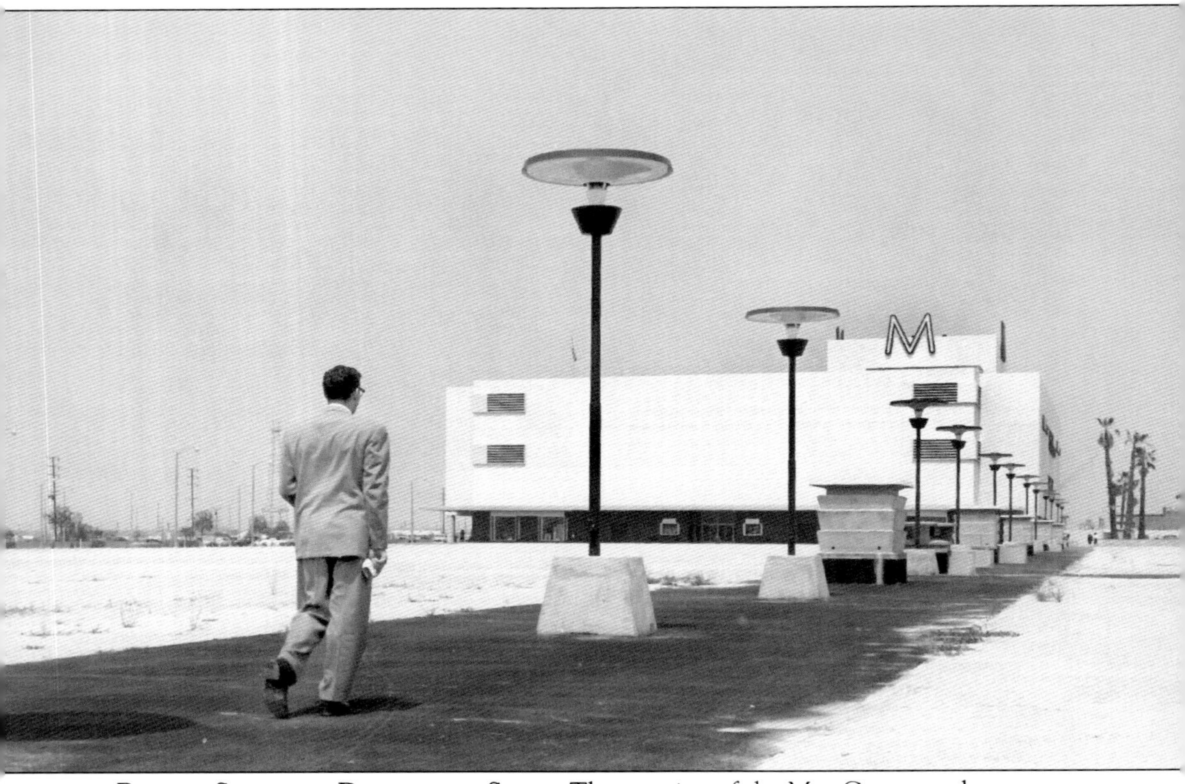

Biggest Suburban Department Store. The opening of the May Company department store on February 18, 1952, filled every available parking space in Lakewood Center's vast lot, with a record-breaking 200,000 customers crowding into the store during its first days. The four-level store featured a tearoom, a hospital with nurses on duty at all times (and a physician at certain hours), and an auditorium available to Lakewood organizations for meetings. Each retail department was decorated in its own color scheme to complement the merchandise. Among its departments was the Youth Center, "the West's largest youth department" and "the largest of its kind in a suburban area, planned deliberately on the basis of the vast number of children in this family community." Perhaps too futuristic was a traffic control tower on the building's roof so that a spotter could direct cars to empty parking spaces through a system of colored lights. The system was not a success.

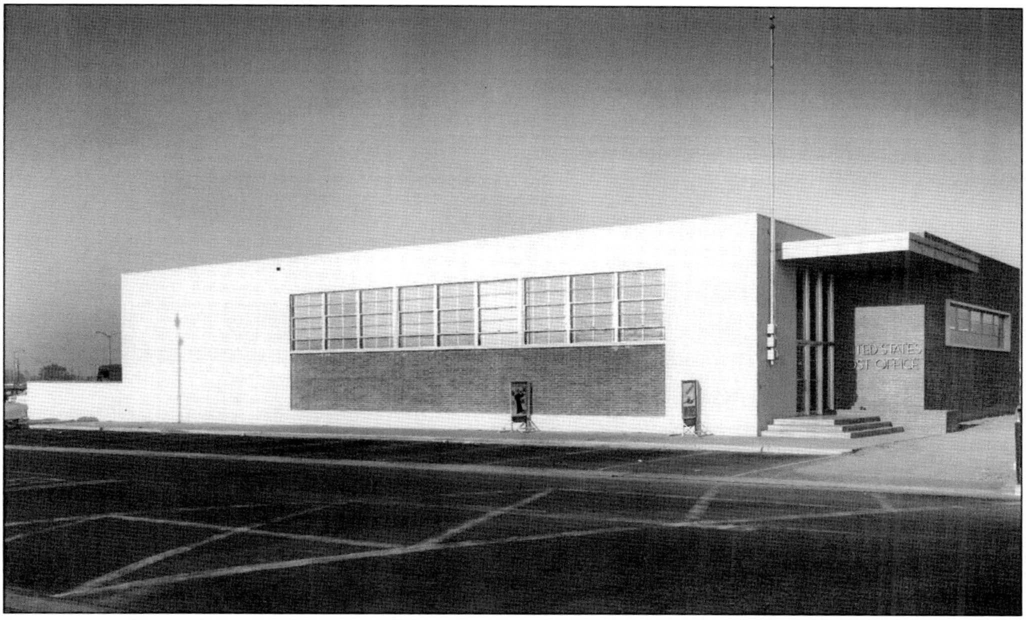

LAKEWOOD POST OFFICE. Lakewood Center was planned as a complete "shopping city" with services not normally found in other retail centers in 1950. Among the first was the Lakewood Post Office, originally located on the center's eastern edge. The post office moved to the Lakewood Civic Center on Clark Avenue in 1964.

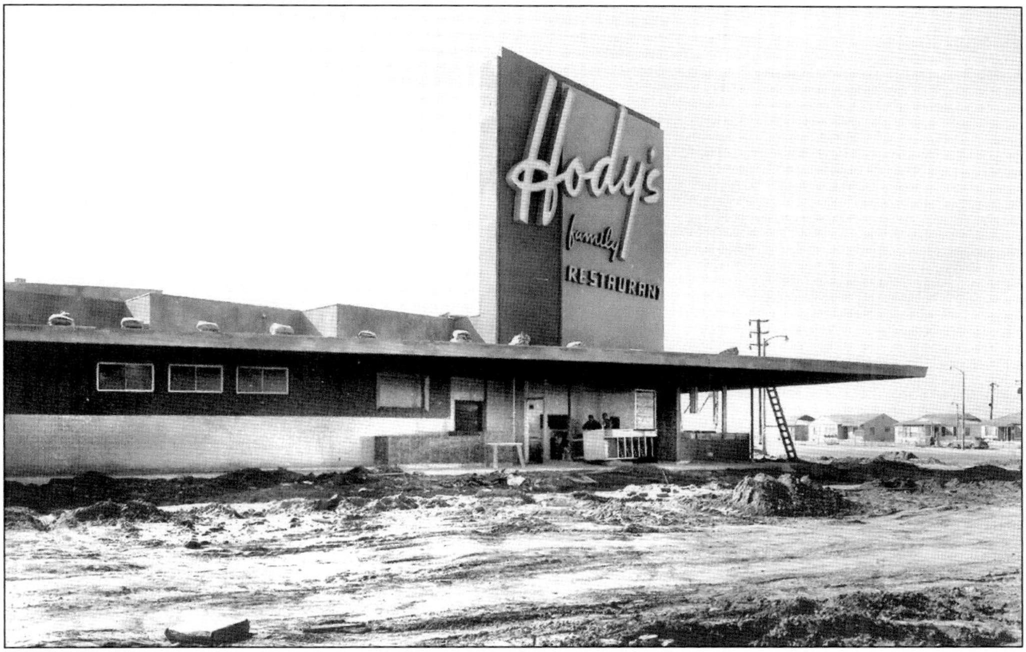

HODY'S FAMILY RESTAURANT. The Hody's chain of coffee shops was one of the first to come to Lakewood Center in 1951. Popular among casual diners—Hody's in Lakewood even had carhop service—the restaurant was designed by Wayne McAllister, famous today for the restaurants he designed in the mid-1950s in the Googie style of swooping roofs and towering signs.

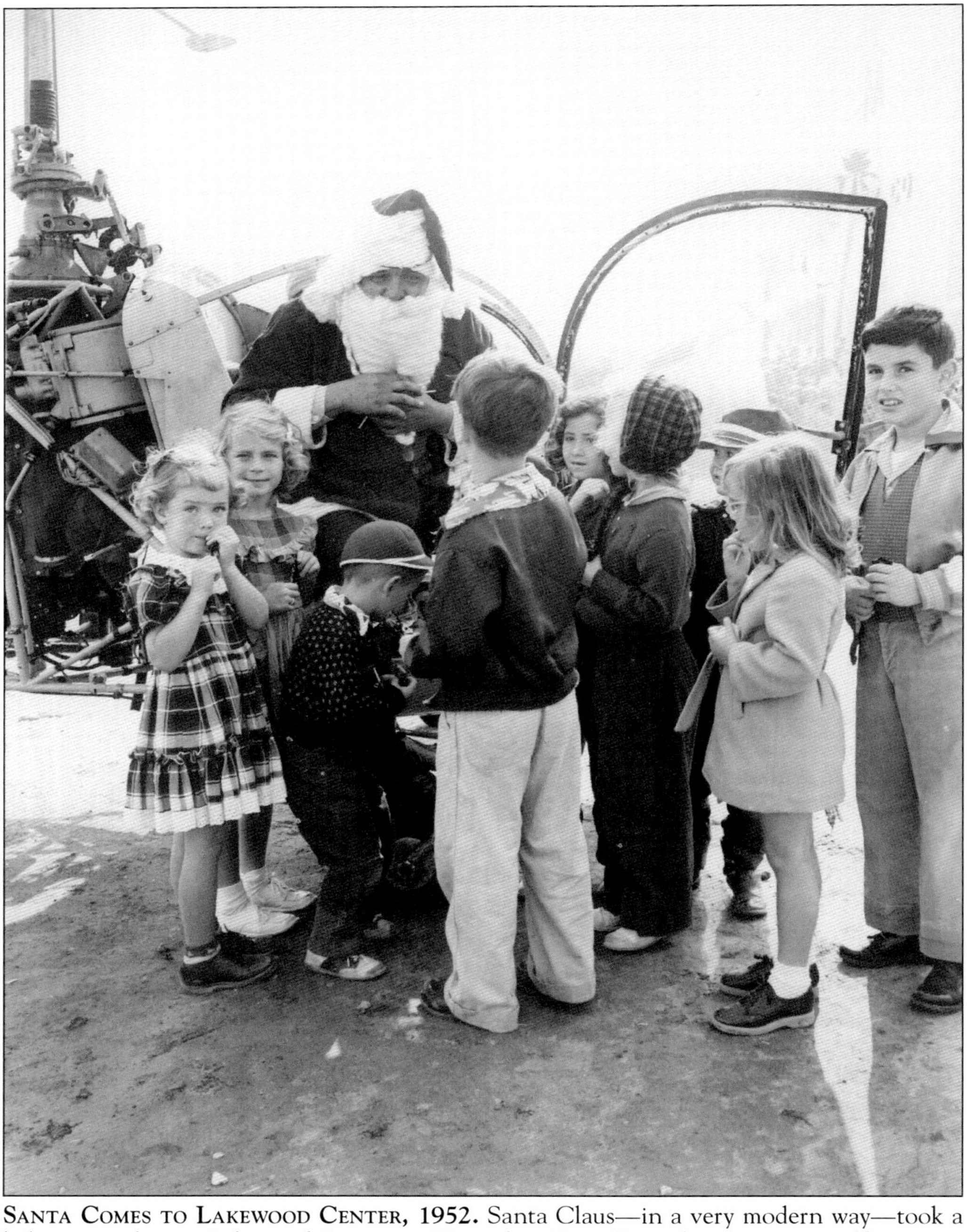

SANTA COMES TO LAKEWOOD CENTER, 1952. Santa Claus—in a very modern way—took a helicopter ride into Lakewood Center on November 28, 1952, to the amazement of his young admirers. The Lakewood Center Businessmen's Association sponsored many community events apart from a visit from a flying Santa, including Easter egg hunts in the fields west of Lakewood Boulevard, Dollar Days (on which another helicopter dropped empty pie plates redeemable at Boys or Hiram's markets for a frozen fruit pie), Mother's Day gift drawings, Halloween carnivals featuring television celebrities, and nighttime teen dances for which the association donated records as prizes. More than a shopping center, the mall was Lakewood's community center.

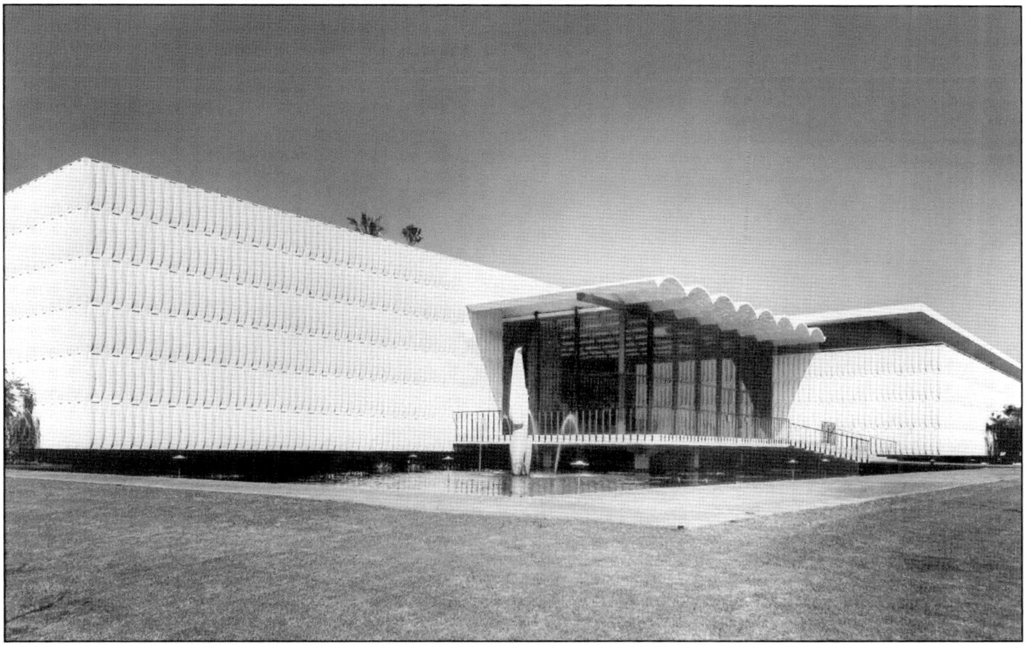

CHANGE COMES TO LAKEWOOD CENTER. Lakewood Center evolved through the 1950s and into the 1960s, adding many new stores, services, and even becoming, for a time, the international headquarters of the Purex Corporation, shown above. The company's starkly modern building was located opposite the Lakewood Sheriff's Station. Bullock's Lakewood, below, stood alone on Clark Avenue opposite Lakewood City Hall until the Bullock's stores closed following a merger. A medical office building, a bowling alley, a meat market, and bank branch offices also came and went as retail trends evolved.

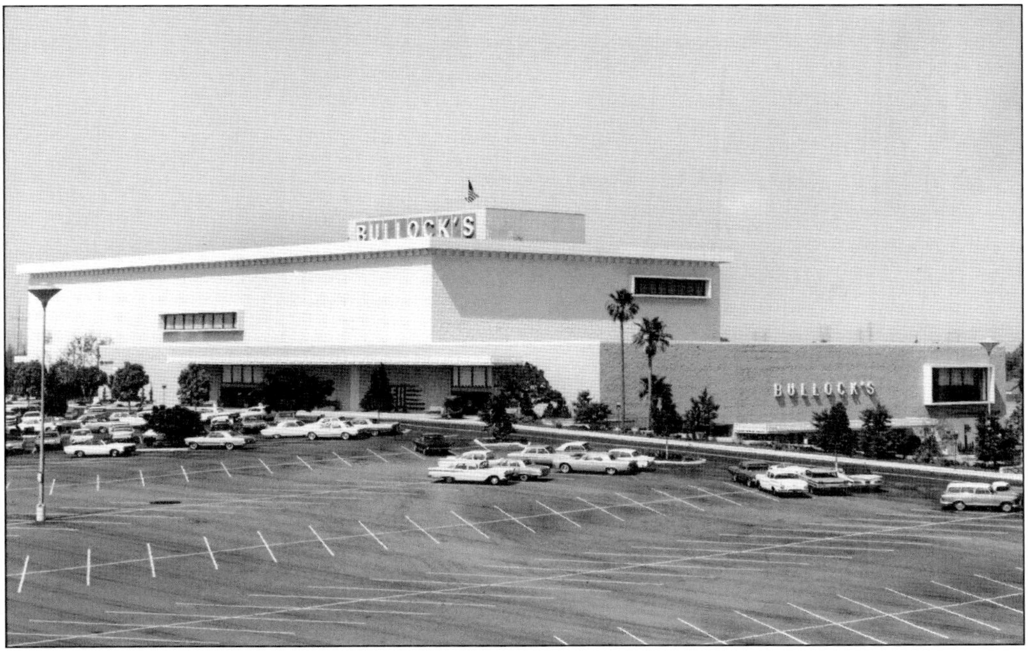

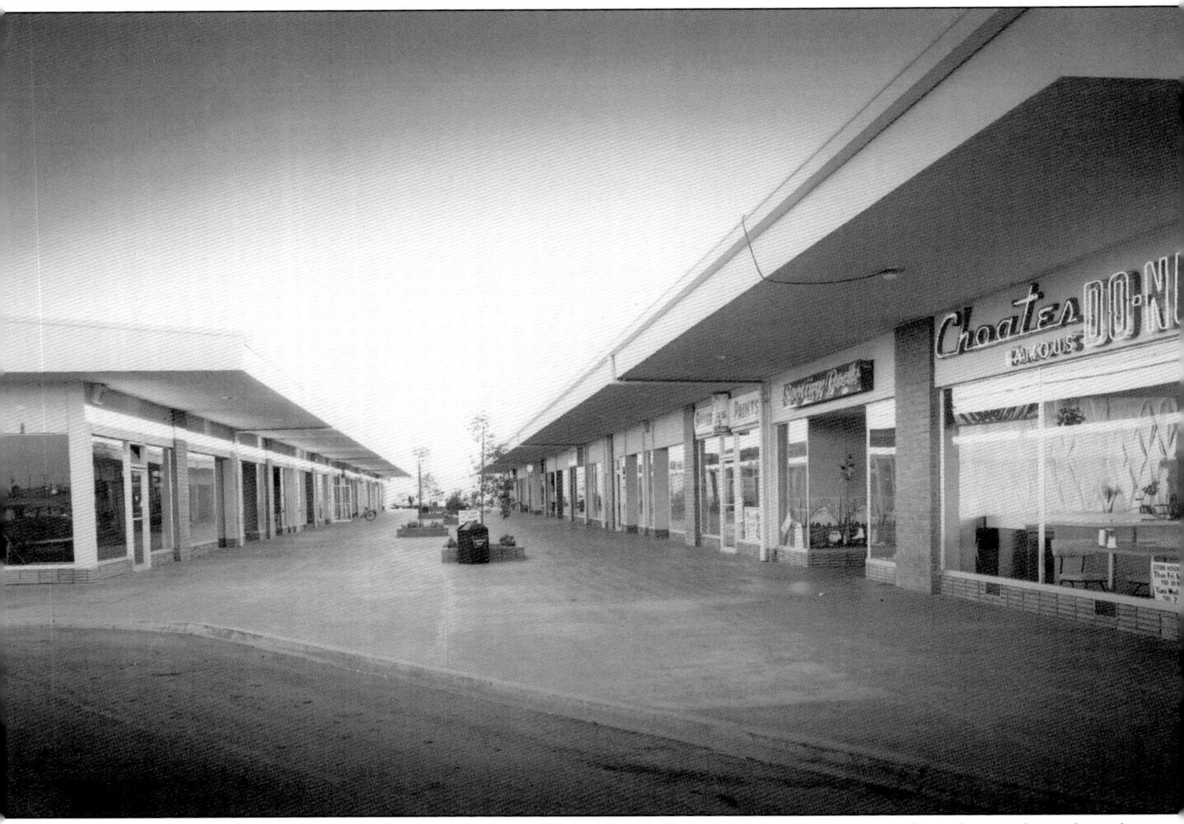

Faculty Shops at Lakewood Center. By 1954, Lakewood Center was so big that a free shuttle transported shoppers between the mall and the Faculty Shops, a two-block-long row of specialty shops across the center's vast parking lot. The Faculty Shops were aimed at local businesses and smaller chain retailers. Among the 36 new stores were an Orange Julius lunch stand, Taylor's Quality Meats, Ranger's Chow Mein to Take Out, Choate's Famous Do-Nuts, Jacqman Paints and Wallpaper, Lakewood Center Stationers, Sav-On Family Shoes, Lakewood Center Tastee Freeze, and De Cannis Hair Styling. The Faculty Shops were eventually demolished to enable the building of the new Bullock's department store. In 1993, Bullock's closed after 29 years in Lakewood Center. The building was demolished in 1995 to make way for a Home Depot and Lucky's supermarket.

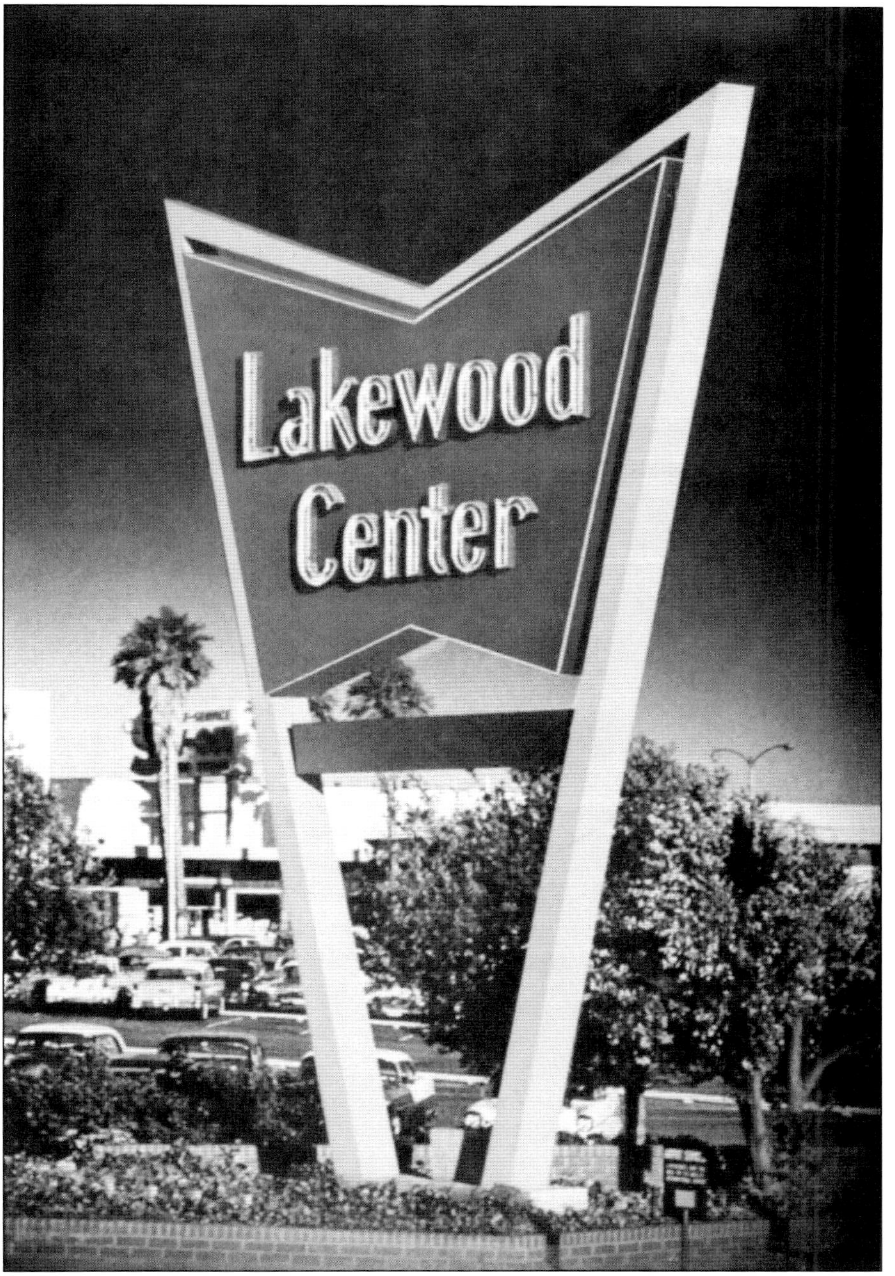

LAKEWOOD CENTER AND LAKEWOOD. Lakewood Center's development really took off between 1964 and 1965, when Buffums, Bullock's, and Desmond's department stores opened, followed by JC Penney's opening in 1967 to anchor the southern wing of the mall. Also that year, Lakewood Center became one of the first shopping centers in the nation to feature motion-picture entertainment with the opening of the Lakewood Center Theatre, a 1,200-seat Cinerama theater. Montgomery Ward opened in 1975. In the years that followed, Lakewood Center evolved into its current incarnation as a superregional shopping center with more than two million square feet of leasable space and a busy and popular restaurant row.

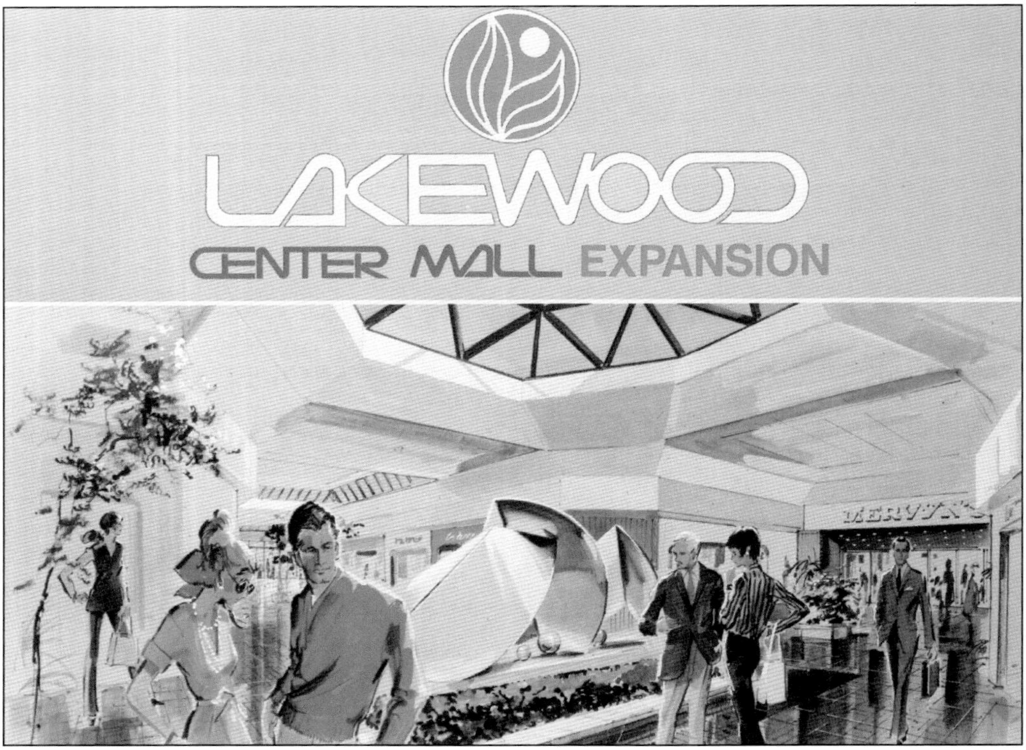

LAKEWOOD CENTER EXPANDS WITH MALL ENCLOSURE. The biggest change for Lakewood Center came in 1975, when the Macerich Company bought and announced plans to enclose the open-air mall, shown above. Two years later, Lakewood Center was enclosed, as seen below, reopening in 1978 with a completely new look—bright skylights, parquet flooring, and colorful sculptures. During the 1980s, the mall expanded several times, including the addition of a center wing of stores in 1983 and an $8 million facelift for the May Company building in 1988.

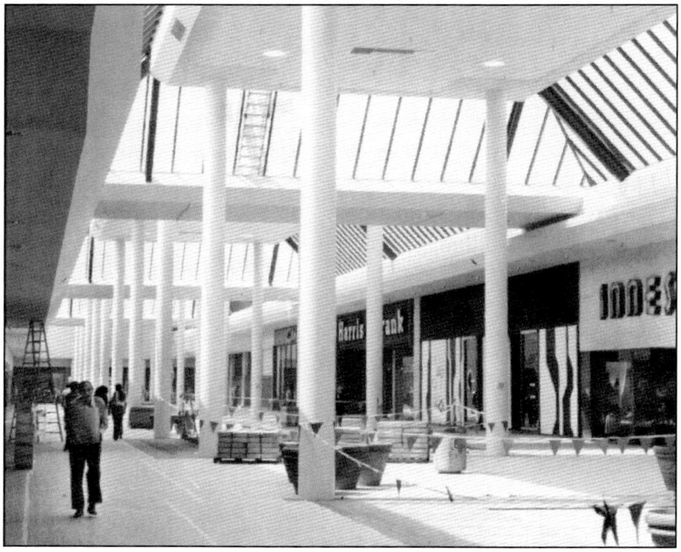

Four

New City Born

Lakewood residents in the years between 1950 and 1954 spent most of their energies making new homes, caring for toddlers and school-age children, supporting the clubs and associations that gave them a sense of community, and sharing their experiences of Lakewood with their new neighbors. Not many of them gave much thought to local politics.

Some did, however, including the members of the Lakewood Taxpayers Association. Among them was a young, energetic lawyer named John Sanford Todd. A World War II veteran with his own young family, Todd was active in advocating for the interests of other Lakewood-area homeowners. He grew familiar with the workings of the Los Angeles County Board of Supervisors that oversaw the county-provided services in unincorporated Lakewood. He knew that his neighbors had concerns about hog farms, open drainage ditches, law enforcement, and recreation programs for youth.

As Lakewood grew, so did those concerns. Todd and others discussed what they could do to aid their new community. The consensus of opinion was conservative—improvements were needed in many areas of Lakewood, but the community's overall situation was just fine.

That changed in 1953 when city officials in Long Beach began a campaign to annex Lakewood neighborhoods piece by piece. Under the so-called Wentz plan, Lakewood was destined to become a district within Long Beach. Todd and those who shared his views about local control disagreed.

Annexation in 1953 was mostly stalled by the delaying tactics Todd advocated, but the status quo was untenable. The threat of annexation remained. The alternative for Todd was incorporation. The movement to make Lakewood a city took fire with the support of the Lakewood Park Corporation and the Southern California Gas Company. Volunteers quickly gathered enough support to put incorporation on the March 1954 ballot.

By an overwhelming majority, Lakewood residents voted for incorporation. They would now determine themselves the kind of city they wanted Lakewood to become.

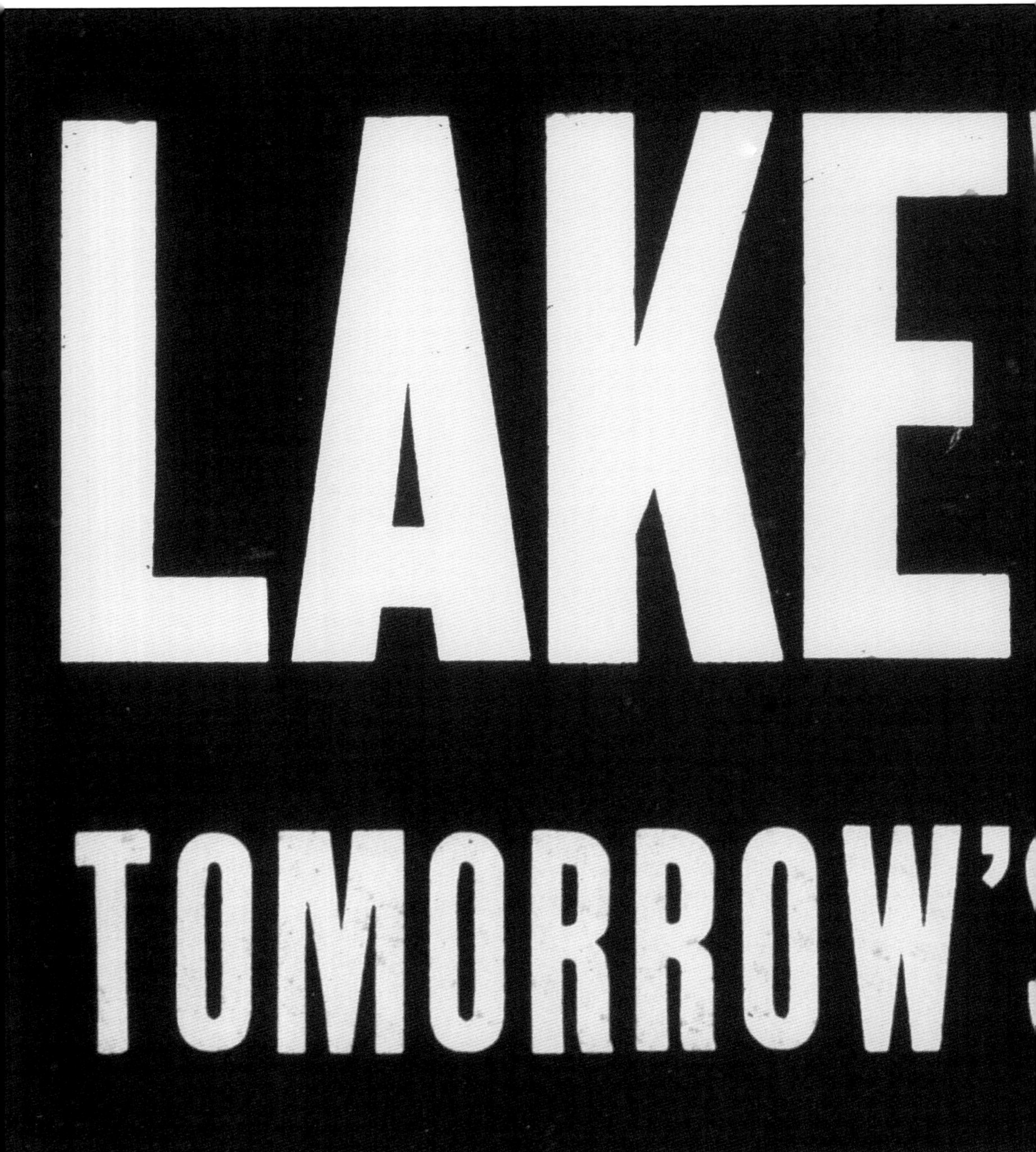

Tomorrow's City. By 1953, the 17,500 homes of Lakewood Park were nearing completion. Lakewood's developers were making Lakewood Center its busy "downtown" shopping district. Lakewood's schools, places of worship, and business offices met the needs of a young population that was nearing 100,000. Jobs at the nearby Douglas plant and at the shipyards and oil refineries of Long Beach and Wilmington employed tens of thousands of workers who called Lakewood home.

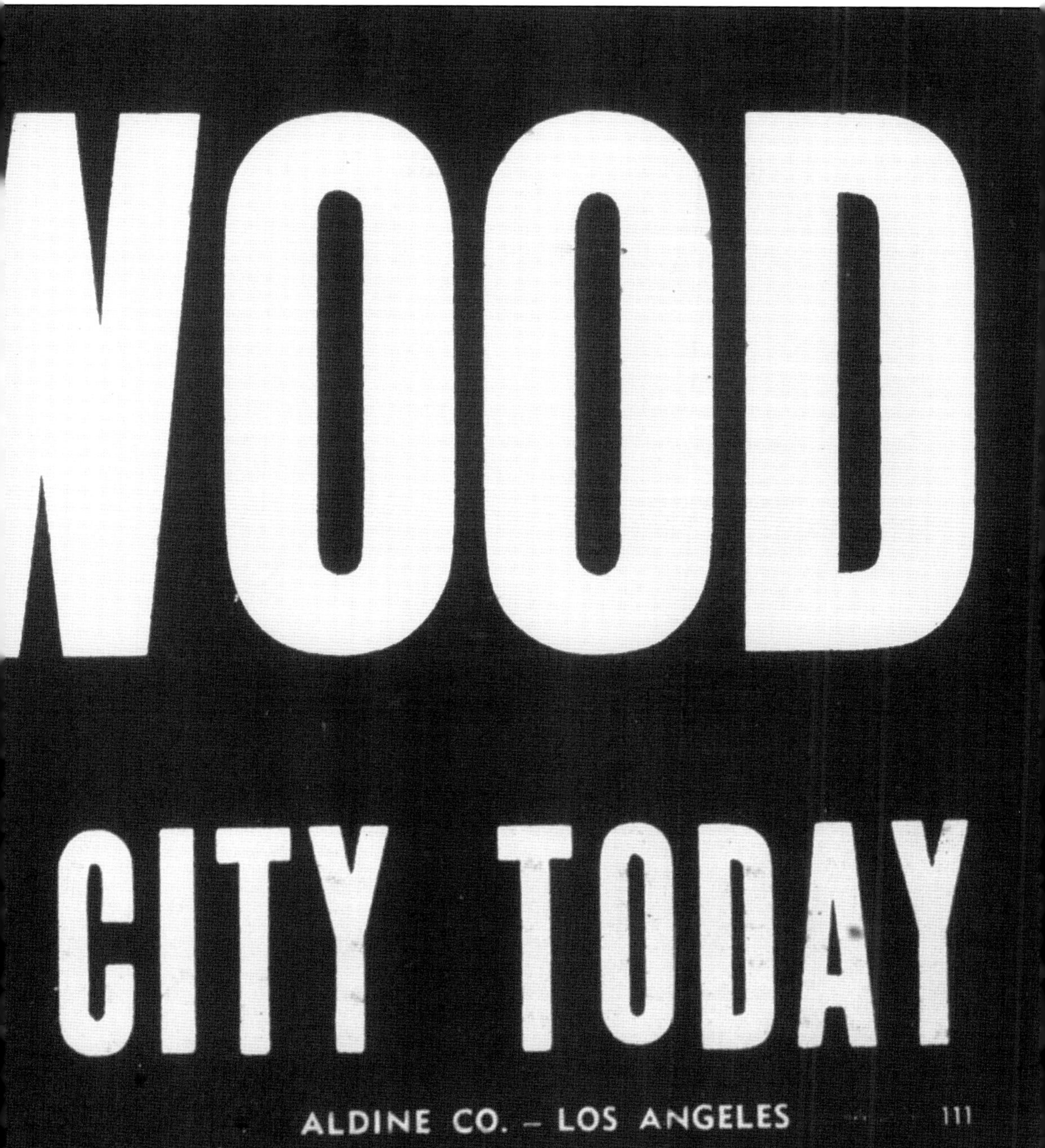

This was "Tomorrow's City." But was it? Lakewood may have been bigger than all but a dozen or so California cities, but Lakewood was, in fact, not a city at all. It was unincorporated territory governed not by an elected city council but by the Los Angeles County Board of Supervisors some 25 miles away.

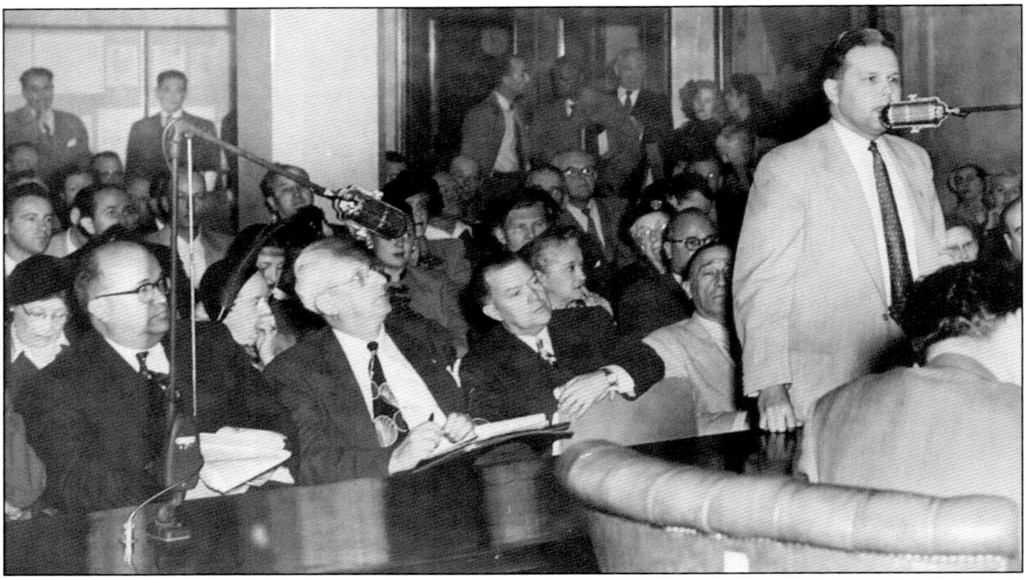

MAKING LAKEWOOD'S VOICE HEARD. John Sanford Todd, standing at the microphone, was one of the leaders of unincorporated Lakewood as a member of the Lakewood Taxpayers Association. In the early 1950s, Todd and other LTA members lobbied the county board of supervisors for the fencing of drainage ditches, for stop signs near schools, and for a zoning ordinance for Lakewood.

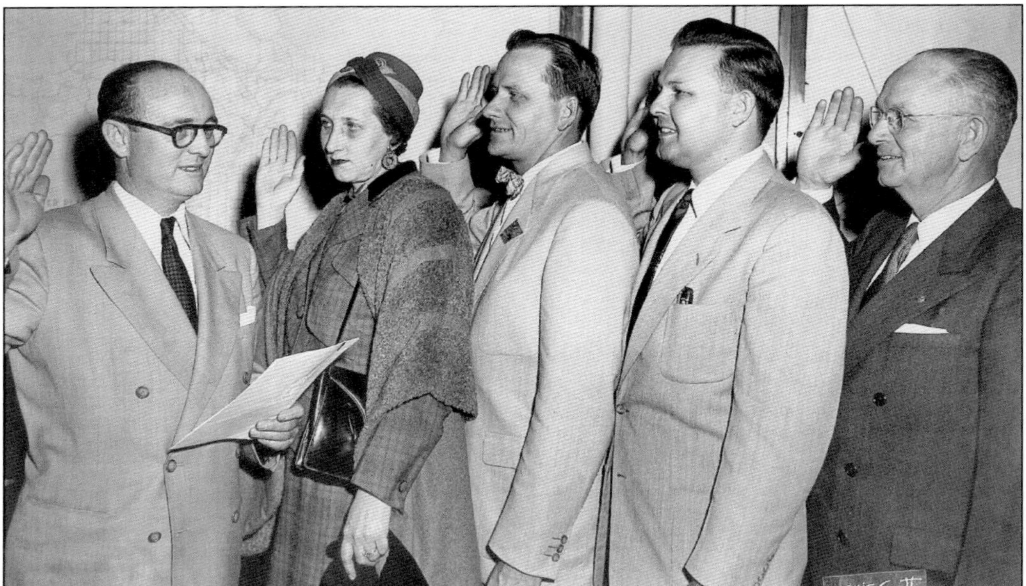

FIRST EXPERIENCE OF LOCAL GOVERNMENT. County officials warned the taxpayers association that the county's purchase of the Lakewood Park Corporation's undeveloped park sites was unlikely unless Lakewood residents established a self-financing park district. Lakewood residents voted overwhelmingly to establish the Lakewood Park, Recreation, and Parkway District in 1953. Being sworn in are board members, from left to right, Ruth Bach, Don Nelson, John Sanford Todd, and Charles Wright.

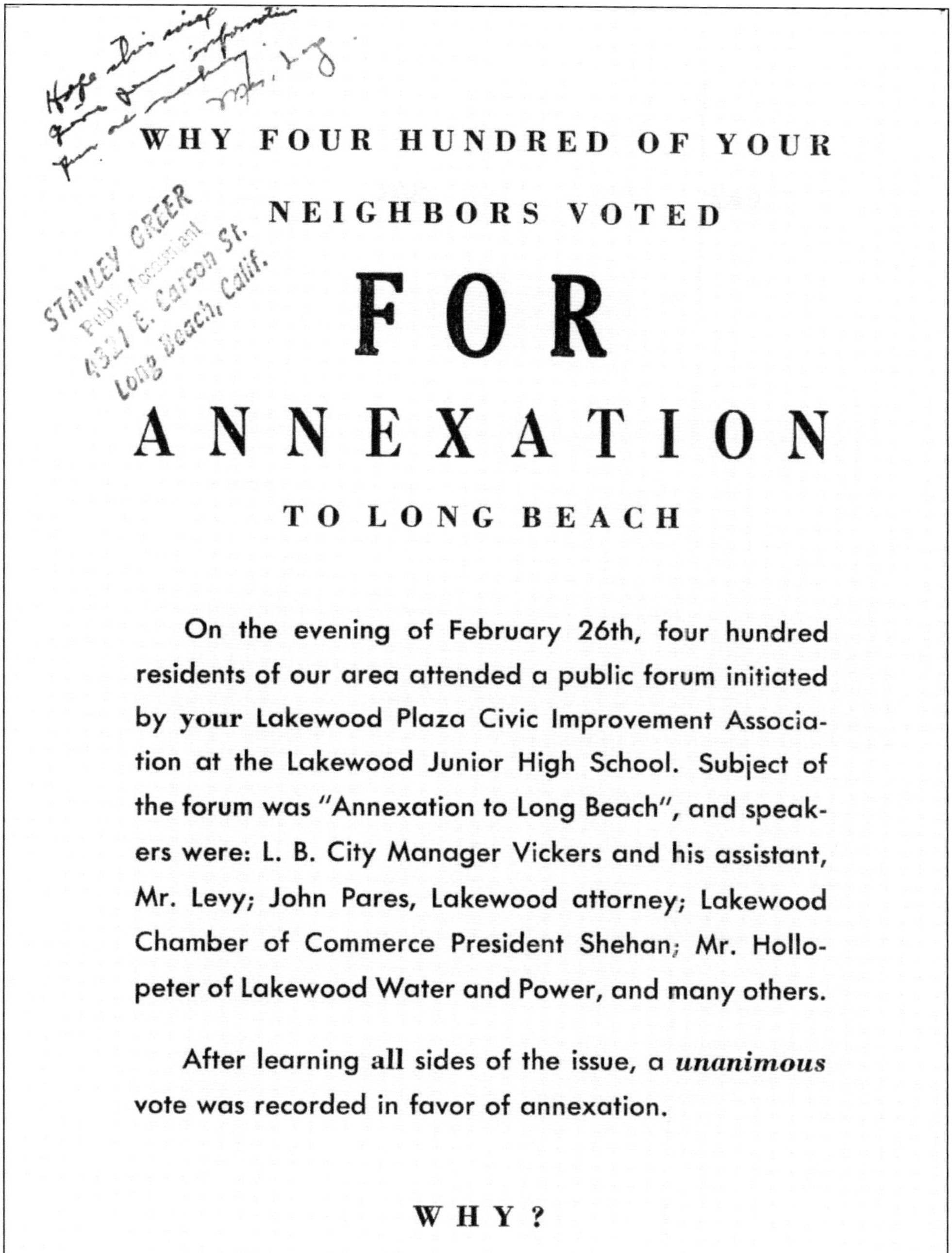

STANLEY GREER
Public Accountant
4321 E. Carson St.
Long Beach, Calif.

WHY FOUR HUNDRED OF YOUR NEIGHBORS VOTED

FOR ANNEXATION

TO LONG BEACH

On the evening of February 26th, four hundred residents of our area attended a public forum initiated by **your** Lakewood Plaza Civic Improvement Association at the Lakewood Junior High School. Subject of the forum was "Annexation to Long Beach", and speakers were: L. B. City Manager Vickers and his assistant, Mr. Levy; John Pares, Lakewood attorney; Lakewood Chamber of Commerce President Shehan; Mr. Hollopeter of Lakewood Water and Power, and many others.

After learning all sides of the issue, a ***unanimous*** vote was recorded in favor of annexation.

WHY?

ARGUMENTS FOR ANNEXATION. The Lakewood Plaza Citizens Improvement Association urged voters to choose annexation to Long Beach in 1953 with an appeal to their pocketbook. "Total savings by annexing to Long Beach would be $25.00 a year" compared to county taxes, the association's flyer predicted. Long Beach also had its oil wealth (from the city's tidelands oil fields) and the advantage of its excellent police and fire services. These arguments worked for the two Lakewood Plaza neighborhoods south of Heartwell Park. They voted to join Long Beach.

PIECEMEAL ANNEXATION: HOW THEY WORK IT

Long Beach is using an ancient technique-- "Divide and Conquer"-- in the drive to annex Lakewood.

Pro-Long Beach forces have rigged a series of separate annexation elections in various Lakewood districts. Their aim: To divide and confuse us, then to move in and knock off one district after another.

If they really had our best interests at heart they would have put the issue before all the people of Lakewood at one time with one election.

Give us one year by defeating annexation now! Let's unite Lakewood and solve the issue all together at one time at one election-- not 8 separate elections.

DON'T LET THEM PUT US BEHIND THE (8) BALL!

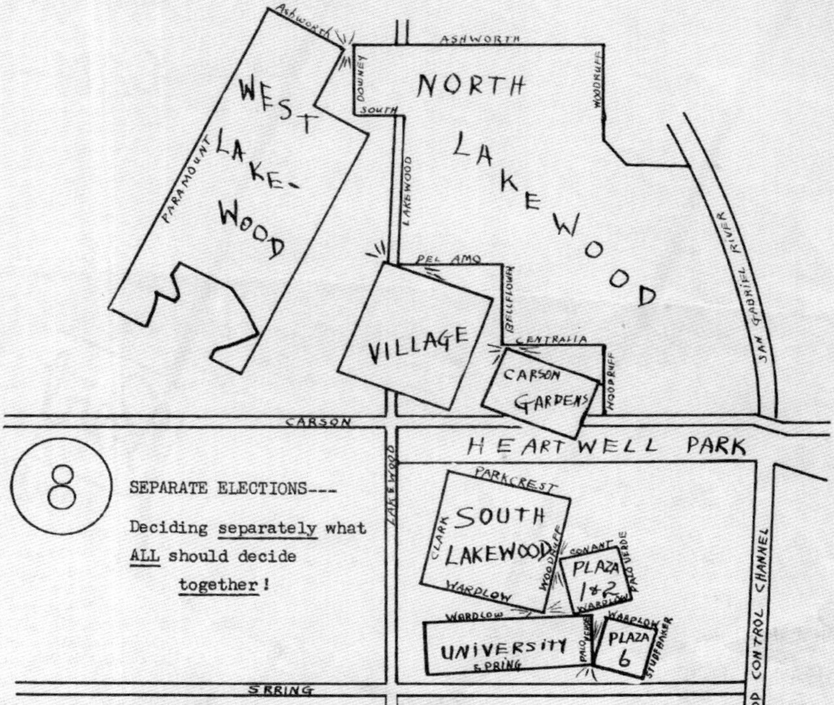

SEPARATE ELECTIONS---

Deciding separately what ALL should decide together!

If you haven't signed a property owners protest petition and want to keep Lakewood united, telephone 519-13 or 393-311 or 589-74 or TO. 705-93 or ME. 382-10 or 597-47.

Join the LAKEWOOD CIVIC COUNCIL -- TODAY -- Membership only $1.00 per year -- Help your neighbors to DEFEAT ANNEXATION.

LAKEWOOD CIVIC COUNCIL, INC.

L.R. Jones, President Telephone 5-9747 Irene Gifford, Exec. Dir.

Battling Against Annexation. John Sanford Todd, later to become Lakewood's first city attorney, had an idea to outfox Long Beach's piecemeal annexation scheme. He advised the Lakewood Civic Council that if a majority of property owners in a neighborhood protested the annexation vote, the election could not be legally called. Long Beach city officials rejected Todd's novel legal strategy and approved annexation elections despite the protests. When they did, Todd struck back with a lawsuit on which he gambled both his reputation and the future of Lakewood. "On August 7, 1953," Todd wrote later, "Judge Frank Swain held that our protests were valid and that the City of Long Beach had failed to give us a fair hearing. Our procedure therefore was valid. Everything I had gambled on had succeeded."

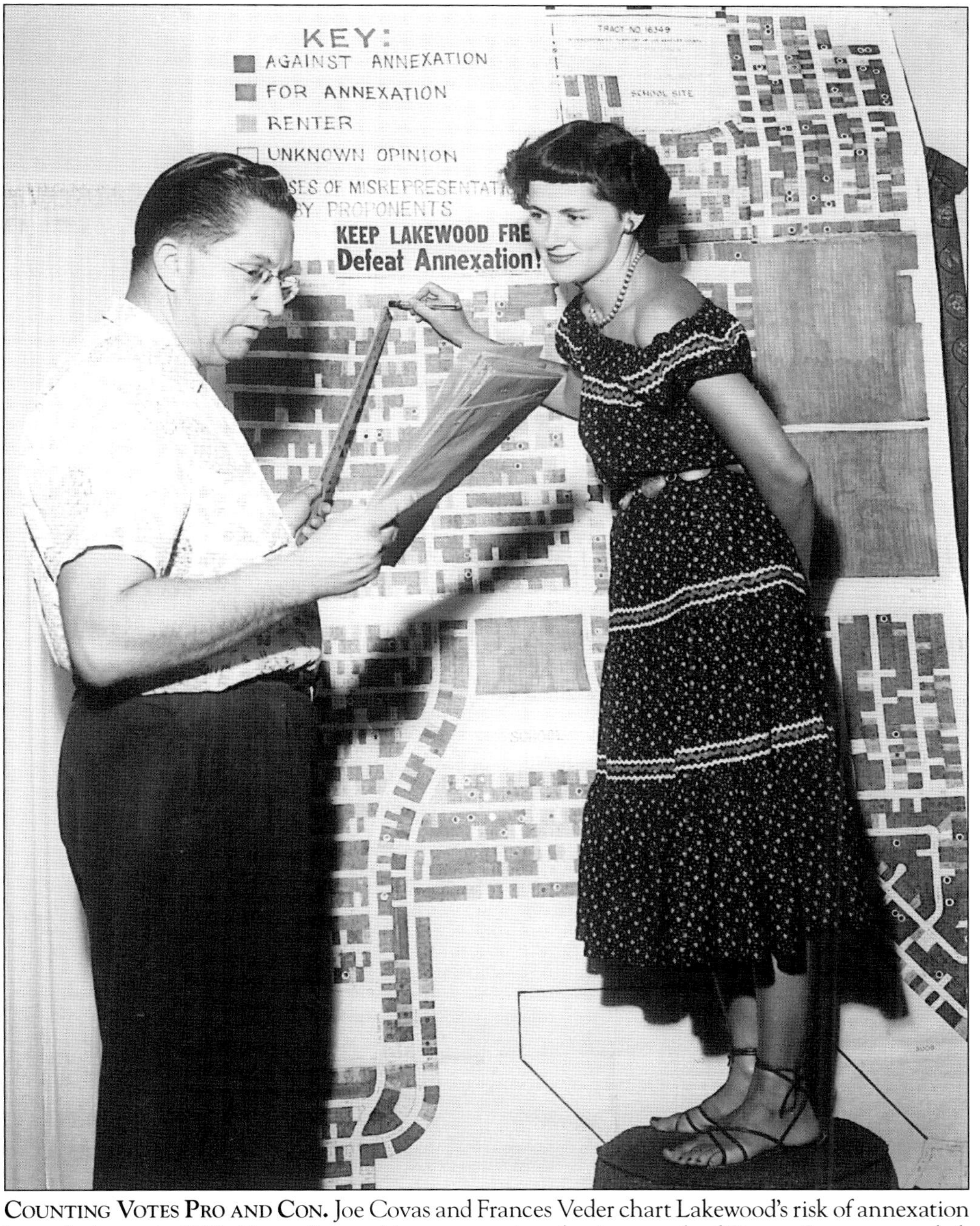

COUNTING VOTES PRO AND CON. Joe Covas and Frances Veder chart Lakewood's risk of annexation house by house in 1953. Generally speaking, annexation elections south of Carson Street succeeded. North of Carson Street, annexation failed except for Lakewood Village. The election there was close, with those in favor of annexation winning by only 76 votes. That left the remaining neighborhoods of what is now the city of Lakewood. According to John Sanford Todd, the Lakewood Taxpayers' Association was being torn apart by a nearly equal division of those in favor of and those opposed to annexation. The Lakewood Civic Council, incorporated by Todd in May 1953, took up active opposition to annexation.

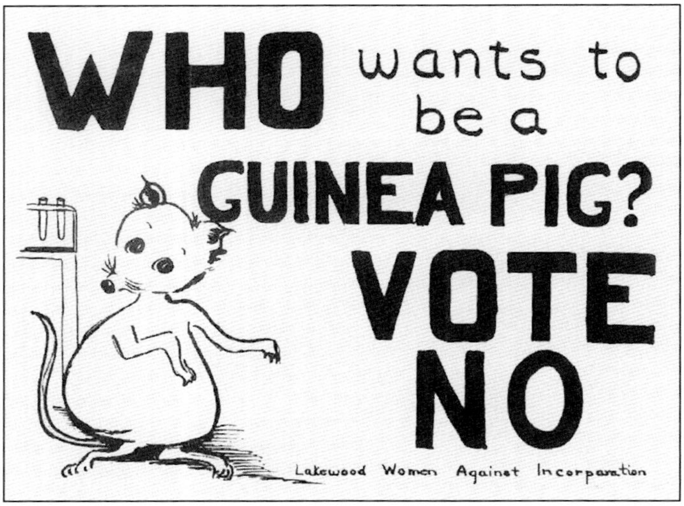

RISKS OF INCORPORATION. Opponents of incorporation highlighted the risks of being the first community in California to incorporate since 1939. They warned of higher taxes and the cost of police and fire stations. The also argued that Lakewood had no industry and only property taxes to keep a city afloat.

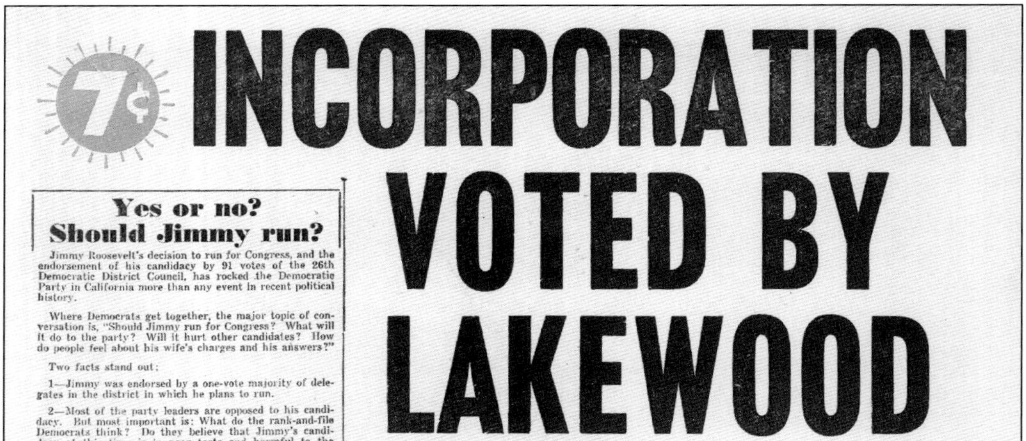

7¢

INCORPORATION VOTED BY LAKEWOOD

Yes or no? Should Jimmy run?

Jimmy Roosevelt's decision to run for Congress, and the endorsement of his candidacy by 91 votes of the 26th Democratic District Council, has rocked the Democratic Party in California more than any event in recent political history.

Where Democrats get together, the major topic of conversation is, "Should Jimmy run for Congress? What will it do to the party? Will it hurt other candidates? How do people feel about his wife's charges and his answers?"

Two facts stand out:

1—Jimmy was endorsed by a one-vote majority of delegates in the district in which he plans to run.

2—Most of the party leaders are opposed to his candidacy. But most important is: What do the rank-and-file Democrats think? Do they believe that Jimmy's candidacy at this time is in poor taste and harmful to the party and to the candidates running for other offices? Or do they believe that this race provides the means for Jimmy to vindicate himself and that it is proper for him to run? As a public service, therefore, the Daily News is going to provide a method of expression for the rank-and-file.

Since the Daily News is the only newspaper in the west that consistently advocates Democratic principles, and since our circulation goes largely to Democratic readers, this newspaper believes that the quickest and surest way of measuring the sentiment of a large segment of Democrats is to provide them with the means to register their approval or protest.

The Daily News, therefore, will publish a ballot on the front page of this newspaper Saturday, March 13.

It will be a simple question: "Should Jimmy Roosevelt run for Congress in the 26th district?"

You can mark your ballot "yes" or "no."

Daily News

WEDNESDAY, MAR. 10, 1954 2★★ LOS ANGELES 54 TEL. RICHMOND 6565

M'Carthy blistered by GOP colleague

VOTE BY PRECINCT

Unofficial Telephonic Returns

Precincts	For Incorporation	Against Incorporation
1	286	210
2	379	172
3	408	223

People pave the way for growth

Amazing Lakewood, which grew from a deserted area to one of the county's largest communities almost overnight after the war, last night took another big step by voting to become a full-fledged city.

WITH ALL 27 precincts re-

NEW CITY BORN. On March 9, 1954, Lakewood voters, by 7,524 for and 4,868 against, approved incorporation. The voters also decided which of the 39 candidates would be the city's first council members. When the results came in, bedlam broke out. People shouted, and everyone tried to get in on the celebration, according to newspaper accounts.

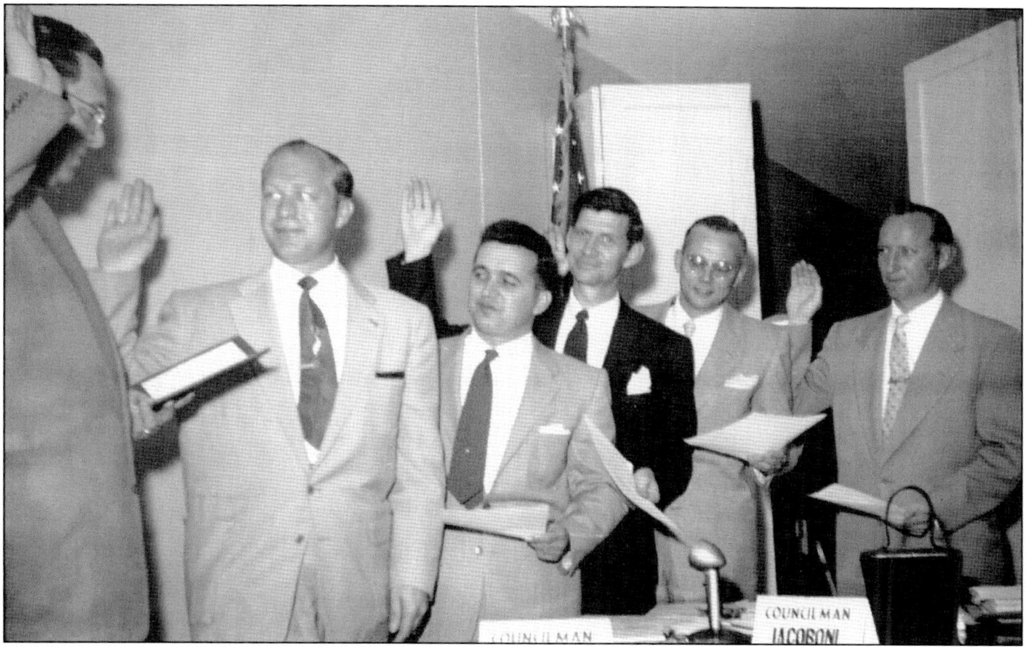

LAKEWOOD GETS DOWN TO CITY BUSINESS. The first city council, shown above, was sworn in on April 16, 1954, at the start of an all-night council meeting by county clerk Harold Ostly. The council members are, from left to right, Gene Nebeker, Angelo M. Iacoboni, George Nye Jr., William J. Burns, and Robert W. Baker. The entire city staff, shown below standing behind the city council, consists of, from left to right, city attorney John Sanford Todd, executive secretary director Guy Halferty, city clerk Nita Burch, and city administrator Robert Anderson. Newspaper's jokingly called Lakewood "the city without a payroll."

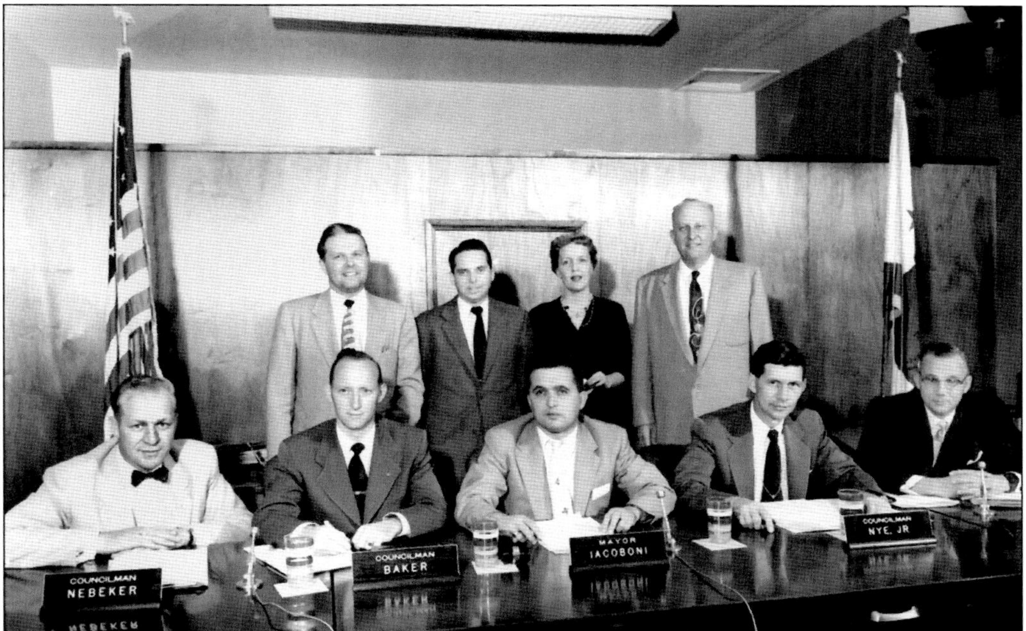

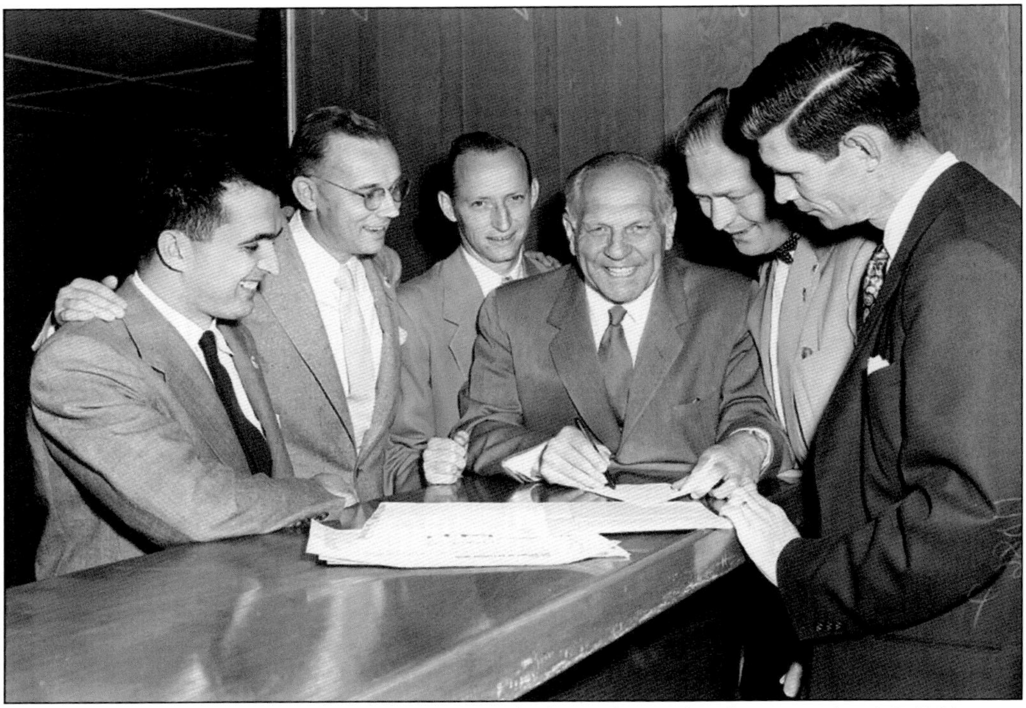

IT'S OFFICIAL. California governor Goodwin Knight (center) signs legislation on April 8, 1954—just days before the first Lakewood City Council meeting—with newly elected Lakewood council members looking on. The measure enabled the new city to receive its share of local tax revenue immediately so that council members could pay for county services.

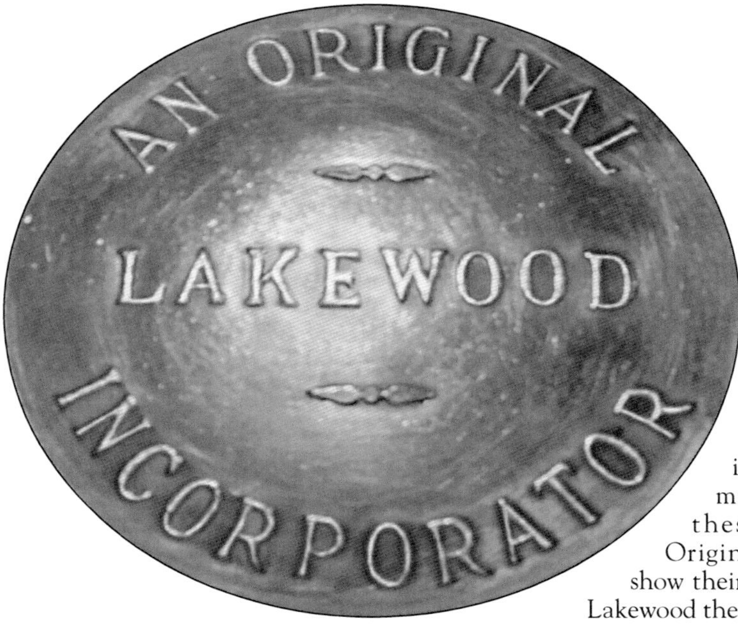

WORN WITH PRIDE. Lakewood residents who had been actively involved in the incorporation movement proudly wore these embossed, copper Original Incorporator pins to show their pride in helping to make Lakewood the state's newest city in 1954.

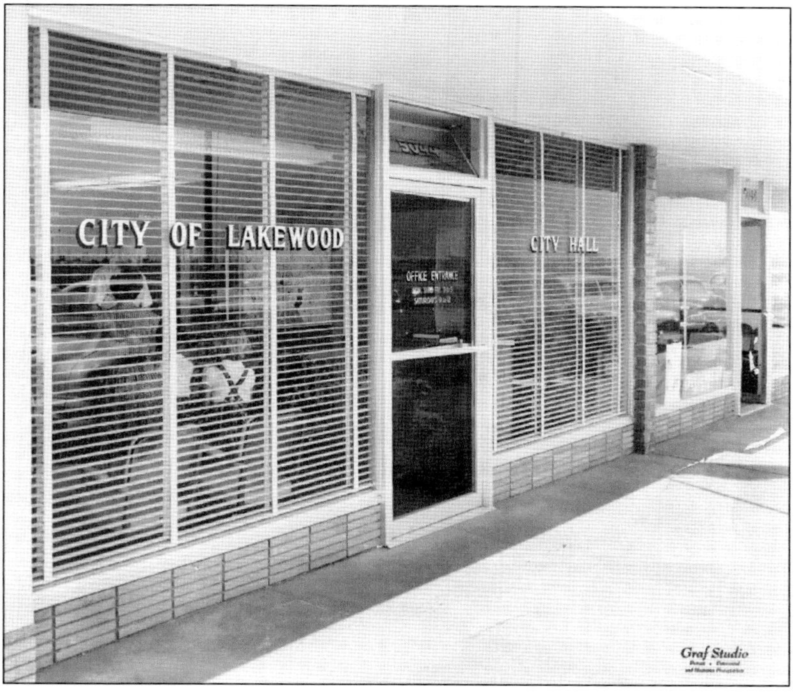

MODEST CITY HALL. Lakewood's first city hall was a rented storefront in the Faculty Shops at Lakewood Center. A few chairs and a table in the back of the room were designated as the city council chambers. The storefront city hall was replaced in 1958 with the Lakewood Civic Center.

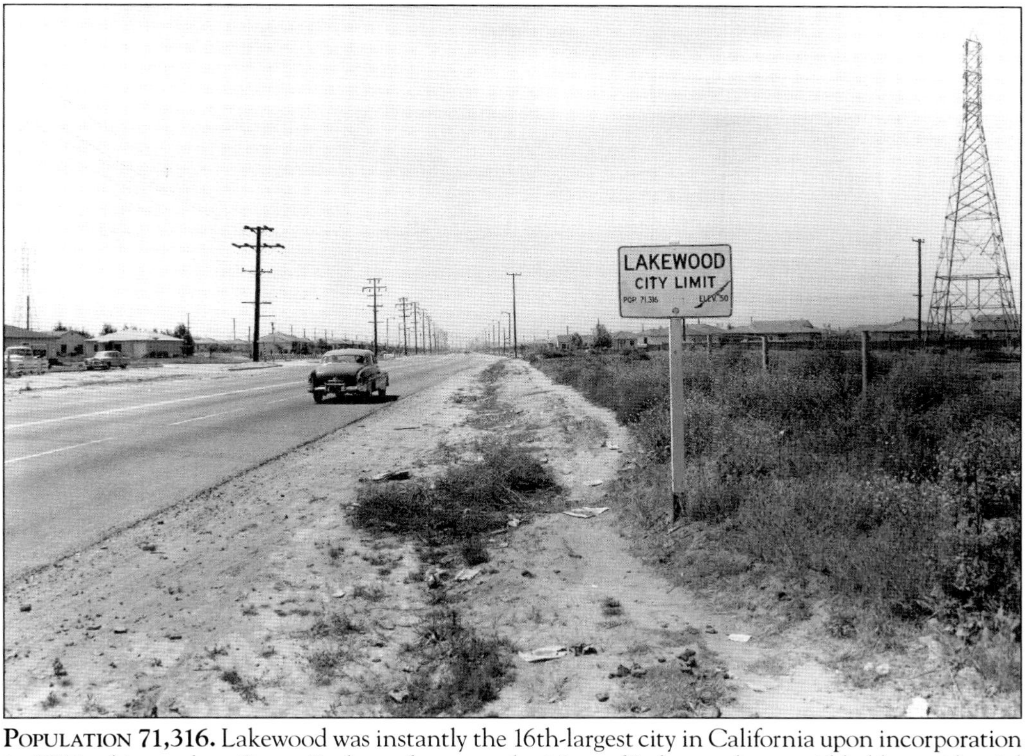

POPULATION 71,316. Lakewood was instantly the 16th-largest city in California upon incorporation in 1954—bigger than Santa Barbara, for example. Most of Lakewood was gridded by residential streets by 1954, but some undeveloped areas remained for future growth.

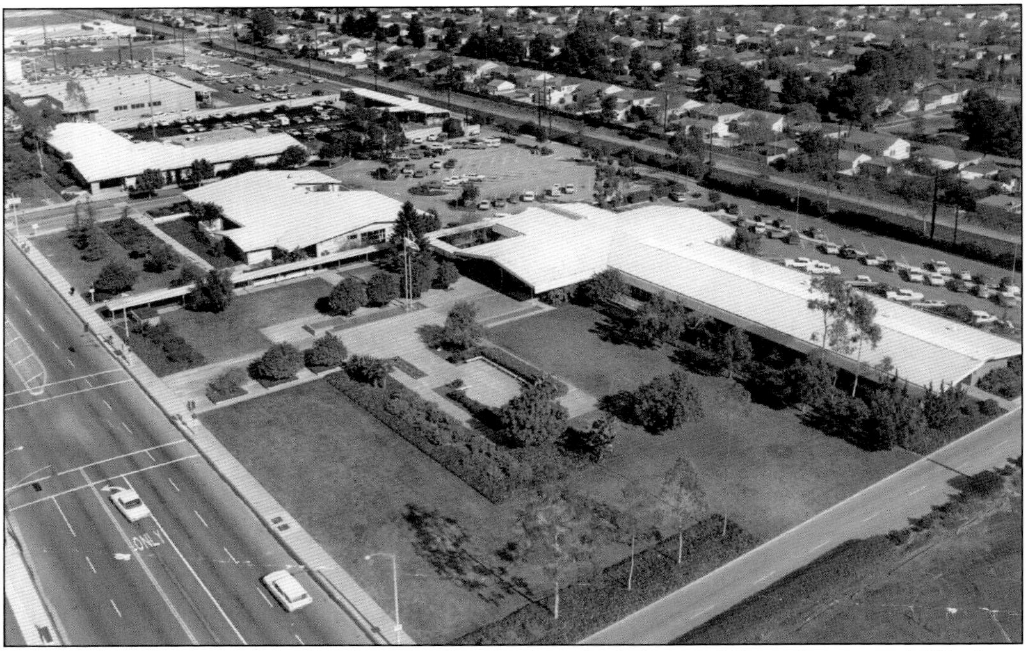

Civic Center Opens. Lakewood City Hall moved to the Lakewood Civic Center in 1958, along with the Lakewood branch of the county library. In 1959, law enforcement services for Lakewood were transferred to the new Lakewood Sheriff's Station, seen in the upper left. A post office joined the civic center complex in 1964.

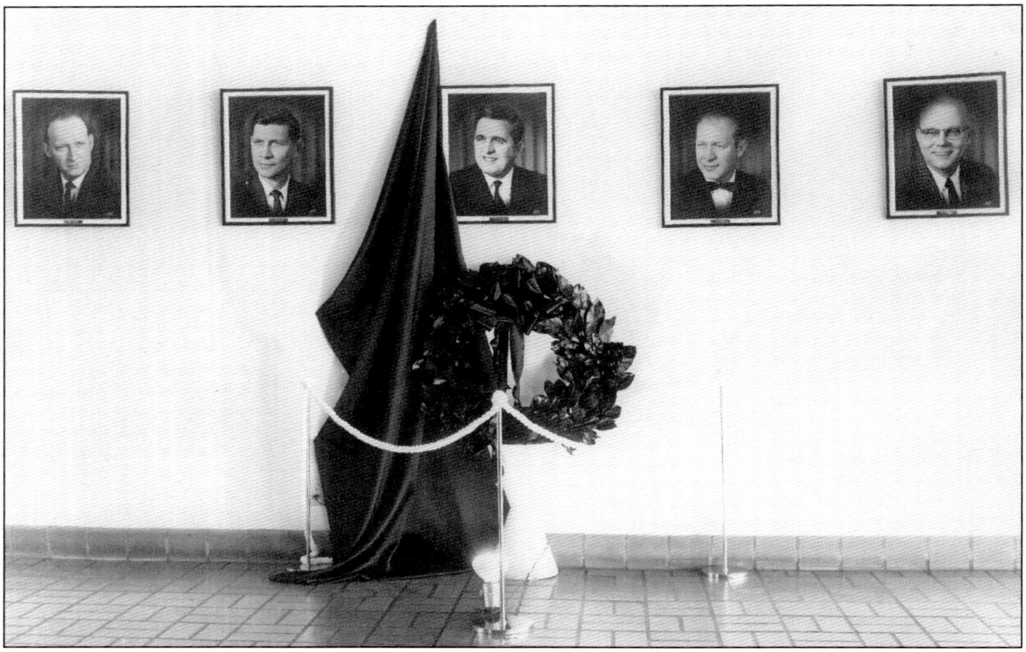

Mourning Lakewood's First Mayor. Already well known as a member of the Lakewood Chamber of Commerce, the Exchange Club, and Sons of Italy, Angelo Iacoboni became Lakewood's first mayor in 1954. In 1964, Iacoboni died of a heart attack while playing tennis at age 46.

Five

The Lakewood Plan

Rather than create its own municipal departments in 1954, the new City of Lakewood contracted with Los Angeles County to continue the services that residents needed. The claim was made—almost true—that Lakewood was "the city without a payroll." There were only three employees after incorporation: a city manager, his secretary, and a public relations representative who handled inquiries from other communities seeking to incorporate under the innovative plan that soon became known as the Lakewood Plan.

The Lakewood Plan made Lakewood the nation's first "contract city." By contracting with the county and with private businesses for services, Lakewood pioneered a model that has been adopted by all but one of the cities incorporated in Los Angeles County since 1954.

Under the plan, the city council sets policies, enacts legislation, adopts an annual budget, and makes land use decisions. The city council also mandates the service levels contractors must provide, monitors the effectiveness of each contract, and selects new contractors.

The city's largest contract is with the Los Angeles County Sheriff's Department. Other county contracts cover street maintenance and building safety services. Contracts with private industry include trash collection and street sweeping.

Fire protection and paramedics are provided by the Los Angeles County Fire Department through a countywide fire protection district. Libraries are similarly provided through a county-governed special district. Other services are supplied through nonprofit agencies based in Lakewood or through contracts with other agencies and joint powers authorities that include Lakewood in their service areas.

Lakewood provides its own recreation programs and operates the water system that serves the western portion of the city.

Contracting for city services made Lakewood possible in 1954, and the contract model continues to provide Lakewood residents with all the benefits of local control along with the cost savings and flexibility that are built into the Lakewood Plan.

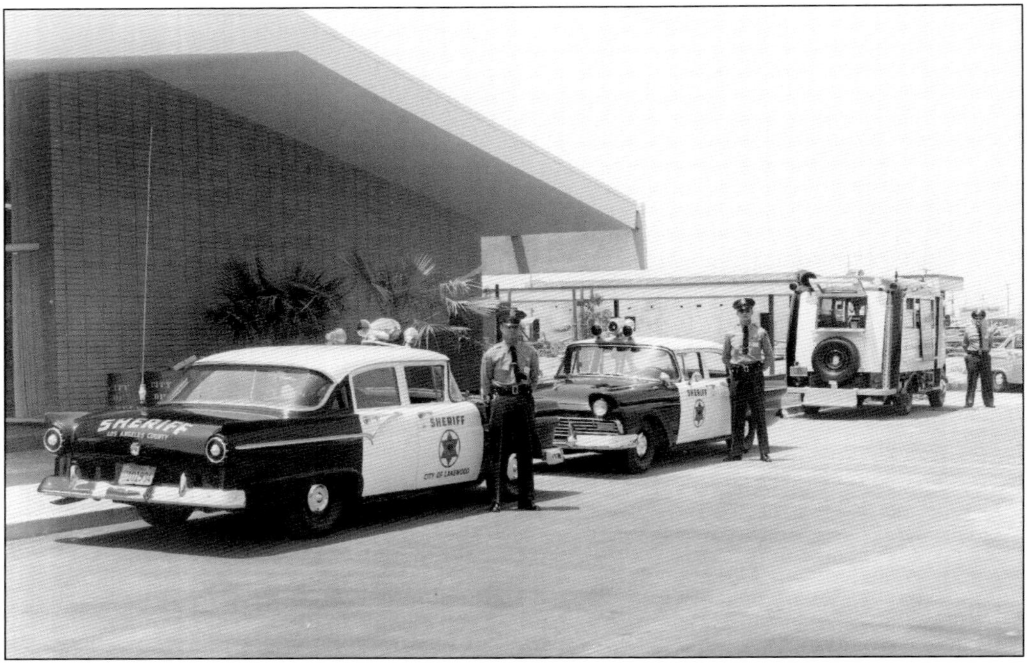

SHERIFF'S STATION OPENS. The Lakewood Sheriff's Station opened in 1959, bringing law enforcement services—provided under contract with the sheriff's department—to the Lakewood Civic Center, seen at the top. The station was the headquarters for a regional law enforcement plan that initially included Lakewood and unincorporated county areas. The station's forces, shown in the image below, grew with the incorporation of Artesia, Bellflower, Cerritos, Paramount, and Hawaiian Gardens. Today's larger and technologically advanced sheriff's station continues to provide regional law enforcement.

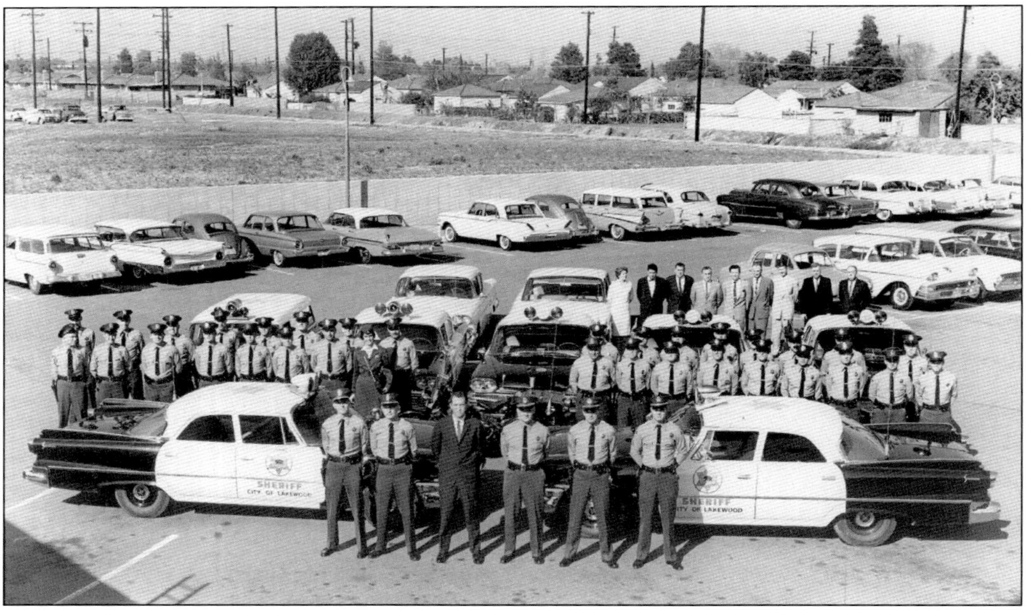

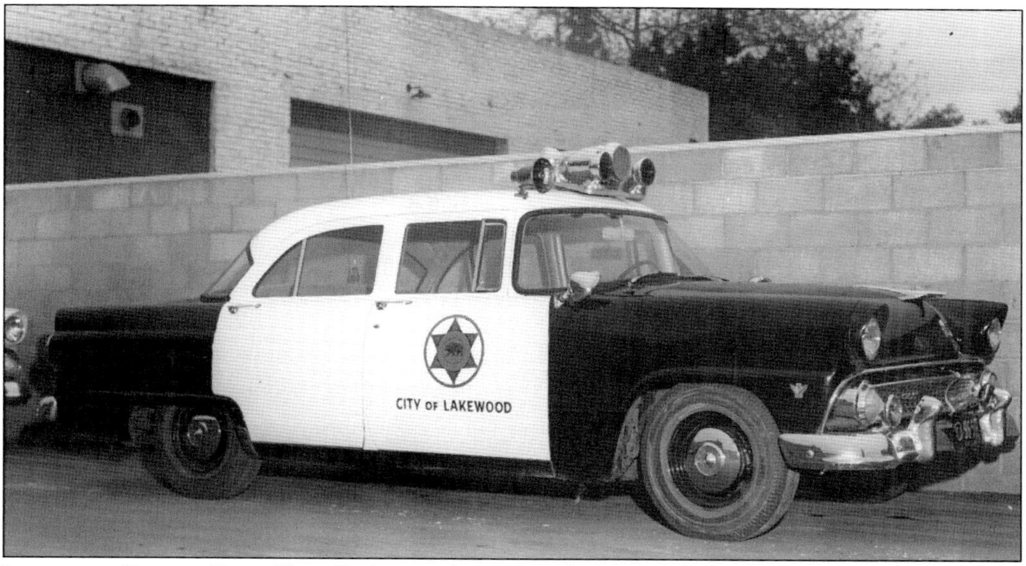

Lakewood Patrol Cars. Sheriff's deputies have patrolled Lakewood's streets in an array of vehicles adapted to law enforcement use. In the early years of regional deployment from the Lakewood station, deputies rode in mid-1950s Ford Crown Victorias, shown above, and early 1960s Dodge Dart Senecas, shown below. The Dodge is posed next to a city entrance sign with the motto "Lakewood—Tomorrow's City Today" in the distinctive "bow tie" shape that distinguished city entrance signs until 2006. The city limit sign in this photograph has upped Lakewood's population to more than 74,000.

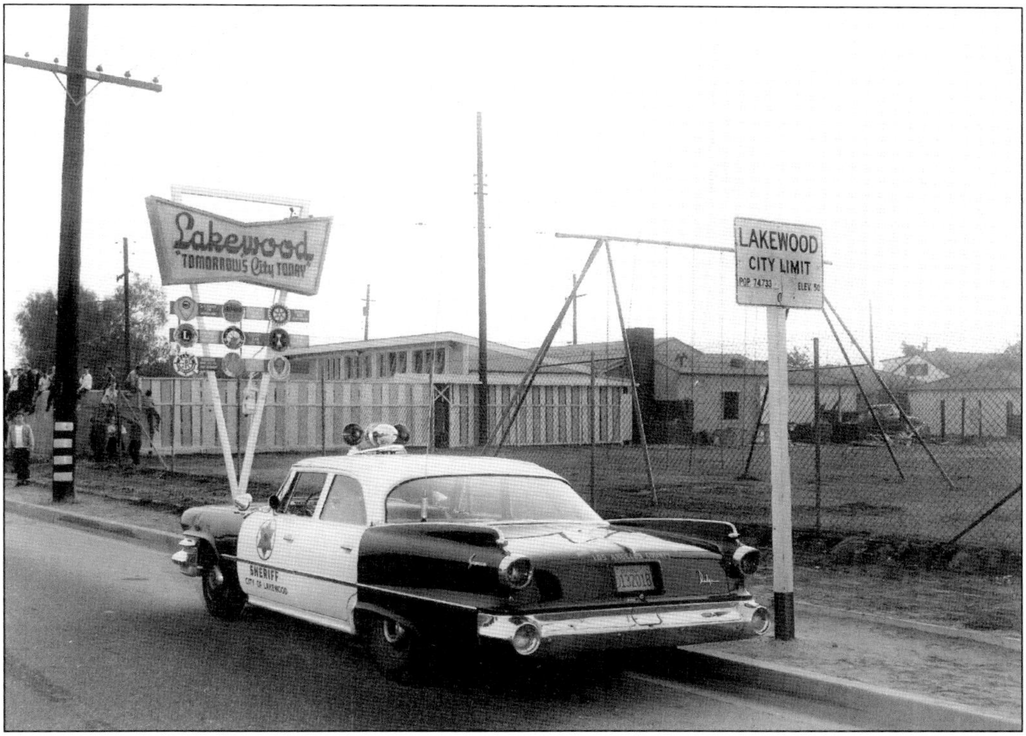

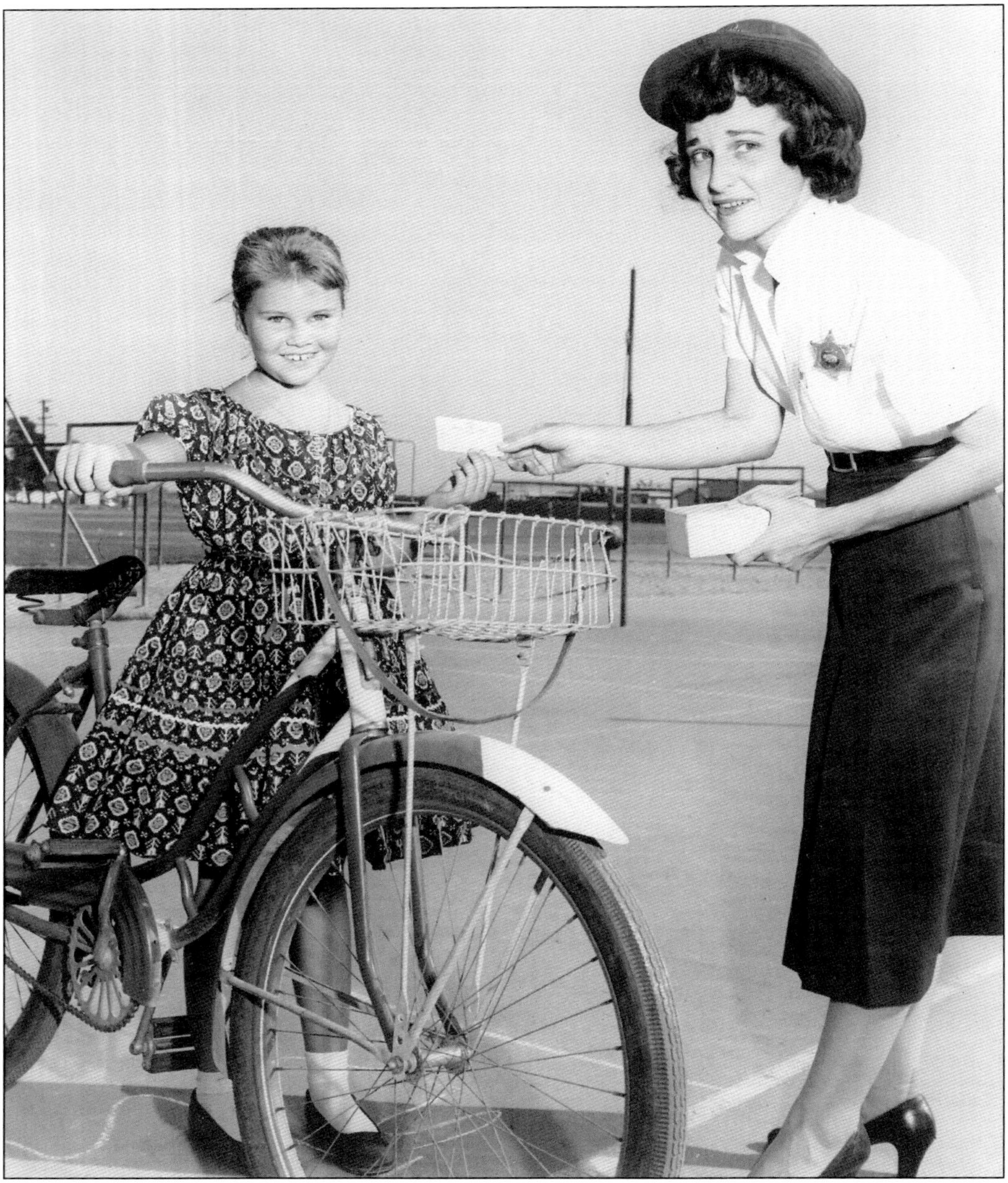

SAFETY FOR LAKEWOOD'S KIDS. Lakewood parents worried about the safety of their sons and daughters in 1954. So did city officials. Among the earliest programs the city council began were visits to Lakewood schools by a county fire safety officer, who taught youngsters the dangers of playing with matches. Deputies from the Lakewood Sheriff's Station reached out to young bike riders through a city-sponsored program of traffic safety education. Programs like these educated generations of school-age youth, and continue today to offer lessons in personal safety, good bike and pedestrian habits, and the dangers of addiction.

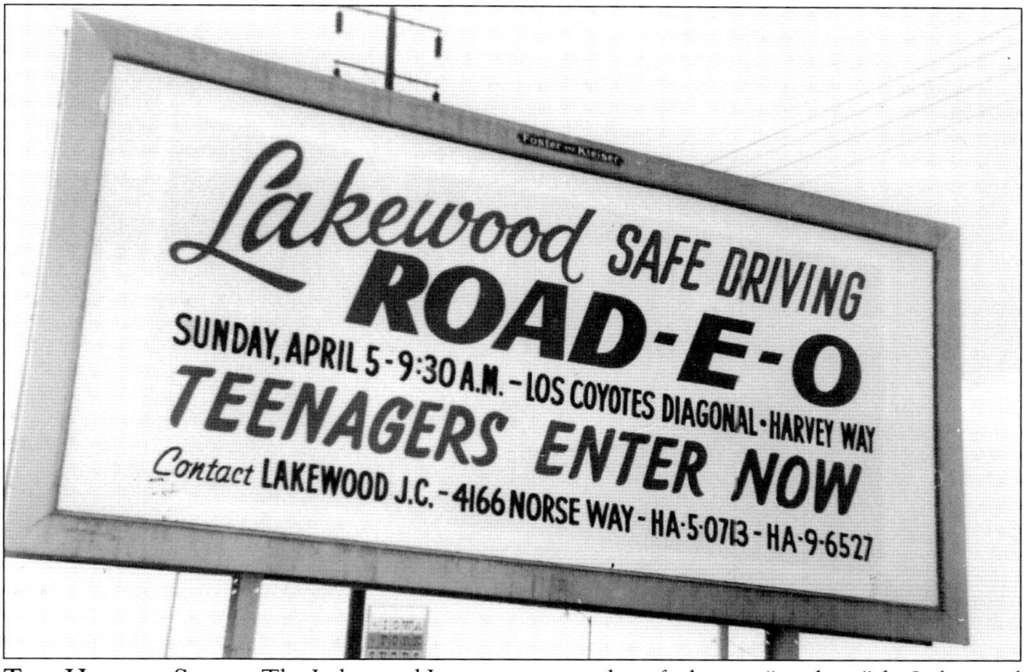

Teen Highway Safety. The Lakewood Jaycees sponsored a safe driving "road-e-o" for Lakewood area teens in the early years of Lakewood. The young drivers competed for points in tests of their skills behind the wheel, including parallel parking, driving in reverse, braking, and signaling.

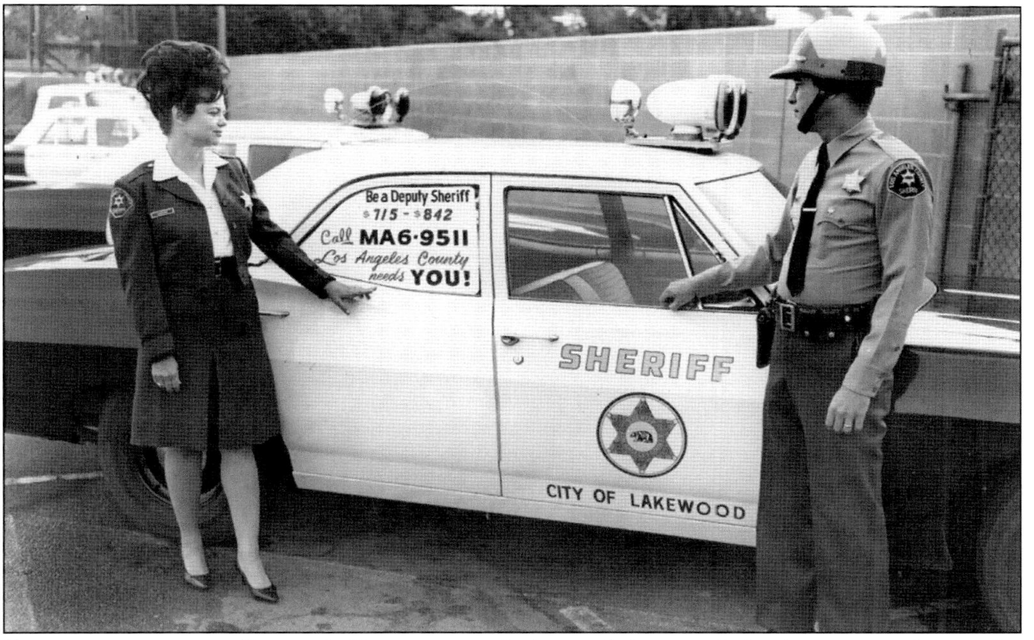

Recruiting for the Sheriff's Department. Lakewood deputies helped recruit applicants for a fast-growing sheriff's department. The crash helmet and bouffant hairstyle suggest that this photograph was taken in the early 1960s, when the Lakewood Station served the law enforcement needs of seven cities, with more than 180,000 residents.

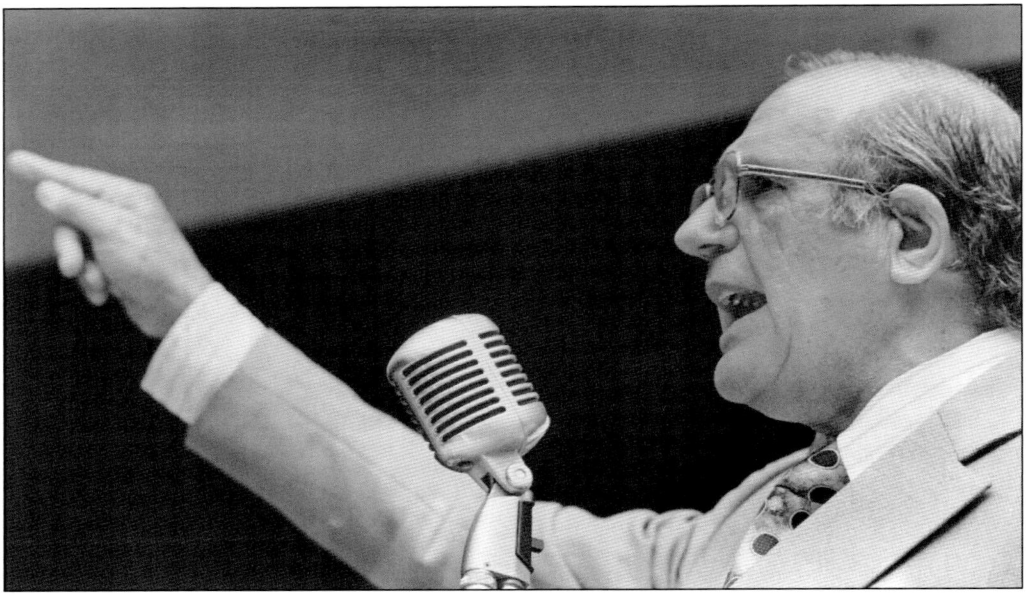

CONTRACTING FOR LAW ENFORCEMENT. Sheriff Peter J. Pitchess, shown above, championed John Sanford Todd's proposal that the new city of Lakewood should contract for law enforcement services. While undersheriff in 1954, Pitchess met with Todd to develop a cost model for pricing deputies and their cars. Their solution made contract law enforcement both practical and economical. As sheriff, Pitchess often came to the Lakewood Station, shown below, and to the city's Award of Valor program that continues today to honor Lakewood's public safety heroes.

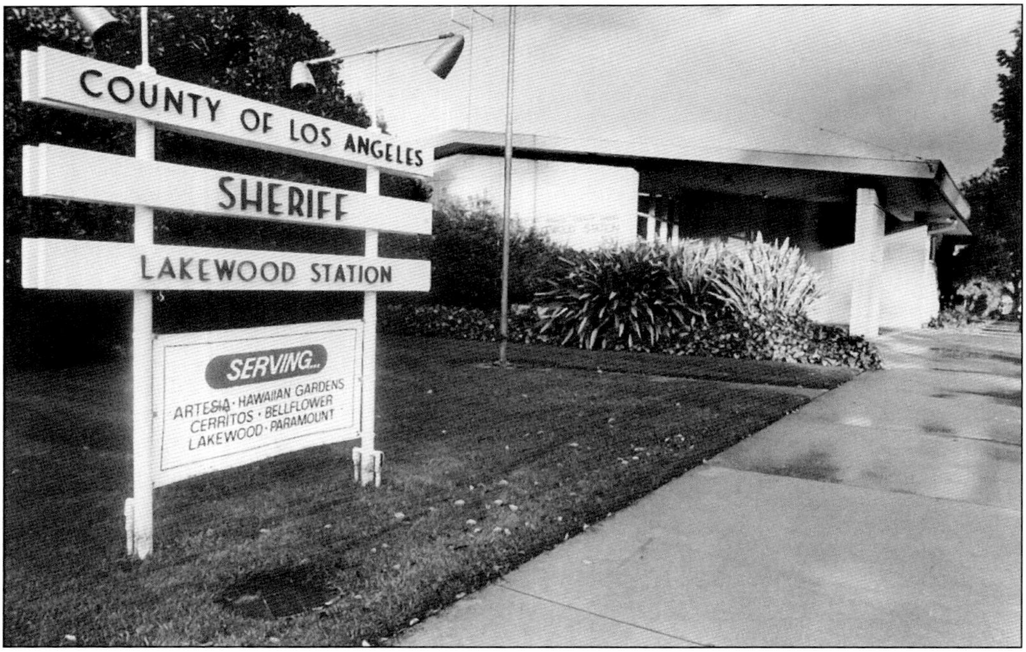

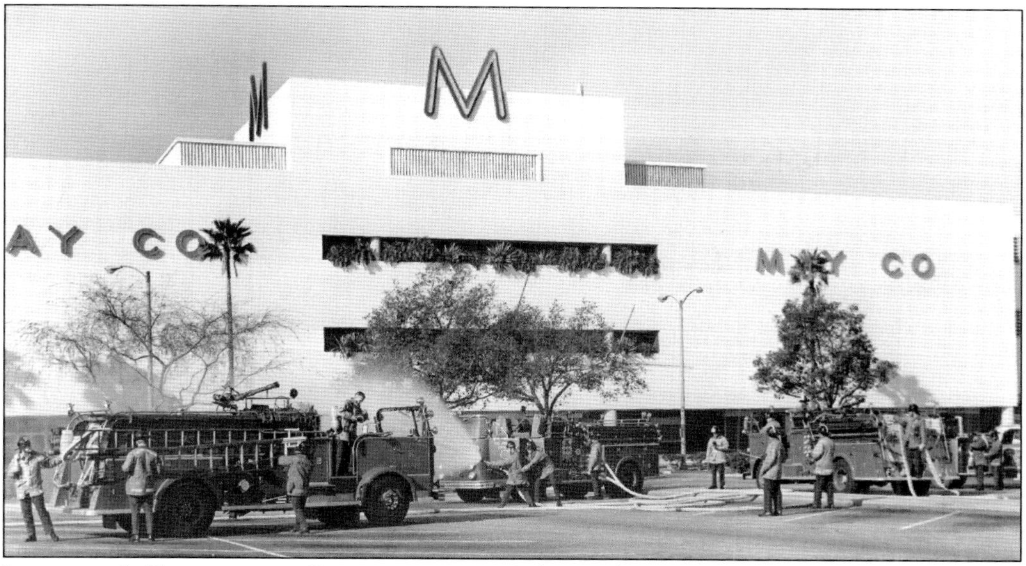

Lakewood's Firefighters. Fire protection in Lakewood is not a contract service, unlike law enforcement. Lakewood is served by the Los Angeles County Fire Department through a countywide fire protection district. The ability to contract for some city services and remain in special districts for others is one of the strengths of the Lakewood Plan. Lakewood's firefighters, shown above, practiced for disaster in front of the May Company building in Lakewood Center. They lined up their equipment for a public review, seen below, in the mid-1950s.

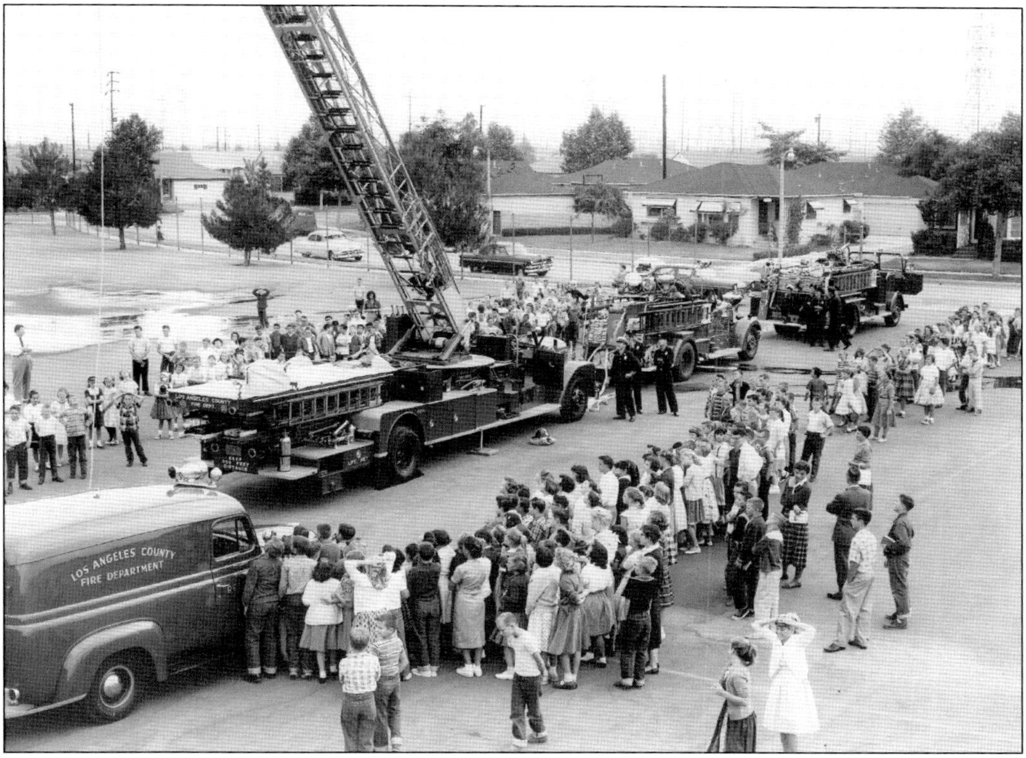

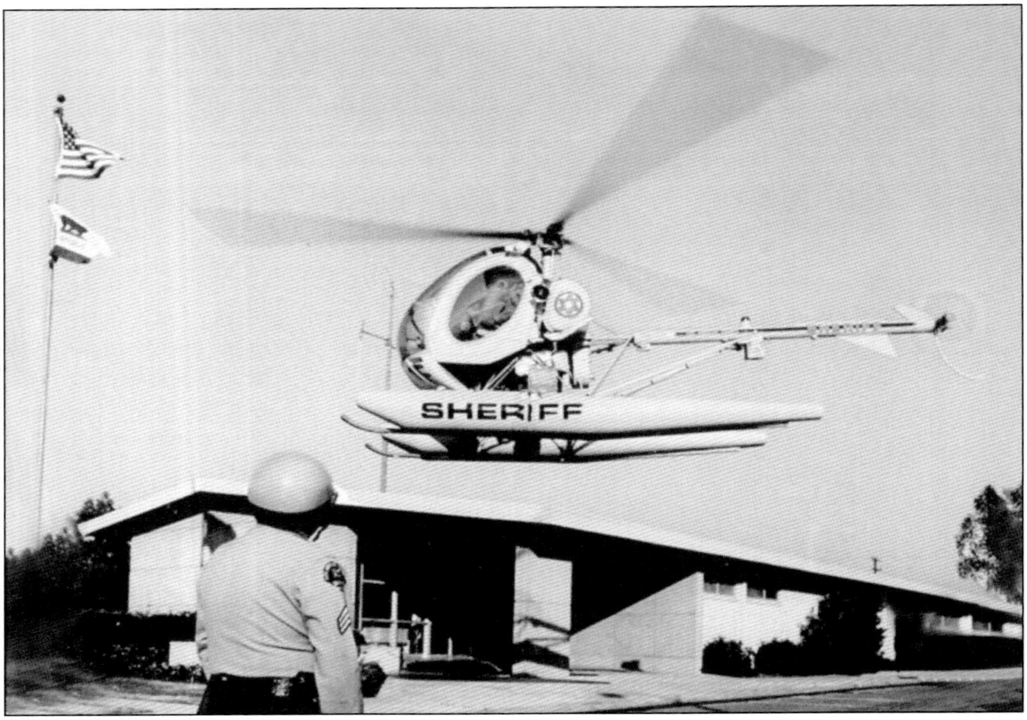

SKY KNIGHT OVER LAKEWOOD. The world's first helicopter law enforcement patrol program began in Lakewood in 1966, as shown above, when the city joined with the sheriff's department and the federal Law Enforcement Assistance Administration in a test of an "airborne patrol car." Named Sky Knight, the program was an instant success and quickly expanded to all the cities served by the Lakewood Sheriff's Station. Day and night patrols became a routine feature of Lakewood law enforcement, pursuing fleeing suspects using its eye-in-the-sky capabilities to monitor a crime scene day or night. Although the program has changed, as shown below, Sky Knight still flies the same helicopter configuration pioneered in 1966.

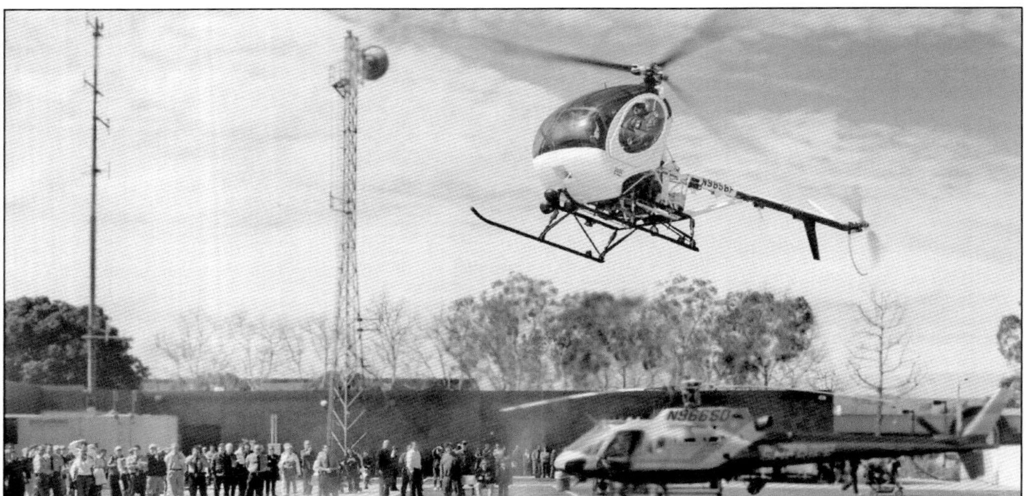

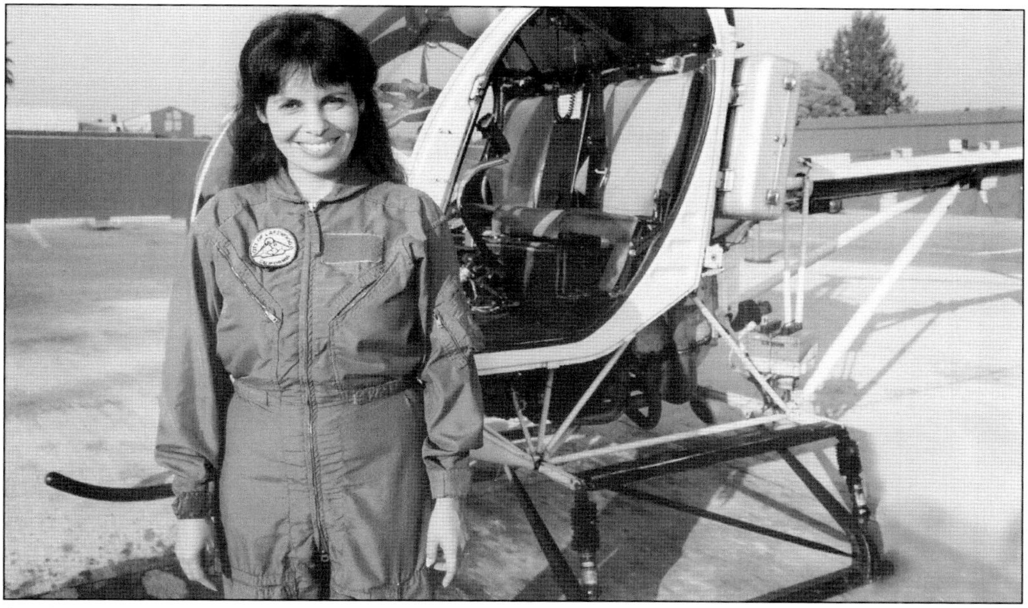

SKY KNIGHT PILOT MONICA MCINTYRE. Former Sky Knight pilot Monica McIntyre was the first women pilot in the program's history and the first in the nation to fly patrols for a law enforcement agency. Sky Knight proved all its abilities in 1986 when it flew continuously over the scene of a crashed commercial jet in Cerritos. McIntyre guided medivac helicopters and positioned news media helicopters away from flight corridors.

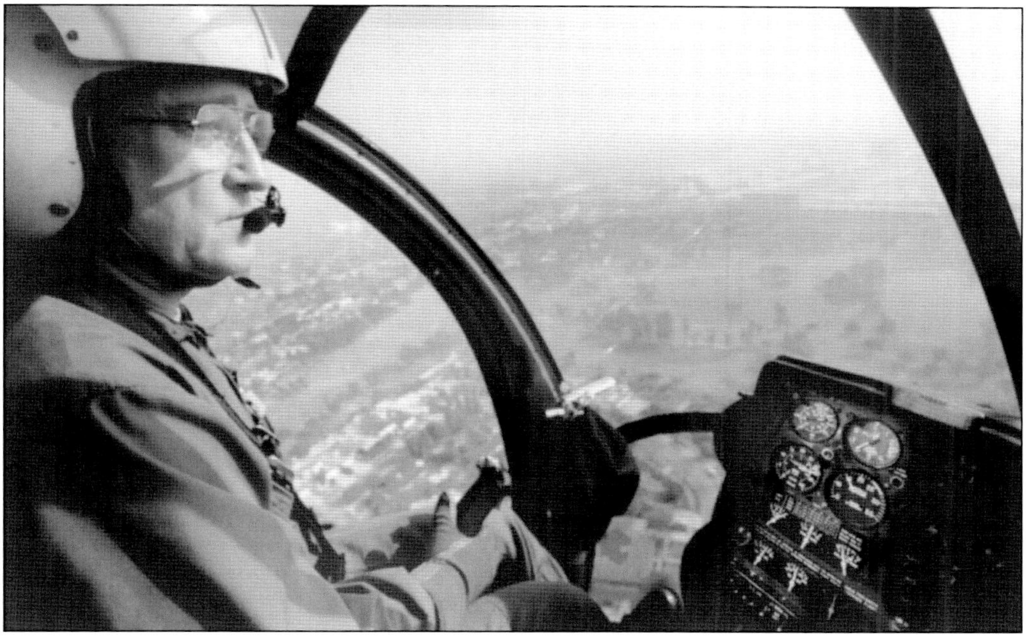

CHIEF PILOT WES PEARSON. Chief Pilot Wes Pearson joined the Sky Knight program in 1976, and was promoted to chief pilot in 1980, earning a remarkable record of flight safety until his retirement in 2010. Sky Knight is one of the few aerial law enforcement programs to combine civilian pilots like Pearson and McIntyre and observers who are deputy sheriffs.

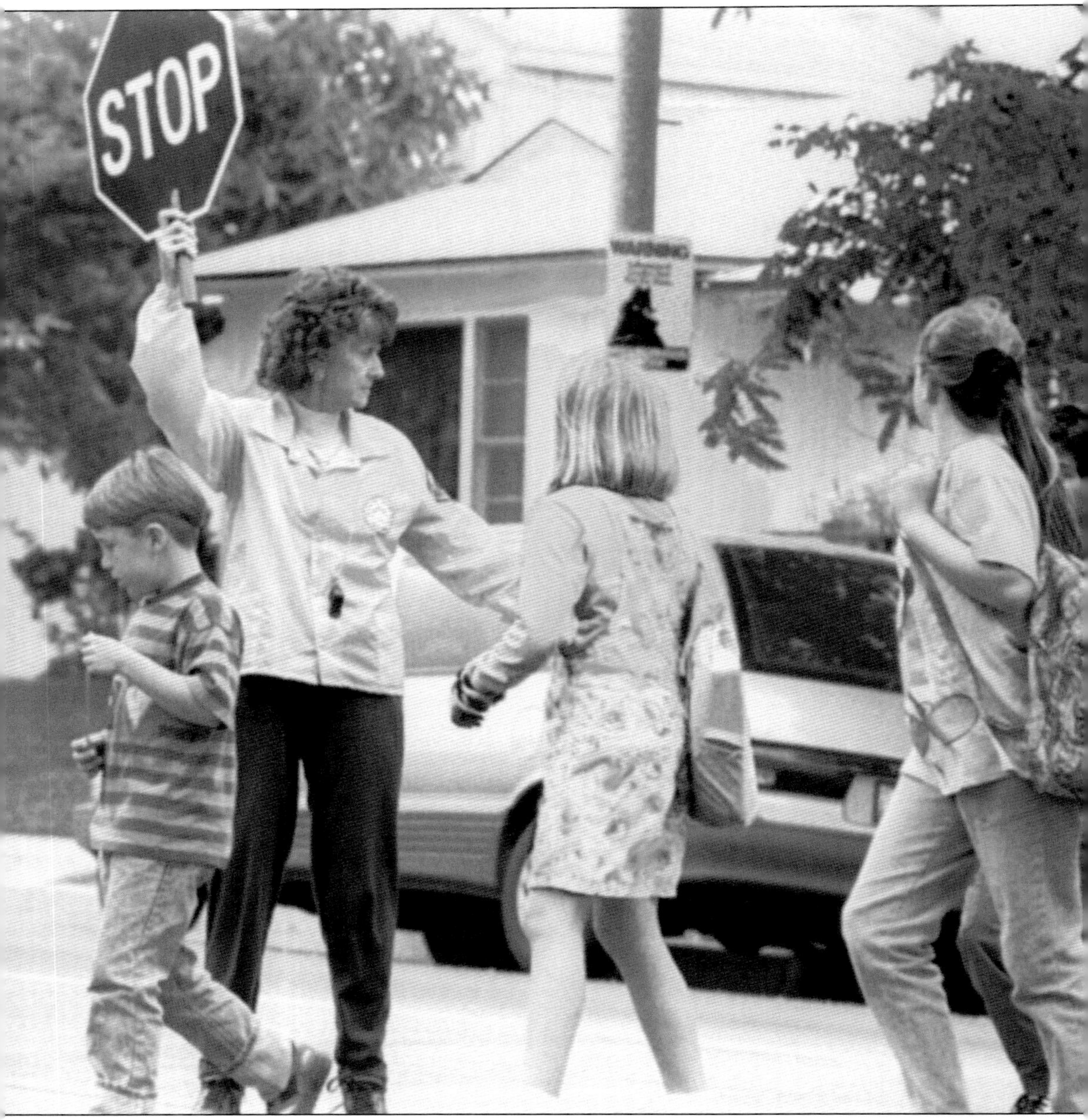

Crossing Guards Protect Students. Concern for its young residents led the city council to establish a crossing guard program to guide students across the major intersections that interrupt routes to neighborhood schools. Lakewood is divided among four school districts, each with different terms and holidays, making a citywide crossing guard program even more necessary. Suggested routes to school are distributed at the start of every school year to show where traffic signals, crossing guards, and crosswalks help make the trip a safe one.

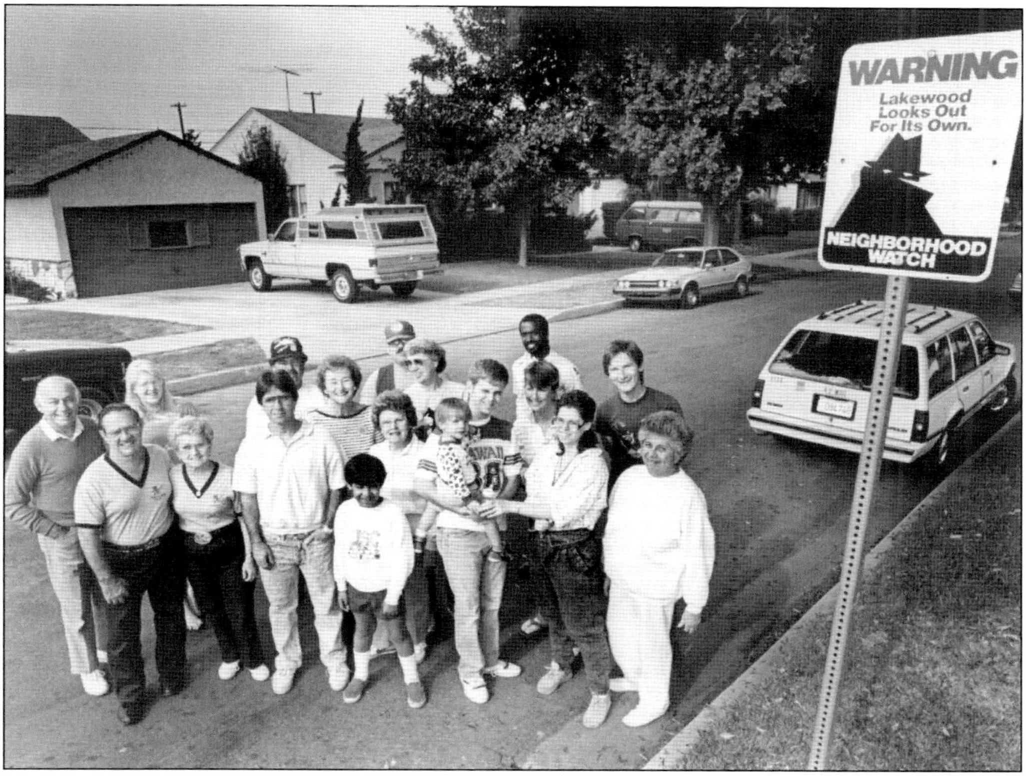

NEIGHBORHOOD WATCH. Lakewood's Neighborhood Watch program took off in the 1980s and soon grew to become one of the largest and most successful in California. Honored by state and county law enforcement leaders, Lakewood Neighborhood Watch members are kept in touch through newsletters, seminars on crime topics, CityTV programs, and an annual picnic.

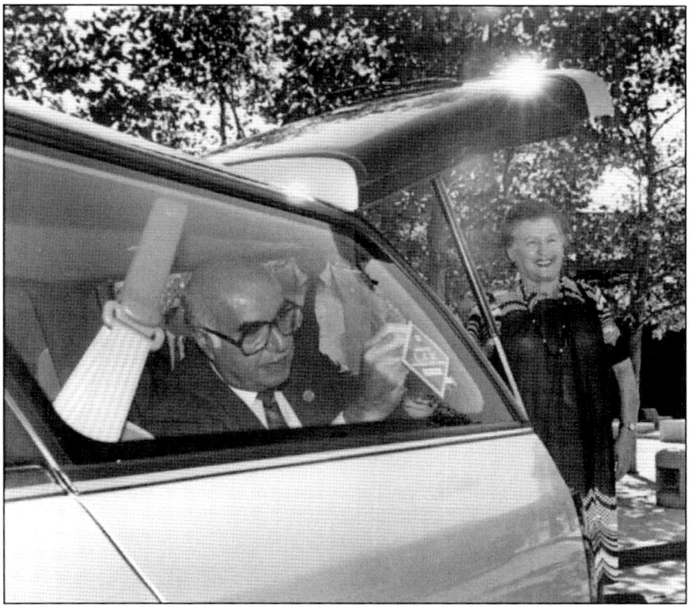

PIONEERING SAFETY PROGRAMS. Sheriff Sherman Block puts up a Lakewood Auto Watch sticker, one of several innovative programs Lakewood began in the 1990s to deal with neighborhood crime. Lakewood Volunteers on Patrol, Lakewood Business Watch, the Special Assignment Officer program, the Lakewood Apartments Nuisance Deterrent program, and other crime prevention initiatives have played a role in keeping the level of serious crime low in Lakewood.

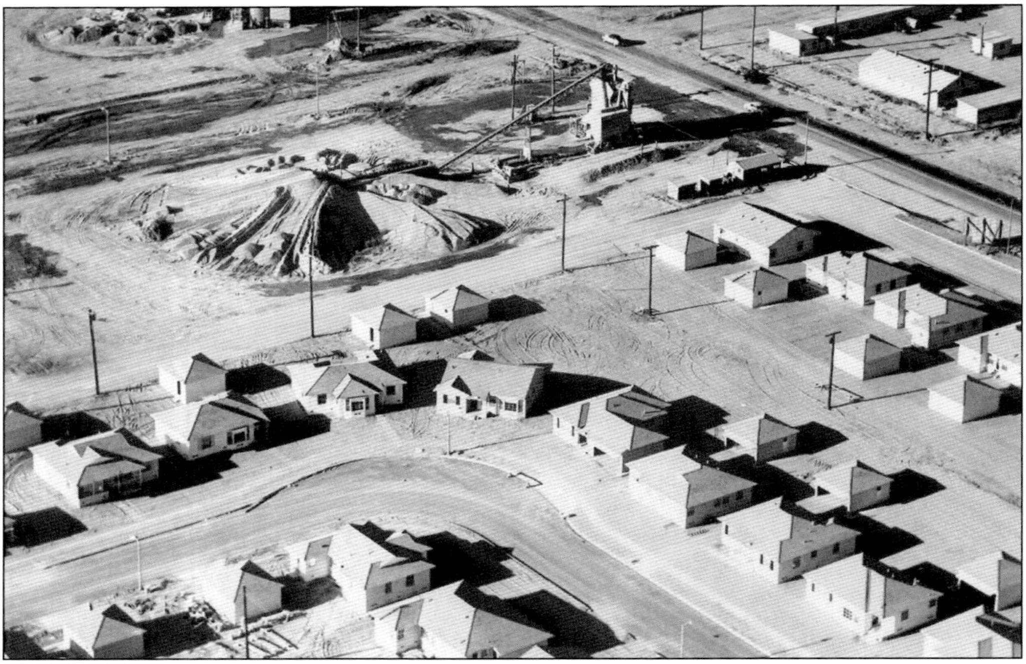

Neighborhood Streets. Lakewood's original developers laid down a network of residential streets, seen above, beginning in 1950. But time and weather have necessitated that the streets be repaved through contracts with paving companies, shown below. Since the 1980s, every major street repair project has included sidewalk, curb, and gutter replacement. In 2000, the Lakewood City Council committed to a multiyear effort to repave every residential street in Lakewood—a significant task in a city with 143 miles of residential roadways. In early 2013, the "100%-repaved" milestone was reached. Lakewood's residents have consistently expressed appreciation for the high quality of the city's streets.

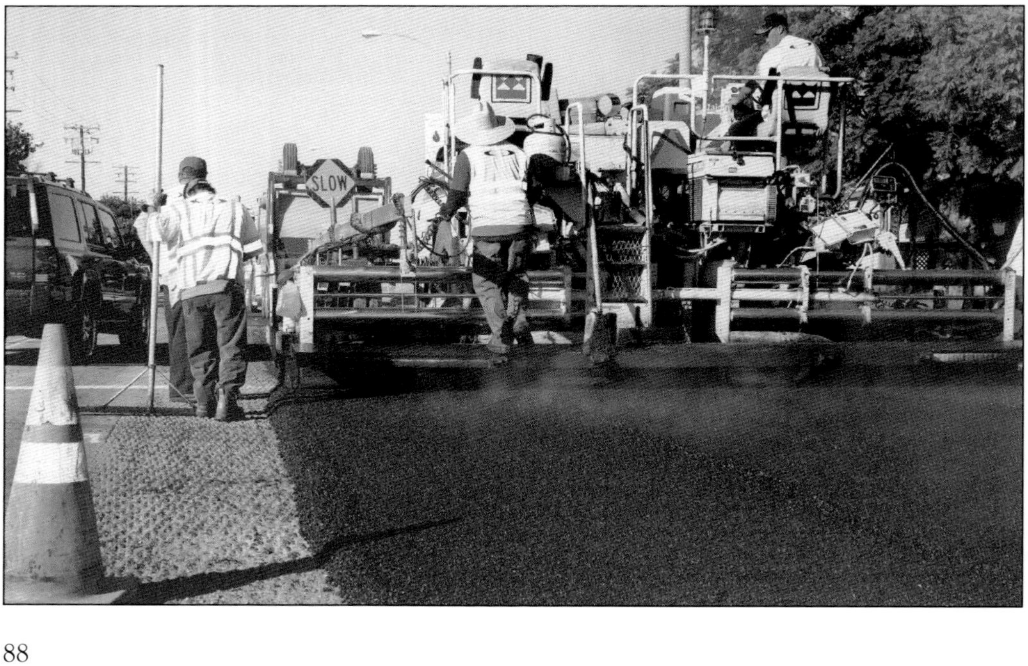

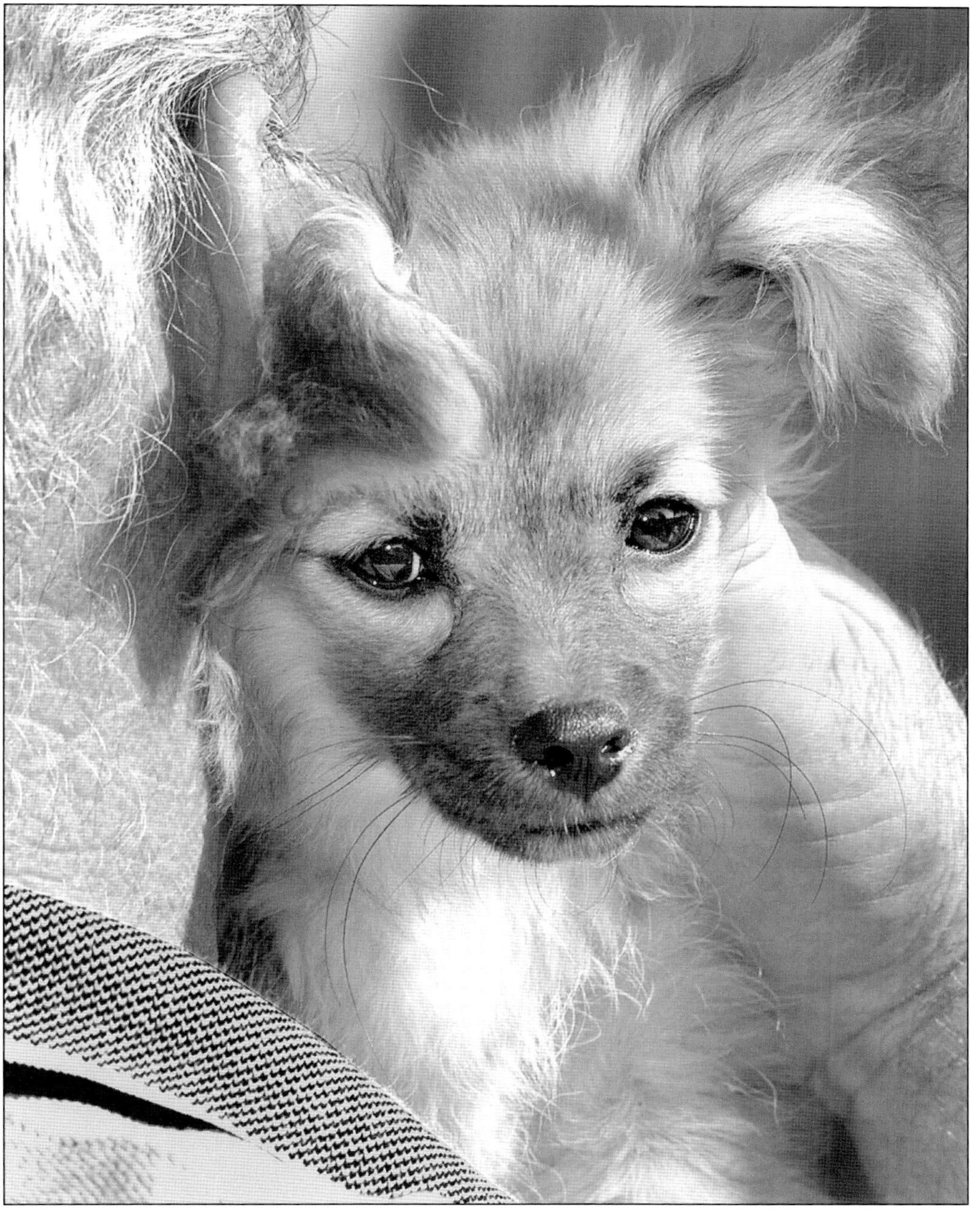

Caring for Lakewood's Pets. Contracting with the county got Lakewood going, but with the need for new programs and with an eye on costs, the Lakewood City Council soon turned to other service providers, like the Southeast Area Animal Control Authority, an agency set up by a consortium of neighboring cities. Under contract with the city, SEAACA cares for Lakewood's lost pets and provides other pet services, such as rabies vaccinations and the annual Bow Wow and Meow Days clinics, where this pup is about to get a vaccination. Lakewood helped form the California Joint Powers Insurance Authority, another consortium of cities, to lower the cost of Lakewood's liability insurance.

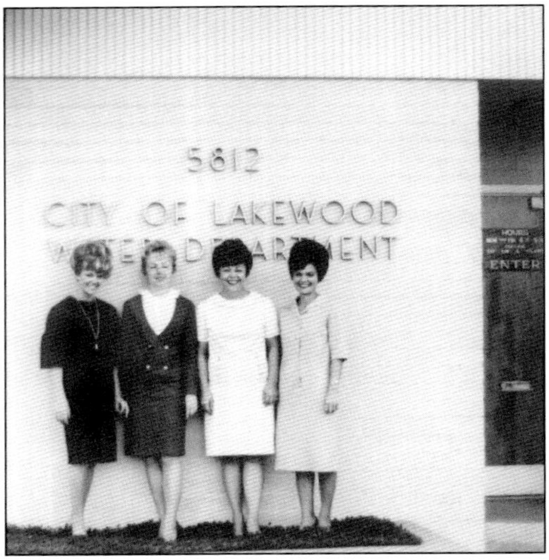

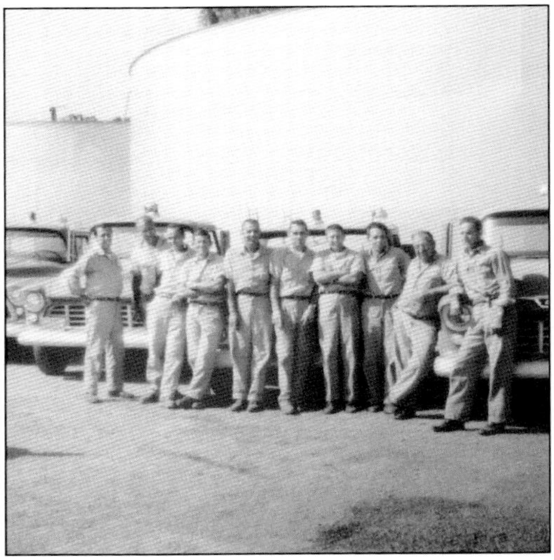

WATER FOR LAKEWOOD'S HOMES. The city acquired the Lakewood Water and Power Company in 1957 from the city's original developers. Office staff members and field employees, shown above, took over the company's former headquarters on Arbor Road. When water mains began their inevitable deterioration 40 years later, the Lakewood Department of Water Resources began the systematic replacement of mains, reservoirs, and pumps. All of water pumped by the city-owned system still comes from Lakewood's own wells.

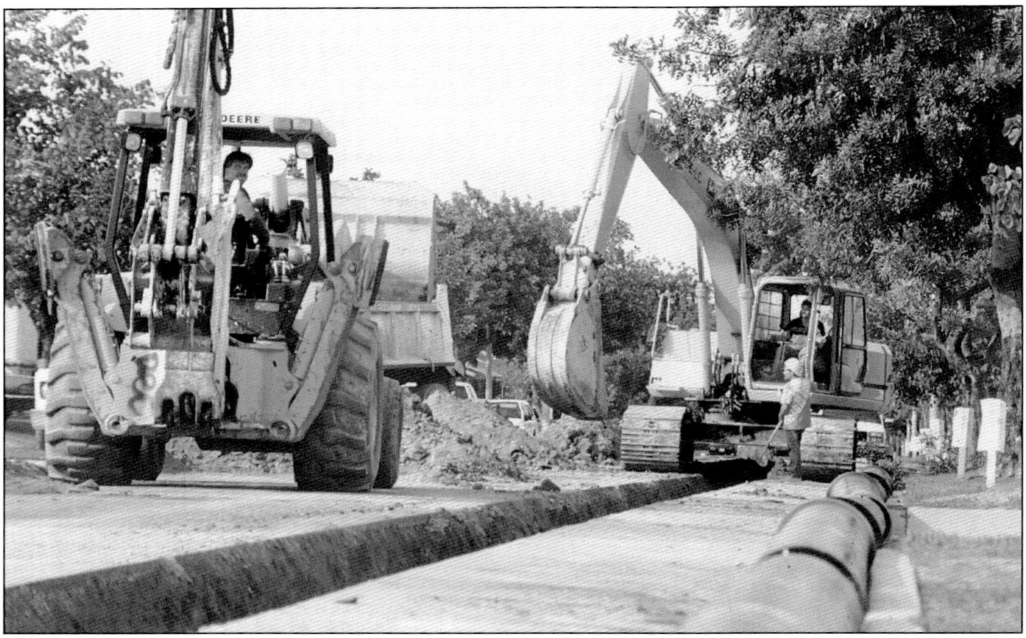

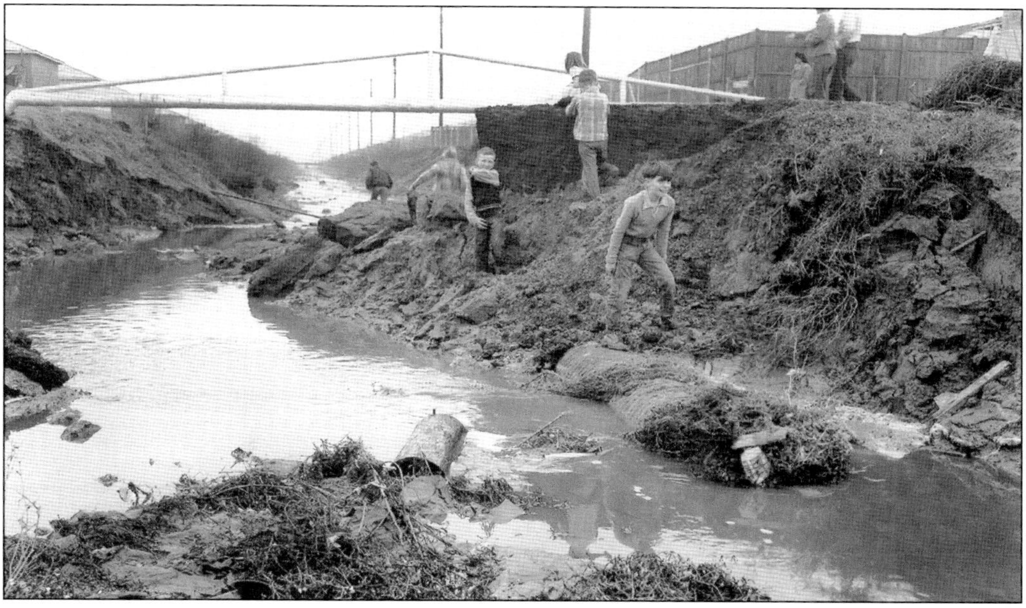

Dangerous Ditches. Nearly every year in the early 1950s, at least one child had to be rescued from open drainage ditches. The Lakewood Taxpayers Association launched a "Make Our Ditch Safe for Kids" campaign to cover the Heather Ditch in 1951. The ditch issue would play a role in the incorporation campaign in 1954, as revealed by one Lakewood Civic Council pamphlet entitled *What About The Ditches?*

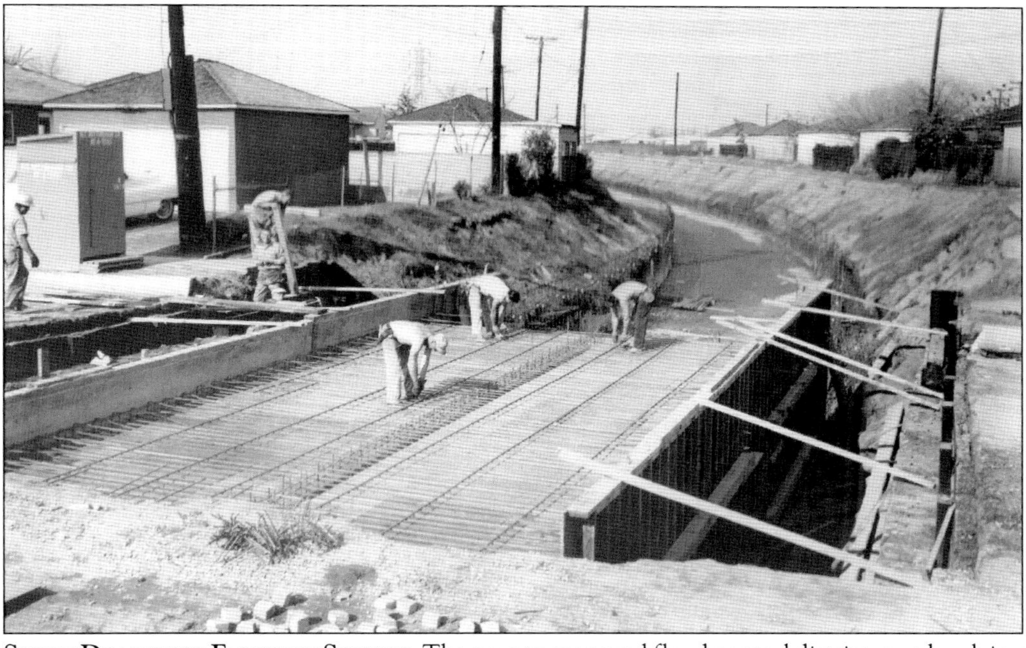

Storm Drains for Flooding Streets. The county-managed flood control district gave low-lying Lakewood priority for new storm drains in the 1960s. Many longtime residents can recall the days before storm drains, when it was common for some streets to be awash after a heavy downpour. Storm drains and sewers are the responsibility of county-governed special districts.

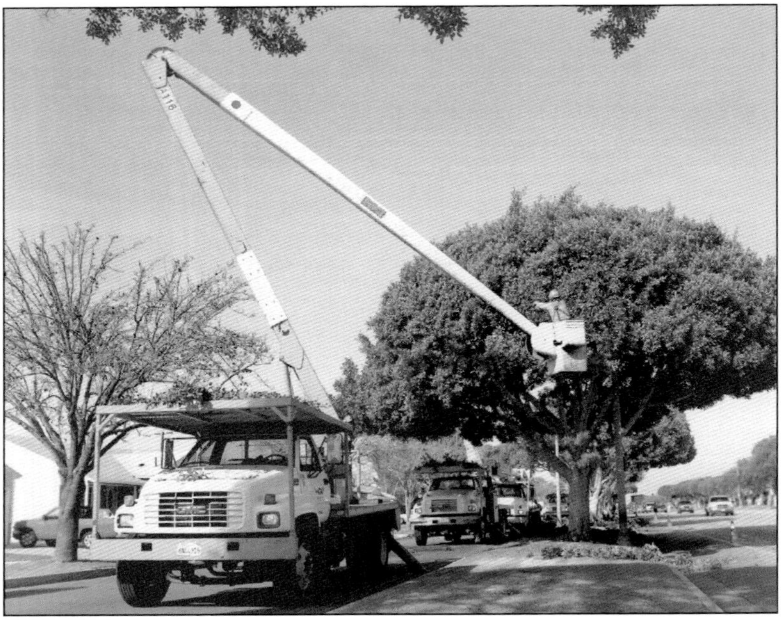

A City of Trees. Lakewood is nationally recognized as a Tree City USA for the care with which the City of Lakewood manages Lakewood's "urban forest," with trees trimmed under contract. First-time visitors to Lakewood typically comment on the canopy of mature trees, many planted more than 50 years ago, that shade residential streets.

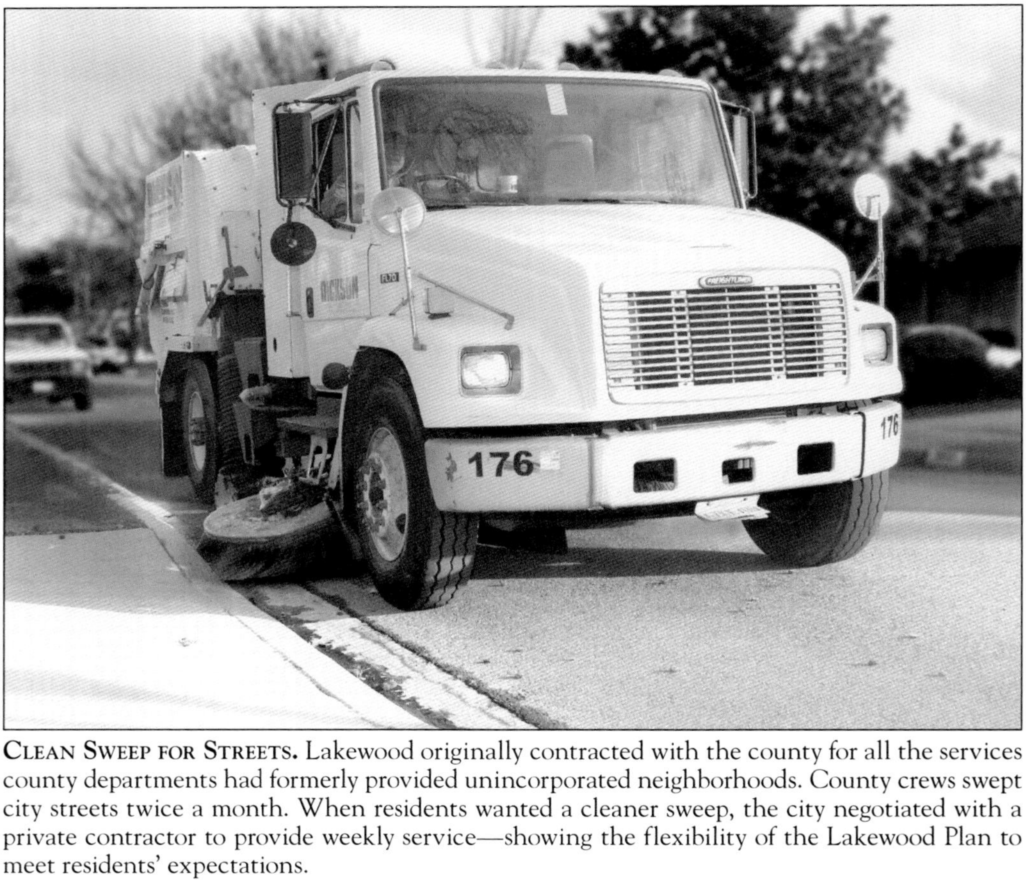

Clean Sweep for Streets. Lakewood originally contracted with the county for all the services county departments had formerly provided unincorporated neighborhoods. County crews swept city streets twice a month. When residents wanted a cleaner sweep, the city negotiated with a private contractor to provide weekly service—showing the flexibility of the Lakewood Plan to meet residents' expectations.

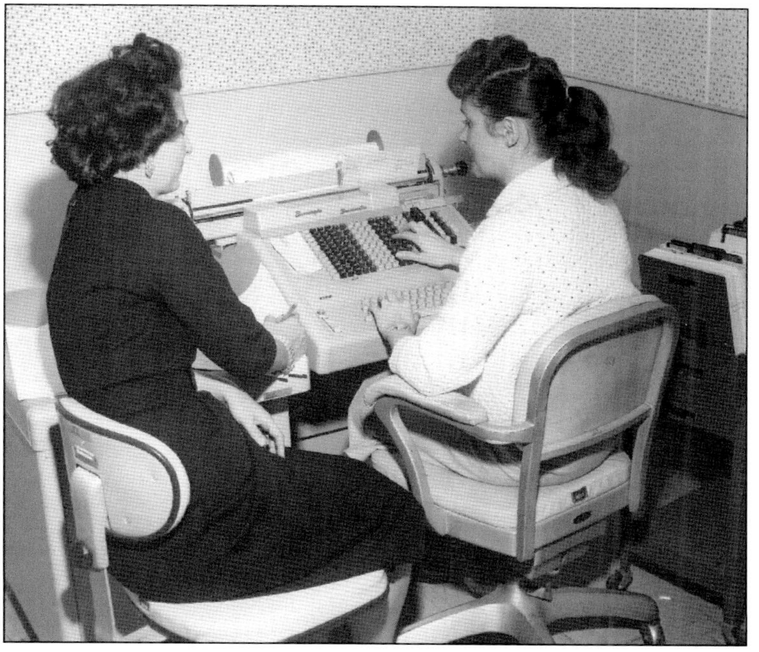

ADDING UP CITY SERVICES. When Lakewood began contacting with a private company for trash collection and purchased the former Lakewood Water and Power Company to supply western Lakewood with water, city hall began billing for both services using one of these massive Burroughs Sensimatic accounting machines. Not a pocket calculator, it weighed in at almost 30 pounds.

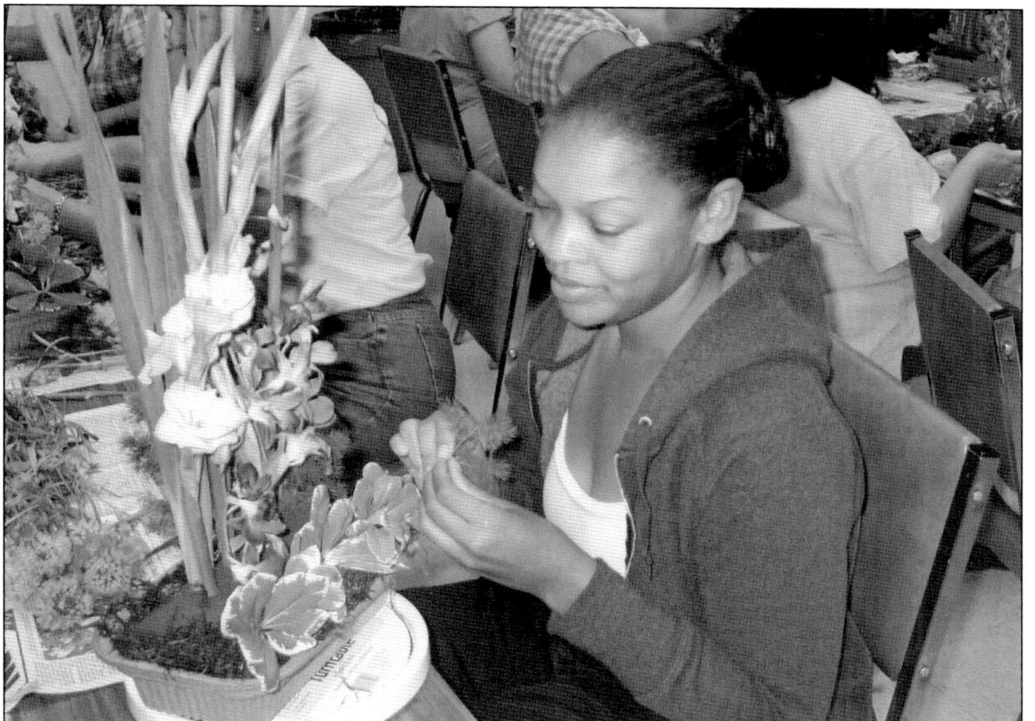

CLASSES FOR FUN. Lakewood's recreation programs include classes for kids, adults, and seniors. The class instructors are contractors, paid from the enrollment fees. Other recreation programs, such as day camps for children, are supervised by city staff members. Volunteers coach park sports teams for boys and girls throughout the year.

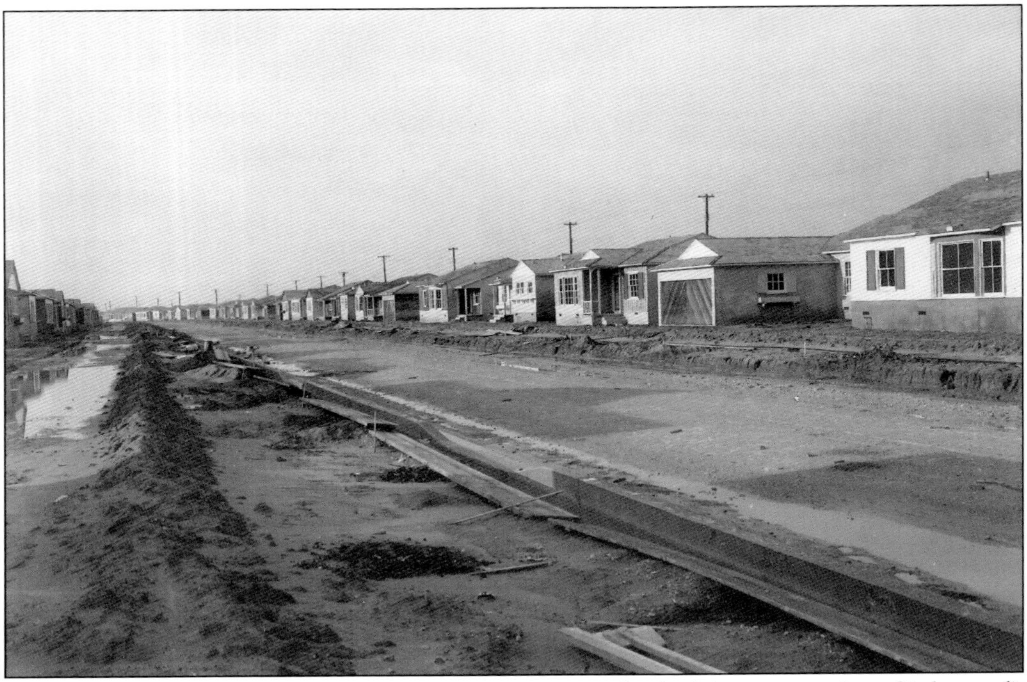

Contracting for Building Services. County inspectors checked the construction of Lakewood's thousands of new homes in 1950, shown above, to ensure the Lakewood Park Corporation met building safety standards. County inspectors continued as the city's building and safety division, under contract with the city after incorporation. Through more than 60 years, the remodeling of Lakewood's homes and the building of new structures, shown below, have been under the watchful eyes of experienced county inspectors.

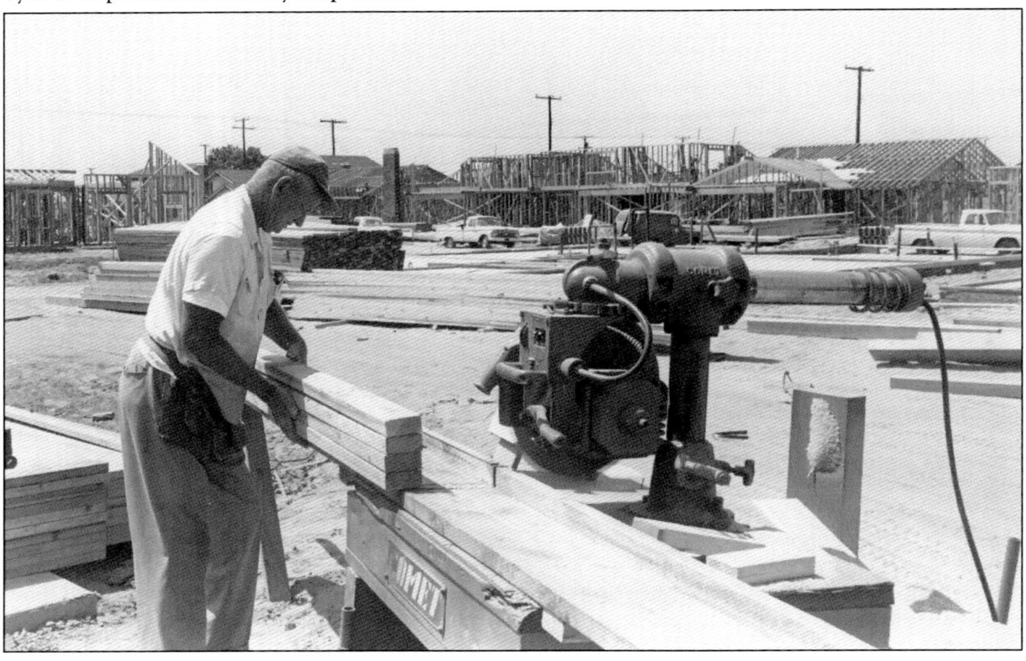

Six

Recreation for Families

During their first year, Lakewood City Council members extended new contracts for municipal services, adopted a "constitution" of codes and ordinances, and expanded public facilities for a growing community. By the end of 1955, Lakewood had a new fire station, acquired Mayfair Park and its pool from the county, and accepted three undeveloped park sites from Lakewood's original developers.

Optimistic Lakewood citizens adopted the motto "Tomorrow's City, Today," and strove to live up to its aspirations by focusing on the needs of Lakewood's thousands of young people.

On a single day in 1957, Lakewood dedicated three new parks with playgrounds, ball diamonds, and picnic areas. To honor Lakewood's tradition of pan-American friendship, the parks were named after Latin American heroes Simón Bolívar, José de San Martín, and José Del Valle. In 1958, Pat McCormick Pool, honoring the four-time Olympic gold medalist diver, was dedicated at Bolivar Park. The following year, Del Valle Park received a new piece of playground equipment: a Douglas Skynight jet fighter. It became the site of annual Memorial Day ceremonies.

By 1964, Lakewood had dedicated four more parks—Biscailuz Park, Monte Verde Park, Mae Boyar Park, and Bloomfield Park, which became the regional park for eastern Lakewood. More recreation facilities—Cherry Cove Park, Rynerson Park, the S. Mark Taper Vista Lodge at Monte Verde Park, the William Burns Community Center, the Weingart Senior Center, the Lakewood Community Gardens, the West San Gabriel River Nature Trail, and the Centre at Sycamore Plaza—were added in subsequent years.

As the city's youth grew from toddlers to school kids to teenagers, Lakewood recognized the need for organized programs to keep young people occupied. The city turned to volunteers in 1957 to staff its park sports leagues. Hundreds of volunteer coaches still staff these programs.

New recreation programs have charted the city's changing demographics, providing dances and clubs for teens, fitness and craft classes for moms, and programs for senior residents—literally something for every member of the family.

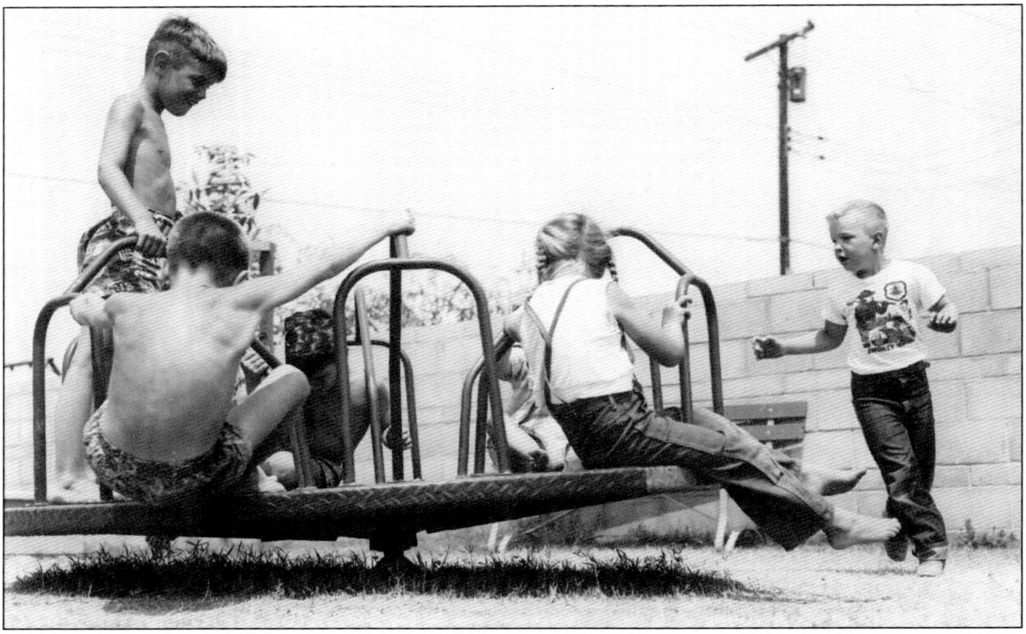

Safe Place to Play. Kids, almost all under the age of 10, were everywhere in Lakewood by 1953. Almost any block would have had as many 80 youngsters bursting with energy. To give kids places to play in their neighborhood, the Lakewood Water and Power Company converted several water well sites into Lakewood's first Tot Lots.

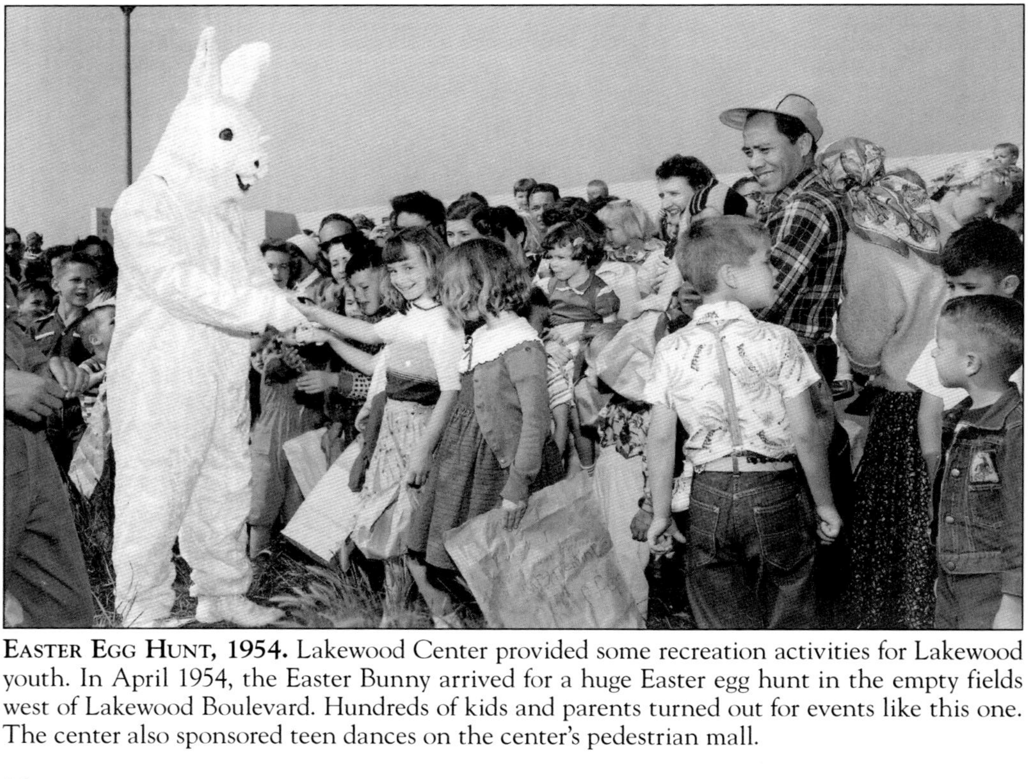

Easter Egg Hunt, 1954. Lakewood Center provided some recreation activities for Lakewood youth. In April 1954, the Easter Bunny arrived for a huge Easter egg hunt in the empty fields west of Lakewood Boulevard. Hundreds of kids and parents turned out for events like this one. The center also sponsored teen dances on the center's pedestrian mall.

RURAL HERITAGE. The Spiller Stables along the San Gabriel River were a popular destination for young riders in the early 1950s. The stables also boarded horses, sold tack, and gave riding lessons along the eastern bank of the river and through still rural Dairy Valley and Artesia.

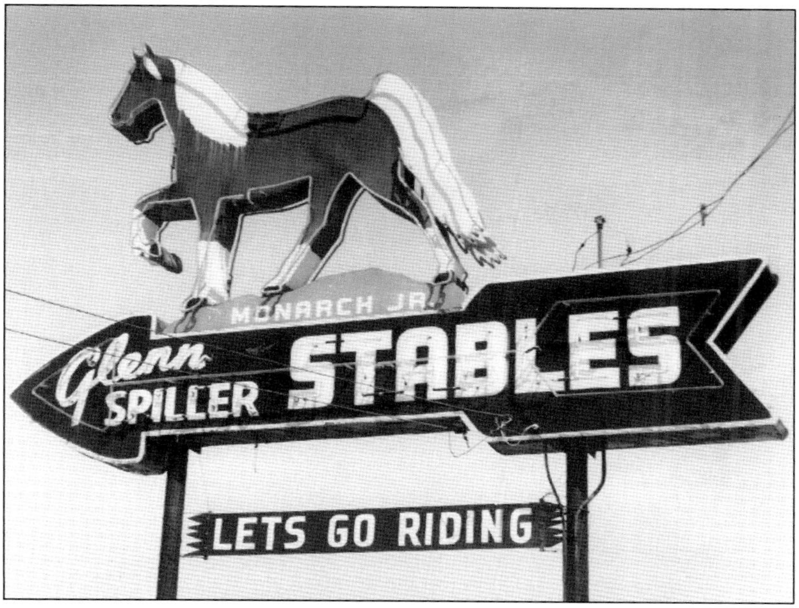

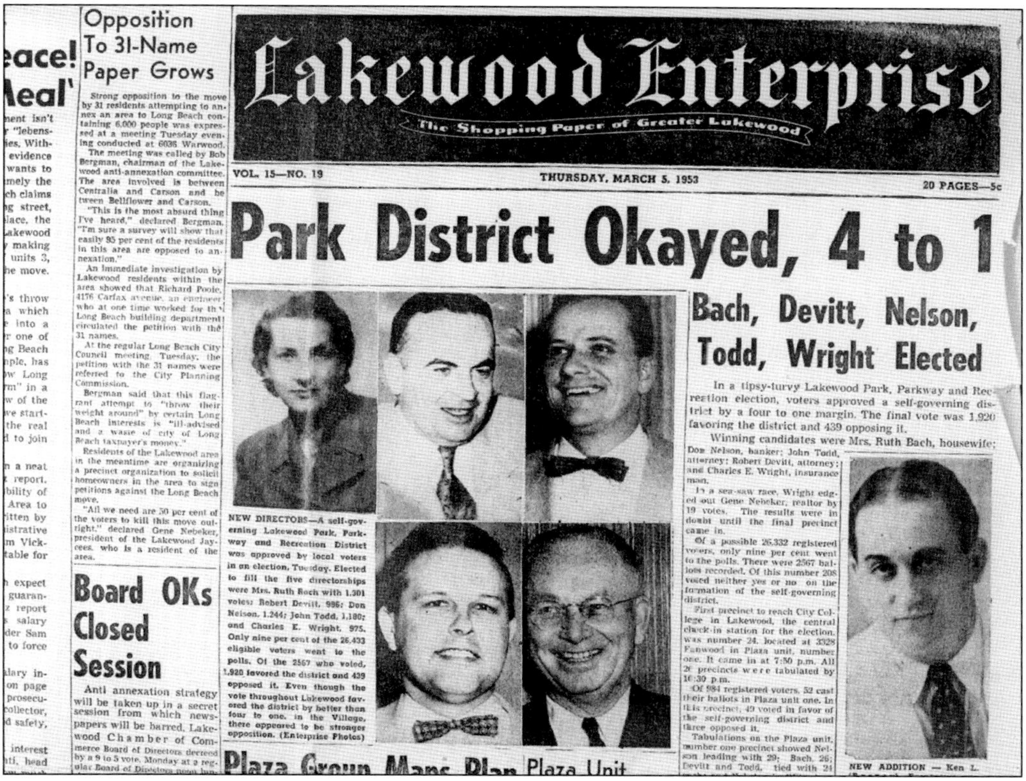

Lakewood Enterprise

The Shopping Paper of Greater Lakewood

VOL. 15—NO. 19 THURSDAY, MARCH 5, 1953 20 PAGES—5c

Park District Okayed, 4 to 1

Bach, Devitt, Nelson, Todd, Wright Elected

In a tipsy-turvy Lakewood Park, Parkway and Recreation election, voters approved a self-governing district by a four to one margin. The final vote was 1,920 favoring the district and 439 opposing it.

Winning candidates were Mrs. Ruth Bach, housewife; Don Nelson, banker; John Todd, attorney; Robert Devitt, attorney; and Charles E. Wright, insurance man.

In a sea-saw race, Wright edged out Gene Nebeker, realtor by 19 votes. The results were in doubt until the final precinct came in.

Of a possible 26,332 registered voters, only nine per cent went to the polls. There were 2567 ballots recorded. Of this number 208 voted neither yes or no on the formation of the self-governing district.

First precinct to reach City College in Lakewood, the central check-in station for the election, was number 24, located at 3328 Fanwood in Plaza unit, number one. It came in at 7:50 p.m. All 28 precincts were tabulated by 10:30 p.m.

Of 984 registered voters, 52 cast their ballots in Plaza unit one. In this precinct, 49 voted in favor of the self-governing district and three opposed it.

Tabulations on the Plaza unit, number one precinct showed Nelson leading with 29; Bach, 26; Devitt and Todd, tied with 24 …

NEW DIRECTORS—A self-governing Lakewood Park, Parkway and Recreation District was approved by local voters in an election, Tuesday. Elected to fill the five directorships were Mrs. Ruth Bach with 1,301 votes; Robert Devitt, 986; Don Nelson, 1,244; John Todd, 1,180; and Charles E. Wright, 975. Only nine per cent of the 26,433 eligible voters went to the polls. Of the 2567 who voted, 1,920 favored the district and 439 opposed it. Even though the vote throughout Lakewood favored the district by better than four to one, in the Village, there appeared to be stronger opposition. (Enterprise Photos)

NEW ADDITION — Ken L.

Opposition To 31-Name Paper Grows

Strong opposition to the move by 31 residents attempting to annex an area to Long Beach containing 6,000 people was expressed at a meeting Tuesday evening conducted at 6036 Warwood.

The meeting was called by Bob Bergman, chairman of the Lakewood anti-annexation committee. The area involved is between Centralia and Carson and between Bellflower and Carson.

"This is the most absurd thing I've heard," declared Bergman. "I'm sure a survey will show that easily 95 per cent of the residents in this area are opposed to annexation."

An immediate investigation by Lakewood residents within the area showed that Richard Poole, 4176 Carfax avenue, an engineer who at one time worked for the Long Beach building department circulated the petition with the 31 names.

At the regular Long Beach City Council meeting Tuesday, the petition with the 31 names were referred to the City Planning Commission.

Bergman said that this flagrant attempt to "throw their weight around" by certain Long Beach interests is "ill-advised and a waste of city of Long Beach taxpayer's money."

Residents of the Lakewood area in the meantime are organizing a precinct organization to solicit homeowners in the area to sign petitions against the Long Beach move.

"All we need are 50 per cent of the voters to kill this move outright," declared Gene Nebeker, president of the Lakewood Jaycees, who is a resident of the area.

Board OKs Closed Session

Anti annexation strategy will be taken up in a secret session from which newspapers will be barred, Lakewood Chamber of Commerce Board of Directors decreed by a 9 to 5 vote, Monday at a regular Board of Directors noon lun…

Plaza Group Maps Plan

Plaza Unit

RECREATION DISTRICT FORMED. Lakewood voters created a park, recreation, and parkway district in 1953 to develop more parks and youth programs. The district's projects included organizing weekend recreation activities at 10 elementary school playgrounds and negotiating for the acquisition of the three sites that the Lakewood Park Corporation had set aside for park development.

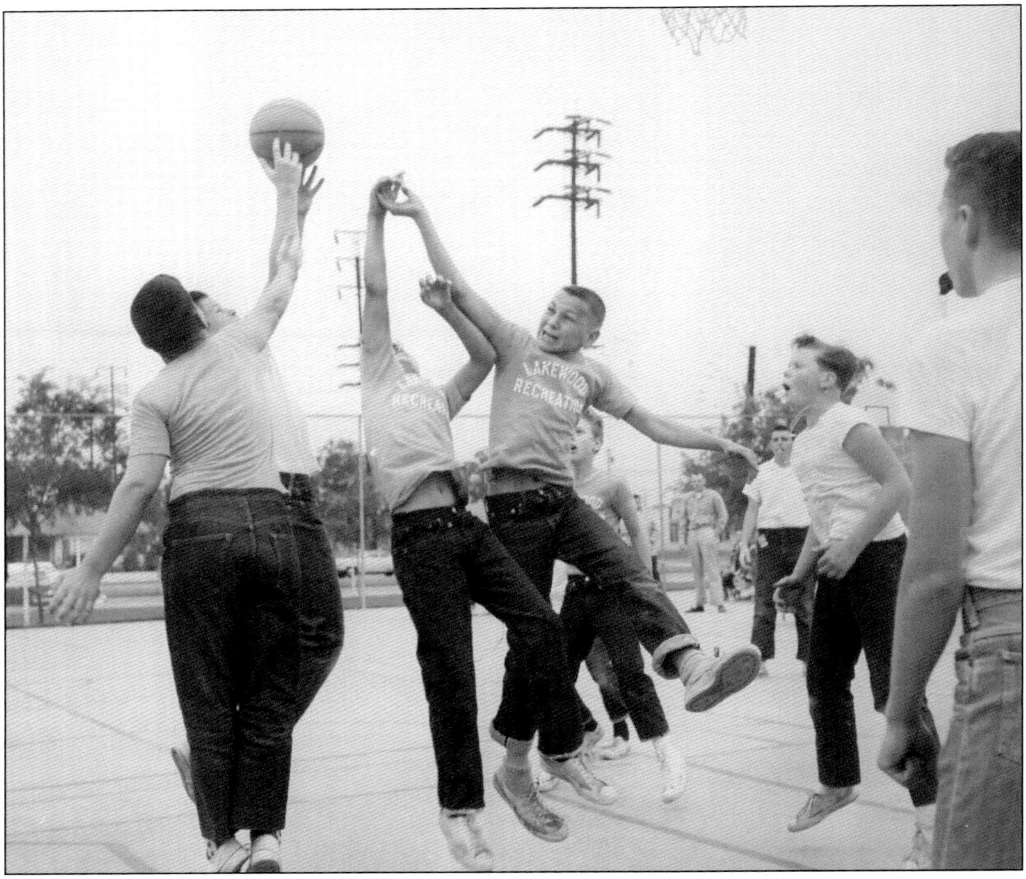

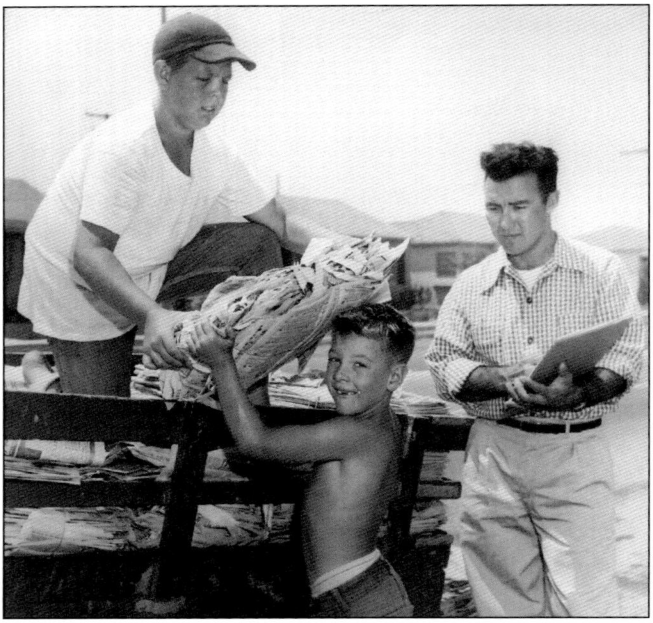

SPORTS FOR ACTIVE BOYS. Lakewood's boys had energy to spare, and playgrounds and parks were among the first desires of moms and dads in forming a recreation district. When the district was dissolved in 1957, the city delivered on the city council's promise of more programs for kids.

FUNDRAISING FOR THEIR TEAM. These eager boys are collecting old newspapers to raise money in 1952 to buy jerseys for their Lakewood sports team. Team sports for both boys and girls are still a core recreation activity at city parks, along with summer day camps, swimming lessons, and a range of classes from karate to dance.

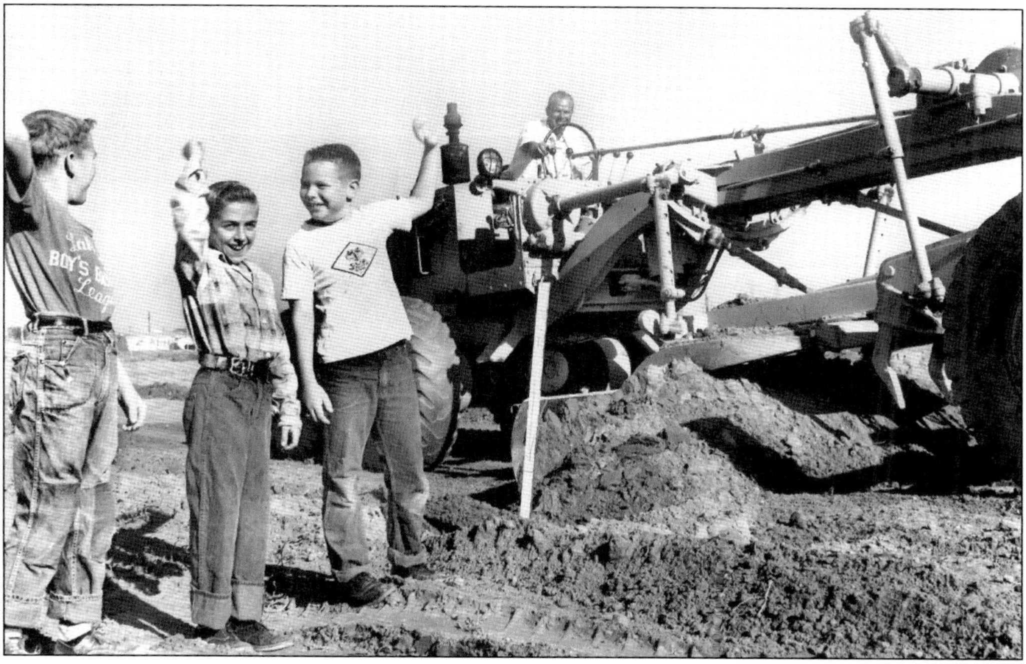

Building Parks for Lakewood Youth. In 1954, the new city council affirmed that park development was a priority and entered into more than three years of negotiations with the Lakewood Park Corporation, culminating in the purchase of three undeveloped park sites at a cost of $276,000. In 1957, Lakewood voters chose to fold the existing recreation district into the city and make the city council responsible for the development of Lakewood's recreation programs. Construction of new parks, shown above, began almost at once. Lakewood's new parks, seen below, soon became every kid's place for fun.

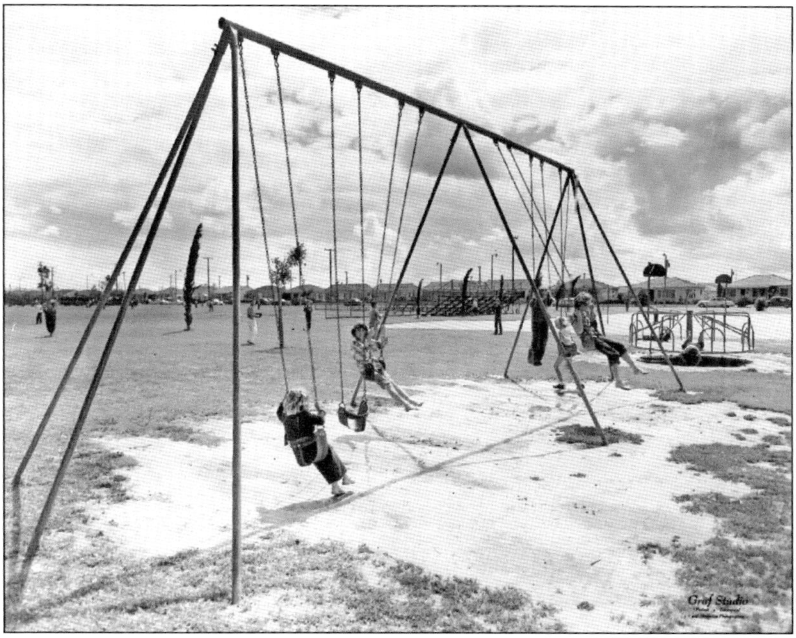

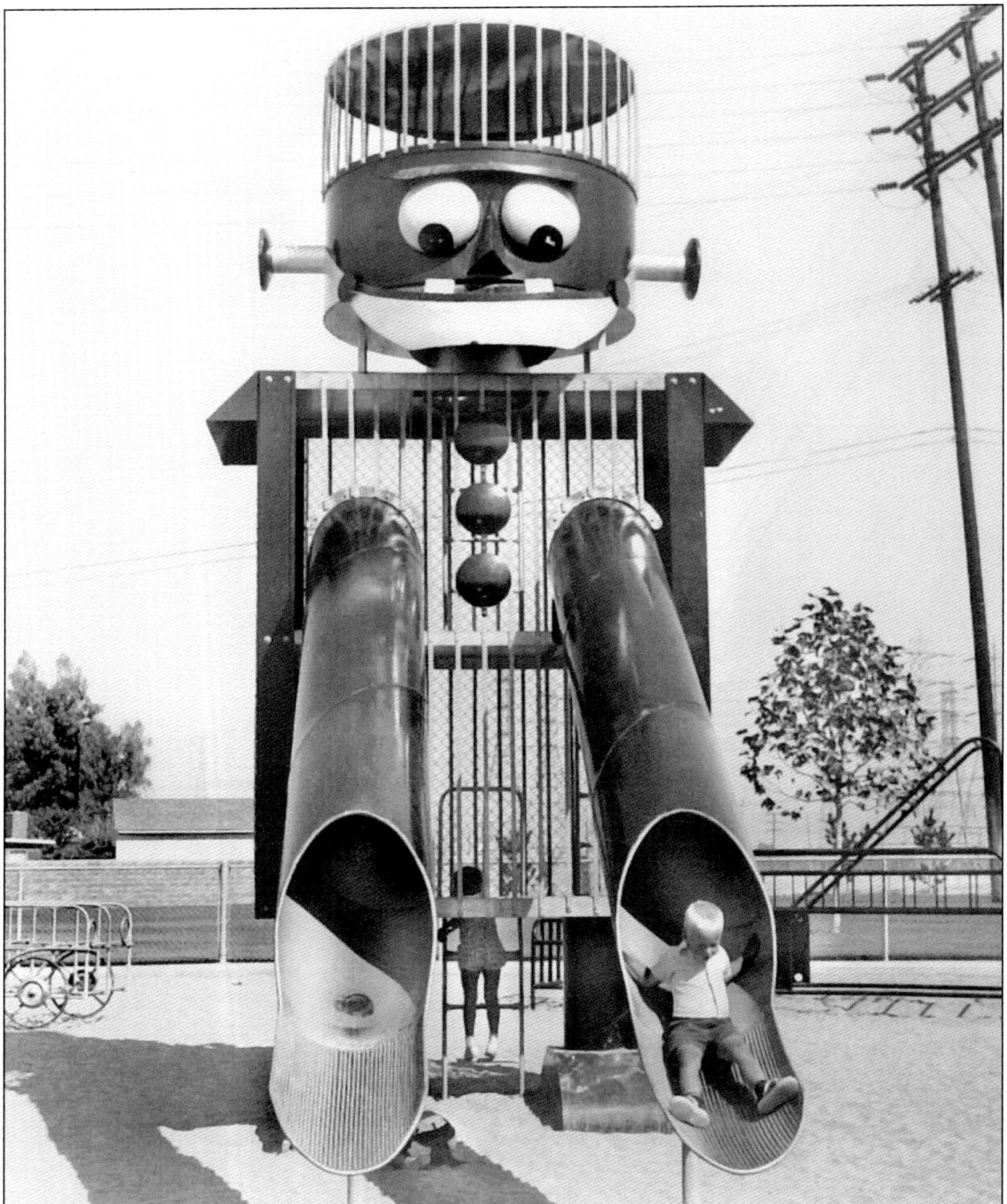

FRIENDLY GIANT. Giganta once stood in Mae Boyar Park, offering thrills for youngsters who climbed into the giant's head or sailed down one of his tubular arms. Boyar Park was dedicated in 1964 in honor of Mae Boyar, the wife of Lakewood developer Louis Boyar, following her death. The city boasted of "an almost unparalleled park development program" that year, averaging one new park each year since 1957, bringing the total to seven. Lakewood's parks were busy all year long, with more than 8,500 youngsters signed up for football, basketball, and baseball programs under the guidance of 900 volunteer coaches. As its park system grew, Lakewood became known nationally for its innovative programs for active families.

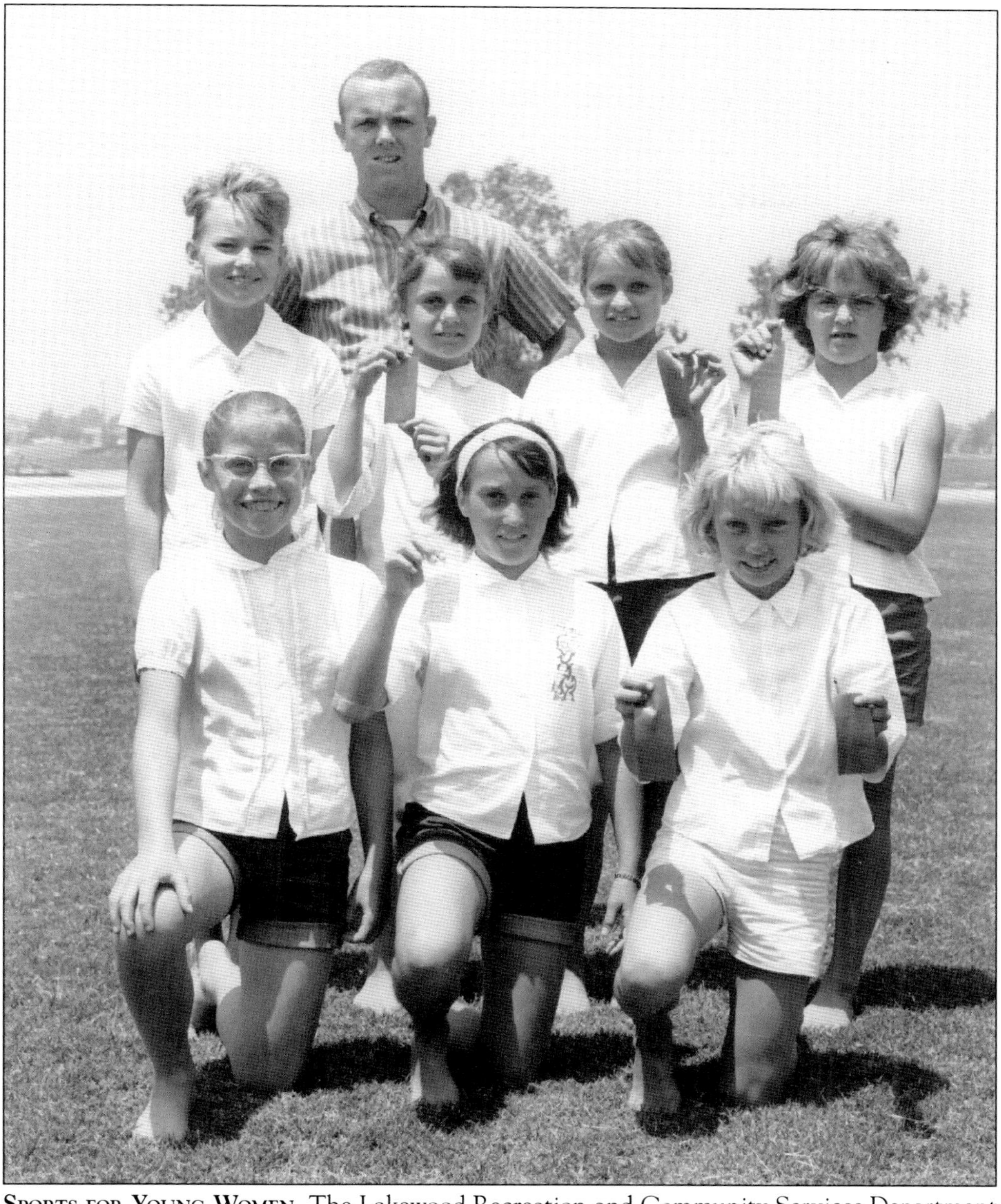

Sports for Young Women. The Lakewood Recreation and Community Services Department began competitive sports programs for girls and young women with the help of Dave Rodda, the young man at the rear in this photograph. Rodda went on to become the coach of women Olympians and the director of the city's recreation department he had joined as a teenager. As Rodda noted, "In 1960, the first girls' softball league was formed. Following the tradition of boys' sports, volunteer coaches were recruited from the women's sports leagues. Every girl had the opportunity to play in every game. We were so far ahead of everyone else. Whatever the boys got, the girls got. Some of the other sports we introduced were different, but the awards were the same. And everybody came to the parks and everybody participated."

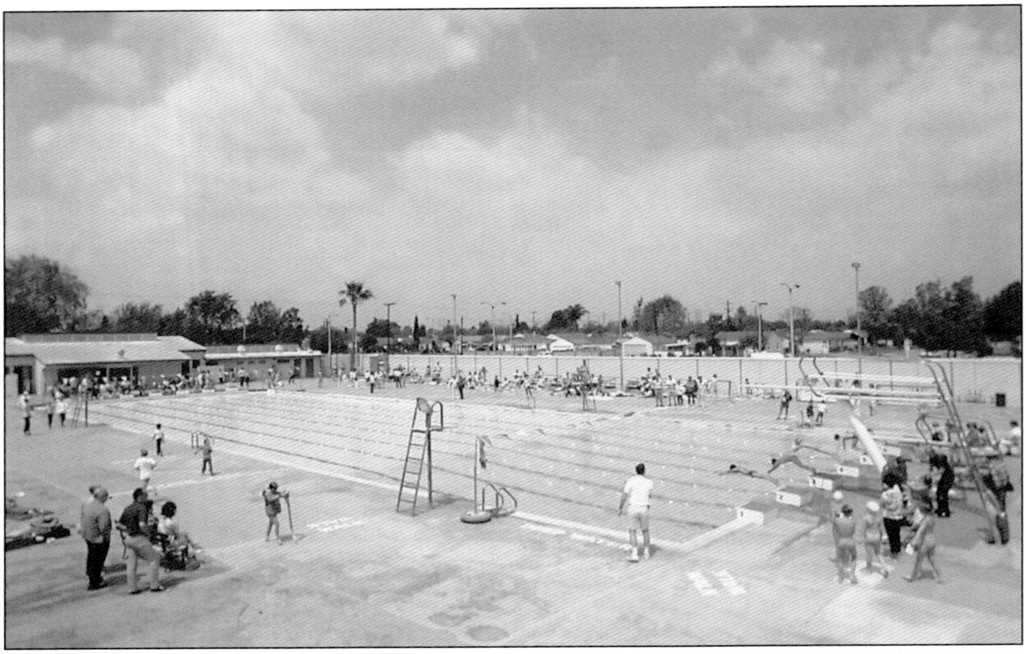

In the Swim. The pool at Mayfair Park, shown above, was the go-to destination on hot summer afternoons in the 1960s. The pool offered swimming instruction, seen below, for school-age youth, adults, and even toddlers. Swimming and diving programs attracted young athletes who went on become national competitors. Mayfair Pool was a gift to the community from the developers of Lakewood as part of the transfer of the Lakewood golf course to the county in 1952.

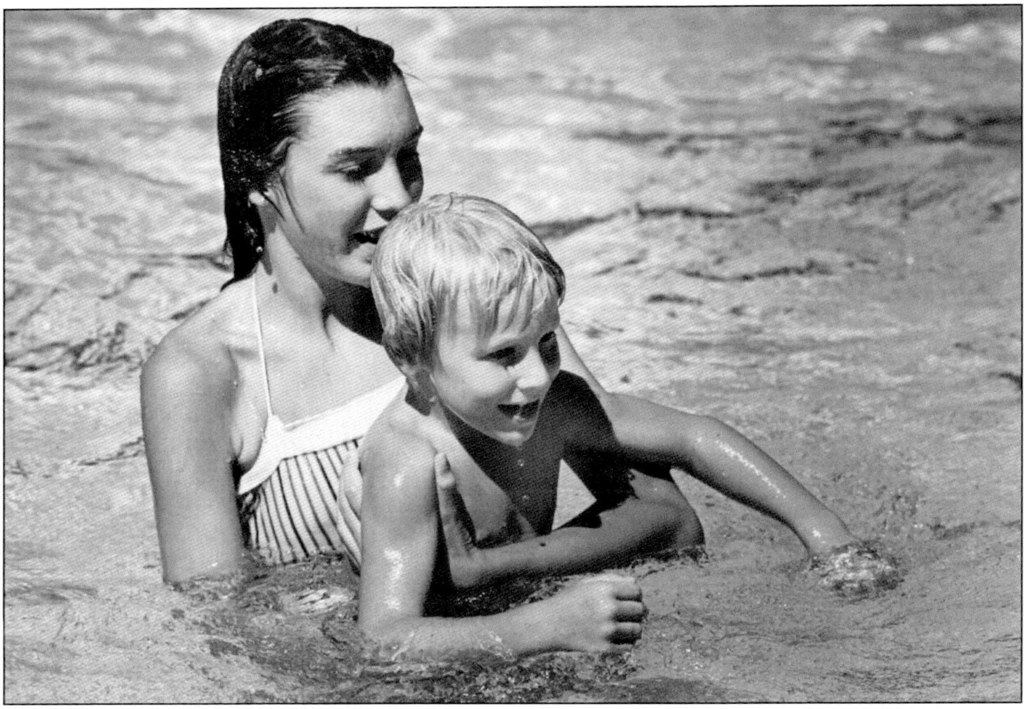

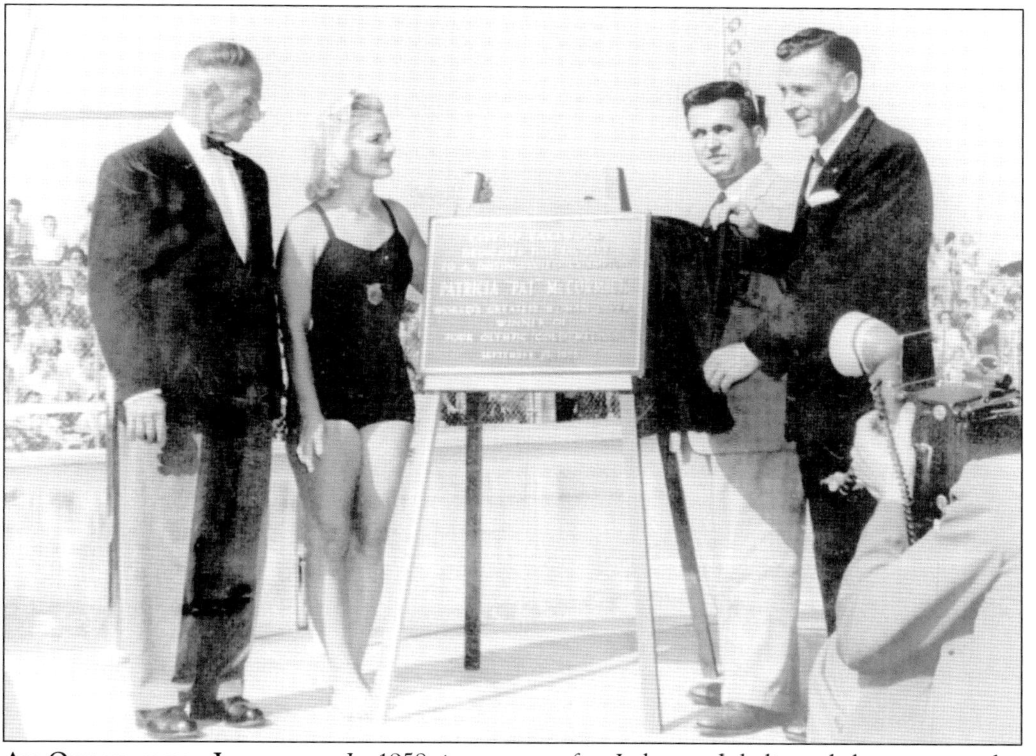

AN OLYMPIAN FOR LAKEWOOD. In 1958, just a year after Lakewood dedicated three new parks, champion Olympic diver Pat McCormick (left), who had grown up in Lakewood, joined Mayor Angelo Iacoboni (holding the plaque) in dedicating Pat McCormick Pool at Bolivar Park as Lakewood's second community swim facility. McCormick thrilled the audience with a demonstration of the diving skills that won her four Olympic gold medals.

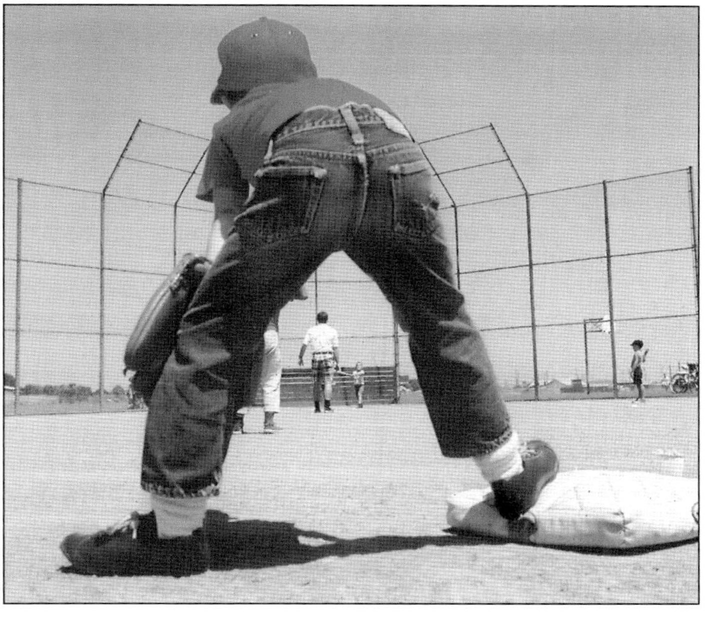

VOLUNTEER COACHES FOR SPORTS TEAMS, 1957. The story of the first Lakewood Youth Sports baseball sign-up day, which took place on a Saturday morning in May 1957, has become Lakewood lore. Instead of the 100 boys expected, 1,500 flocked to Mayfair Park. City recreation staff members quickly called parents all over the city, asking for volunteers. They came and launched what remains one of the city's largest volunteer programs.

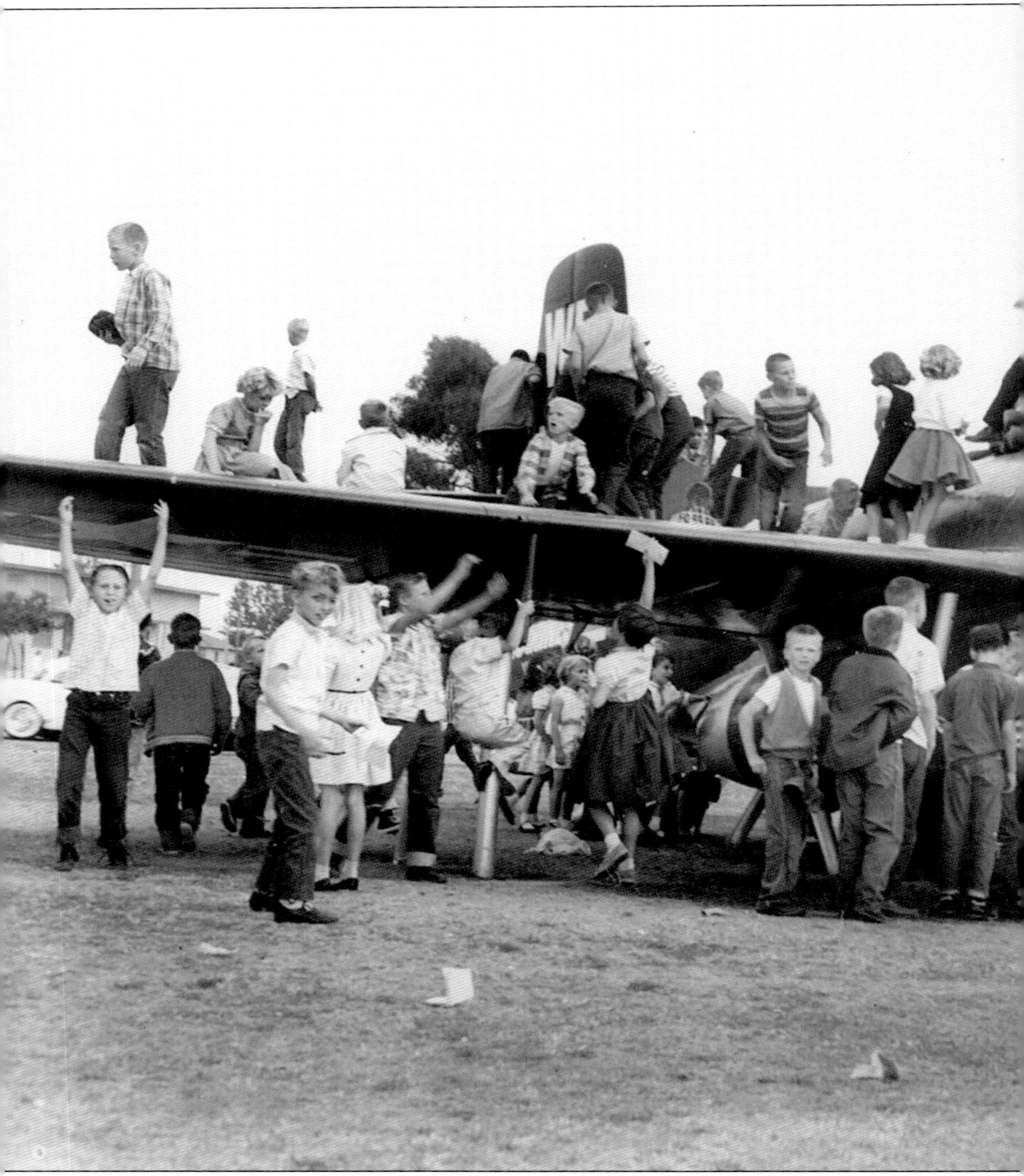

A Jet for Del Valle Park. In 1959, Del Valle Park received an unusual piece of playground equipment, courtesy of the Marine Corps—a Douglas F-3D Skynight jet fighter. The plane was painted black thanks to its night fighter role during the Korean War, but it was stripped of its operating gear. The jet was delivered to the park by the Navajo Freight Lines company, which explains why, for many years, the company's logo of a Navajo portrait was painted on the sides of

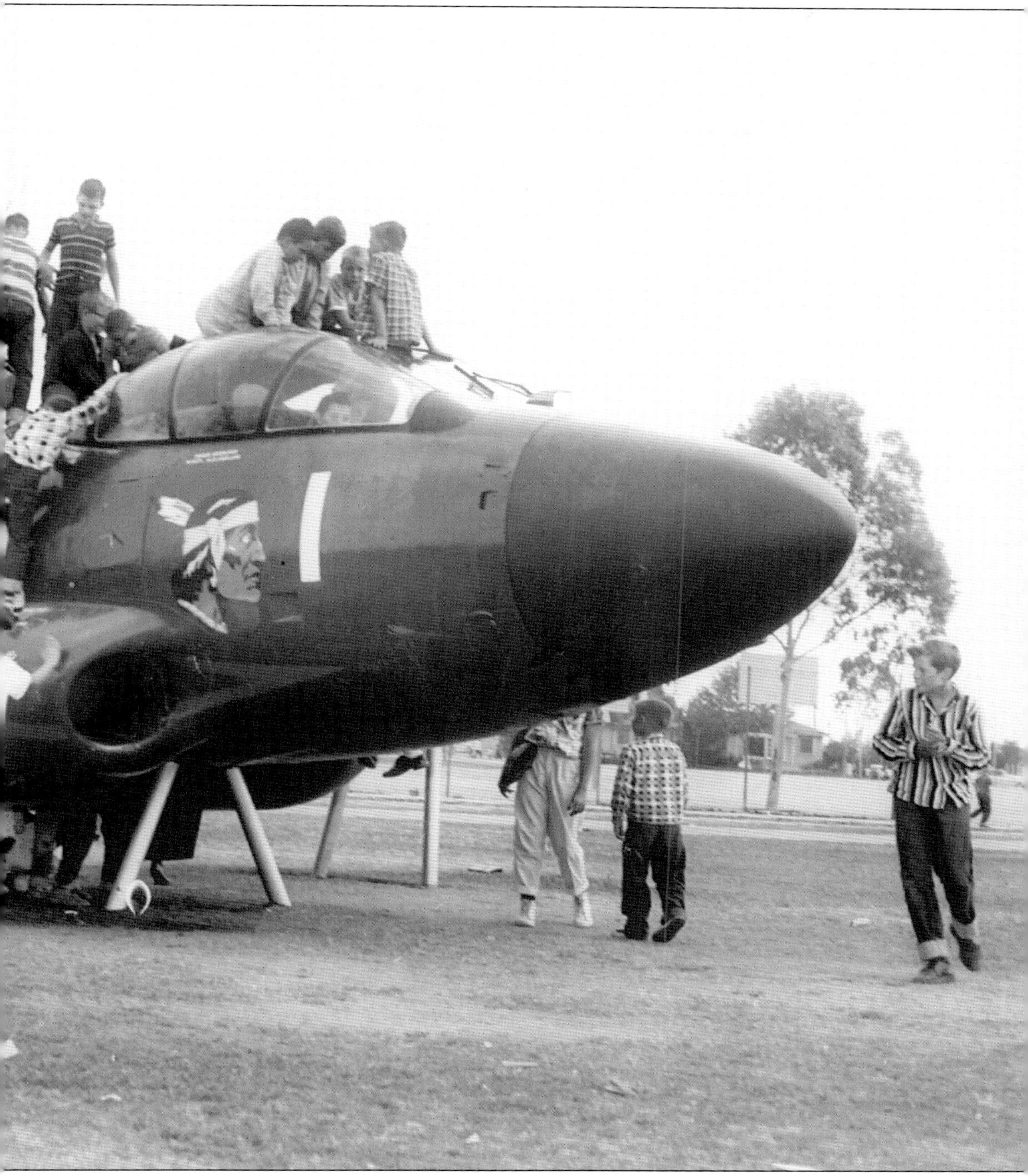

the plane. The park itself, designated as the city's space-age-themed park, featured a rocket ship climbing structure and other futuristic details, but locals soon began calling it Airplane Park. The jet was a popular piece of playground equipment. As longtime resident Dennis Lander remembers, "It was very much a flight of fancy. In other city parks, there was nothing like it."

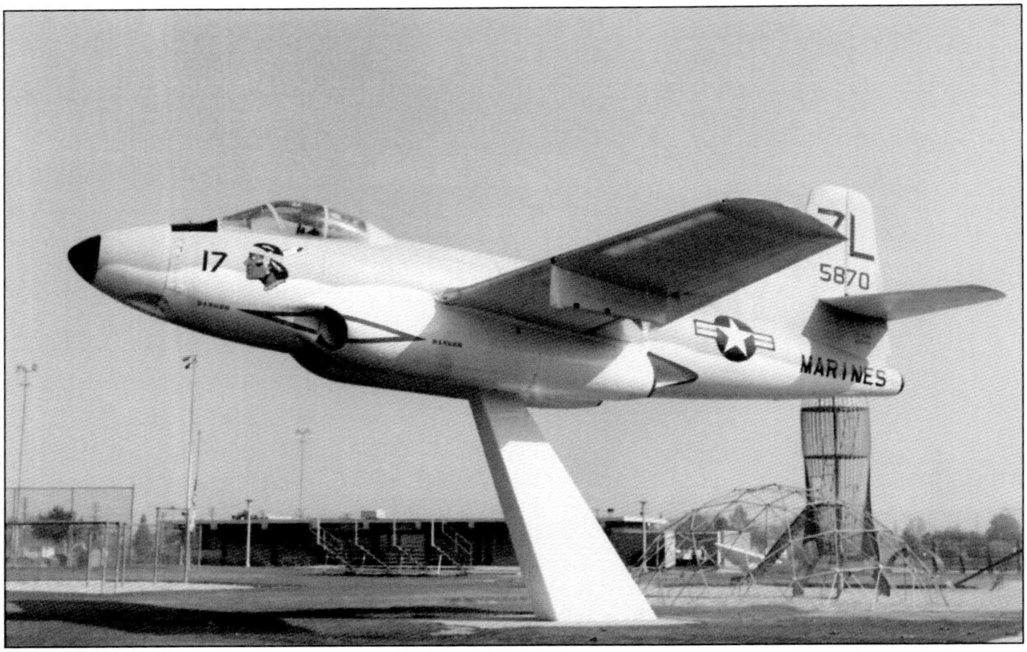

RAISED UP OVER DEL VALLE. The city soon discovered that a warplane was not made for playground use. The refurbished plane was lifted on a concrete pylon, nose up as if taking off over Woodruff Avenue, and repainted. On Memorial Day 1964, the Del Valle jet was officially dedicated as a memorial to those from Lakewood who had fought in the Korean War.

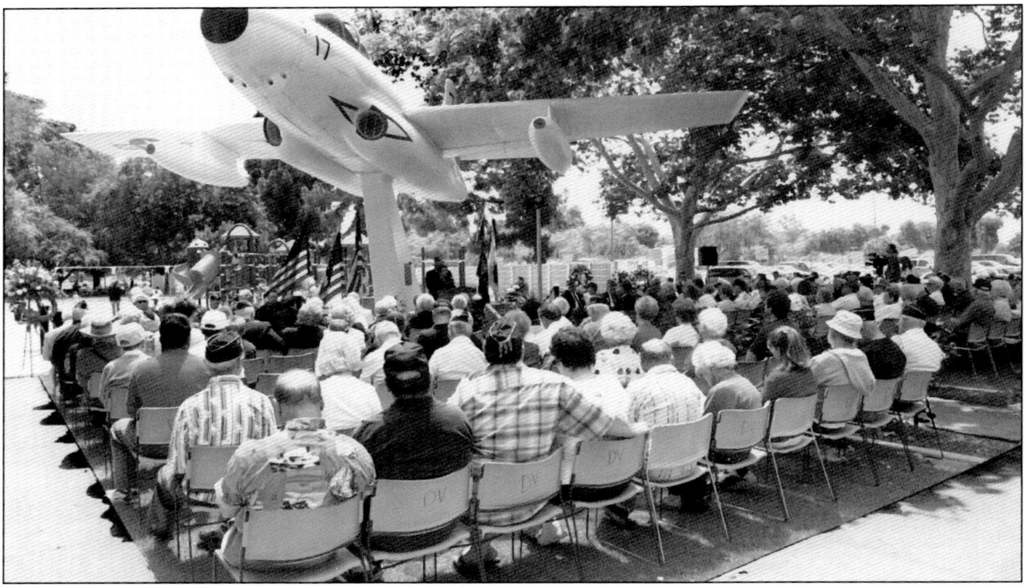

MEMORIAL DAY OBSERVANCES. With the help of American Legion Post 496, Del Valle Park and the jet plane became the location for the city's Memorial Day programs. The city council also began the tradition of recognizing the men of Lakewood who had fallen in Vietnam with a solemn roll call of their names. The family of the Rev. Dr. John Bonner later provided a plaque that recalls the contributions of World War II veterans.

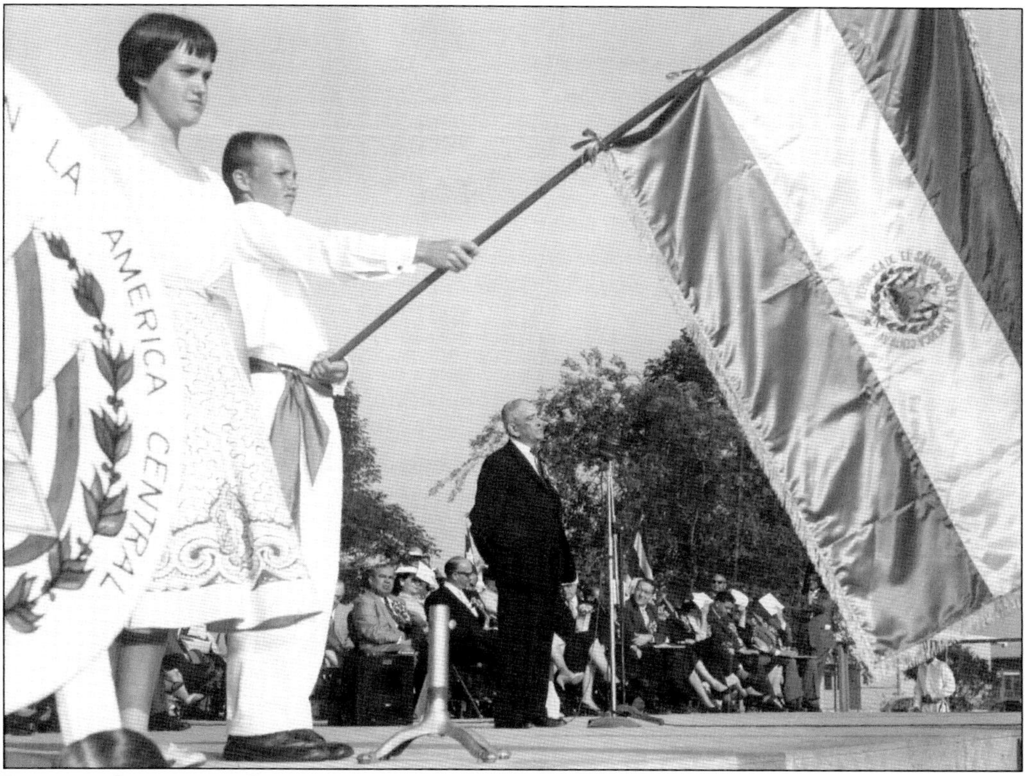

FESTIVAL CELEBRATES PAN-AMERICAN FRIENDSHIP. Lakewood's oldest community event is the annual Pan-American Festival, honoring the peoples and cultures of Latin America. Flag exchanges, shown above, were the highlight of the original festival. The Pan-American Festival Association later hosted the Saludos Amigos parade, shown below, with floats, equestrian units, and marching bands. In 1979, the festival highlight became the three-day Pan-American Fiesta at Mayfair Park. The festival still kicks off with the El Comienzo Luncheon. The Pan-American Fiesta is the nation's only citywide celebration of pan-American friendship outside of Washington, DC.

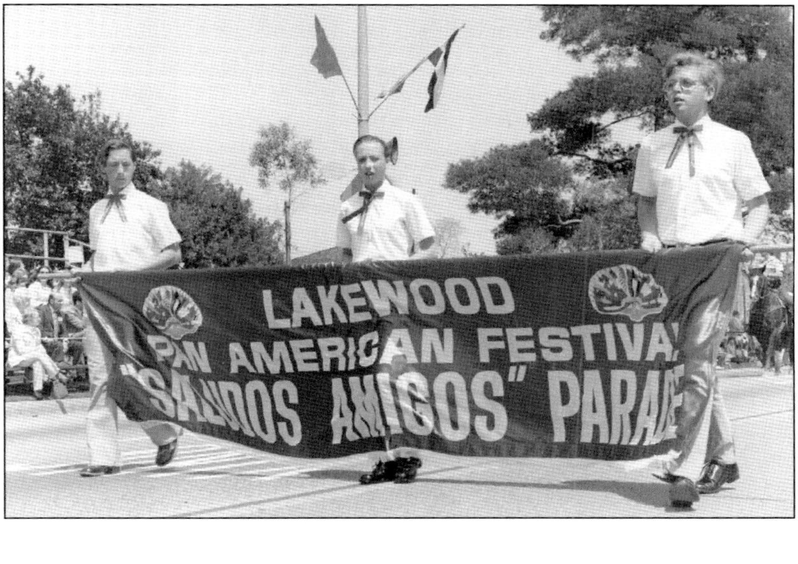

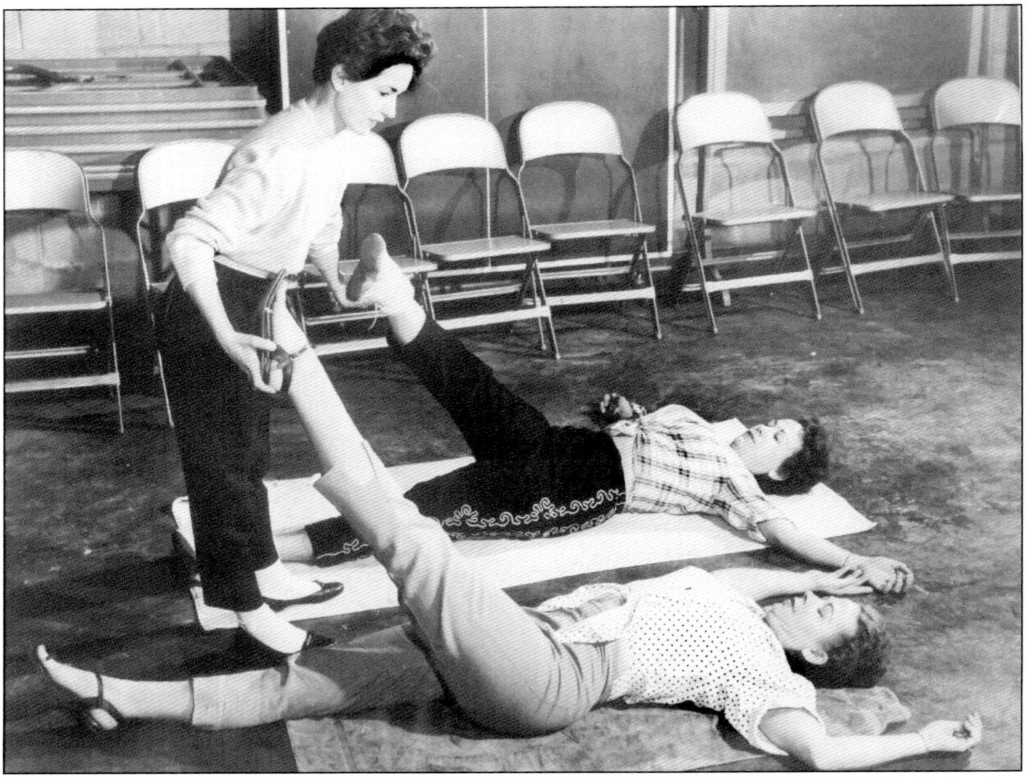

Contract Classes. Lakewood recreation focuses on lifelong fitness for family members, whether young moms in the 1960s, seen above, or fathers and sons in the 1980s, shown below. Specialized classes for adults and youth are still taught by expert instructors who contract with the city. Instruction in everything from yoga to swing dancing is offered today. The city provides the recreation facilities and support services, including seasonal recreation catalogs and online registration for classes and activities. The online system allows users to register for classes 24 hours a day, seven days a week.

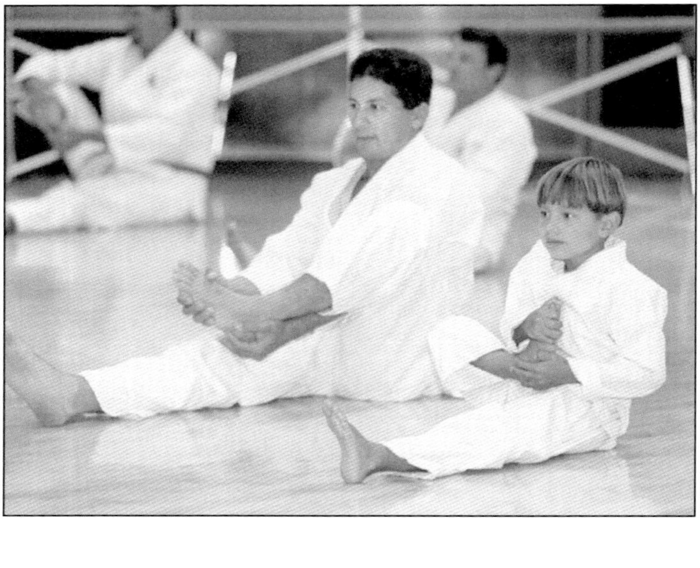

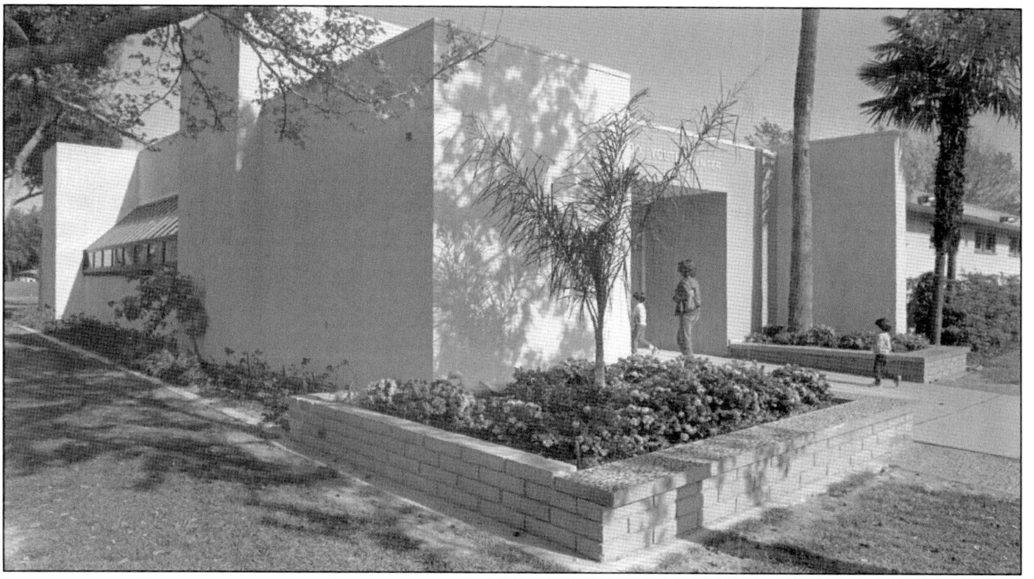

Lakewood Youth Center. Community organizations began a three-year campaign to build Lakewood a teen center in 1955, with the help of the Lakewood Women's Club and 15 other service organizations. When the Youth Center, also known as the Canteen, was dedicated in Del Valle Park in 1958, it became a favorite spot for dances held after Lakewood High School football games.

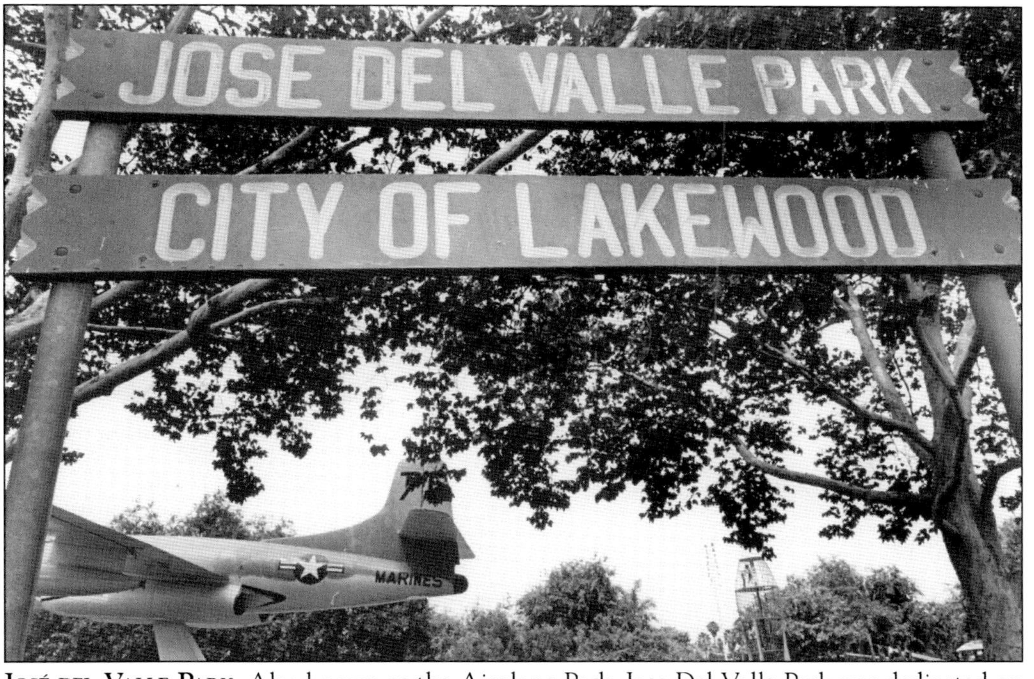

José del Valle Park. Also known as the Airplane Park, Jose Del Valle Park was dedicated on one hectic day in 1957, along with two other parks named in honor of Latin American heroes Simón Bolívar and José de San Martín. Del Valle Park is the site of the Lakewood Youth Center and the grove where Summer Concerts in the Park are performed.

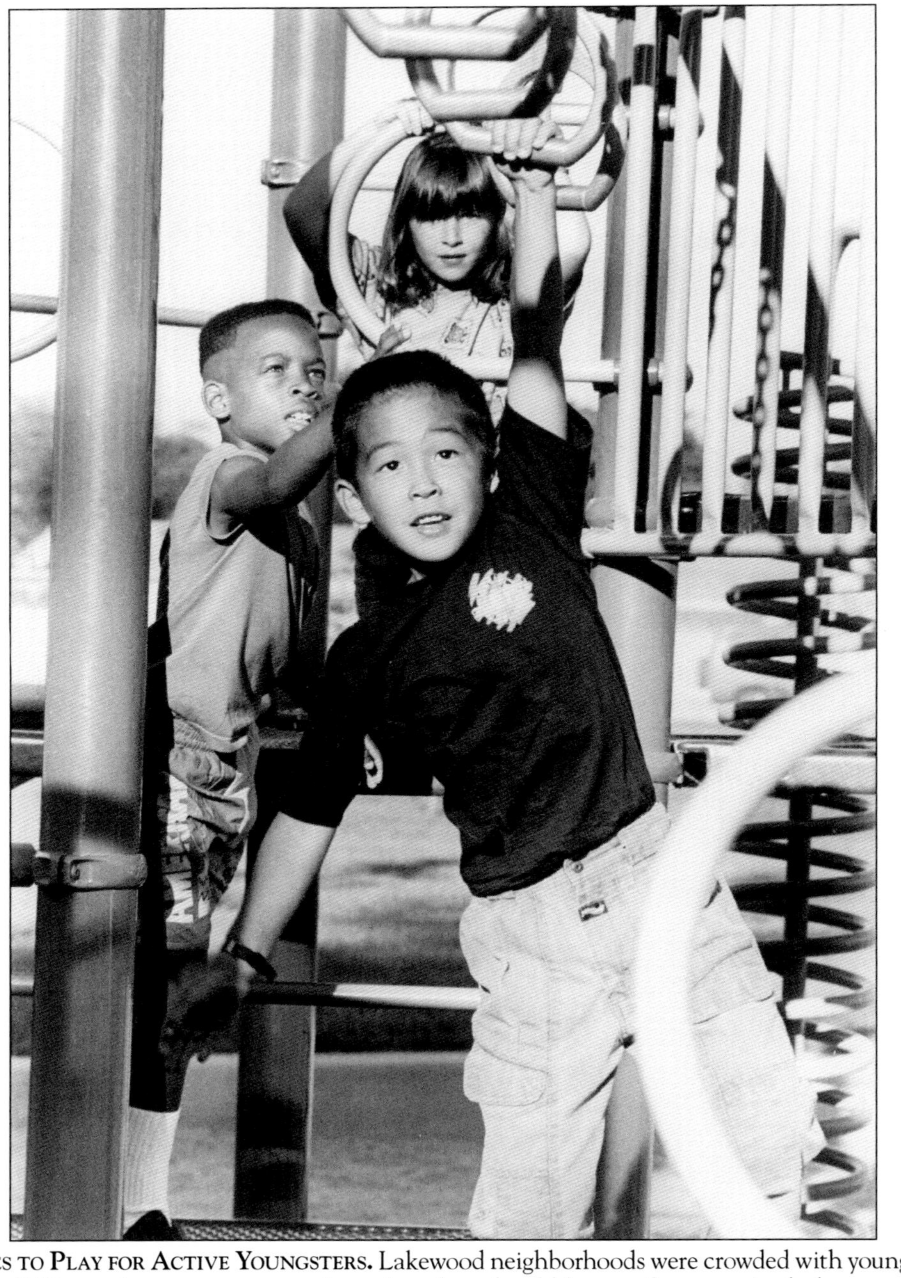

Places to Play for Active Youngsters. Lakewood neighborhoods were crowded with youngsters in the 1950s, and parents were anxious that they should have safe, supervised places to play. Lakewood eventually developed 10 major parks with ball diamonds, multipurpose game courts, sports lighting, playgrounds and playground equipment, activity buildings, and picnic shelters. Demographic shifts in the 1980s brought a new wave of young families to the city's affordable homes. The Lakewood Recreation and Community Services Department responded with new recreation programs and improved park playgrounds, including the parent-cooperative Tot Lots that had begun almost 40 years before. Here, Katie Allen, top, Amiel Givens, middle, and Casey Ung, bottom, try out the new play equipment.

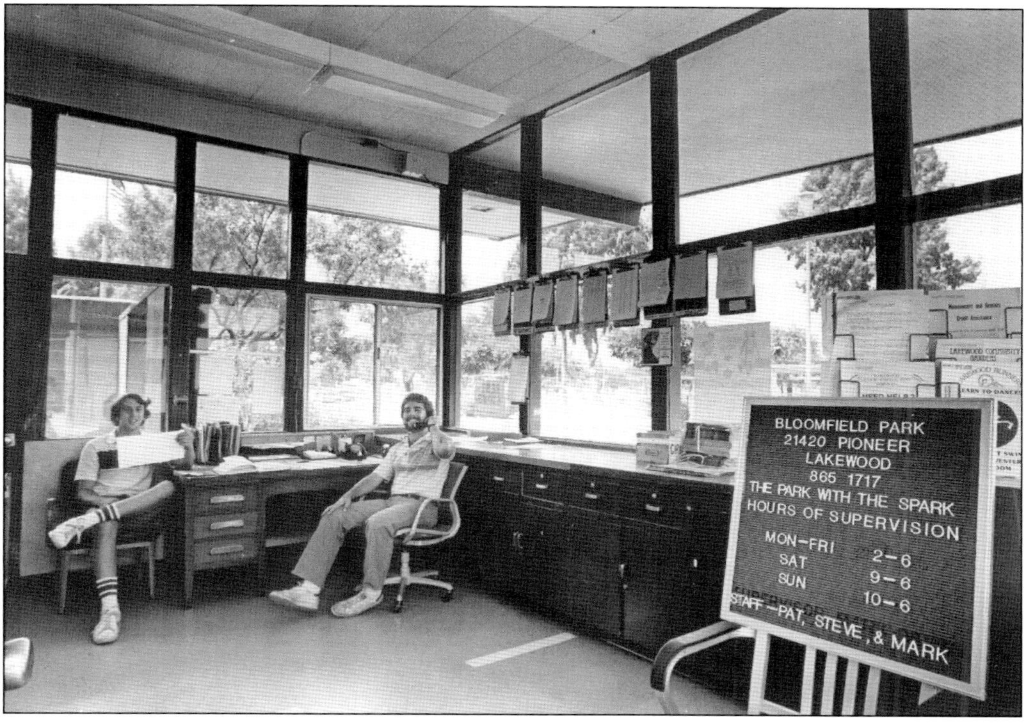

PARKS FOR EASTERN LAKEWOOD. Neighborhoods east of the San Gabriel River joined the city in the 1960s after residents there requested annexation. Their recreation needs were initially met by Bloomfield Park, a large regional park acquired from the county in 1964, shown above with recreation leaders Danny Costley (left) and Tony McKeon (right). The city expanded those facilities through the decades, most recently adding a teen center and new playground equipment. Rynerson Park, shown below, meanders along the east bank of the San Gabriel River. It was dedicated in 1975. In 1990, the park was rededicated as Rynerson Park in honor of three-term mayor Jacqueline Rynerson, a member of the first Lakewood Parks and Recreation Commission.

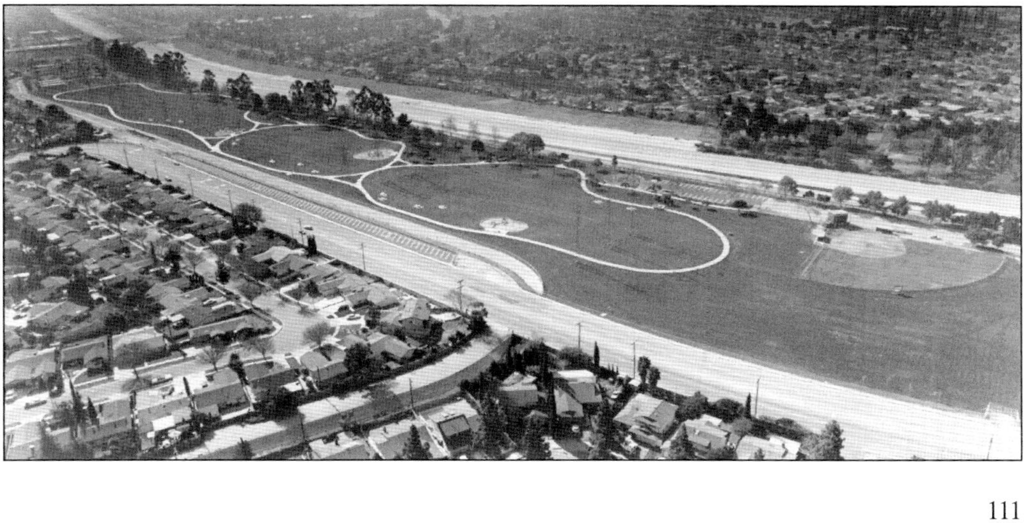

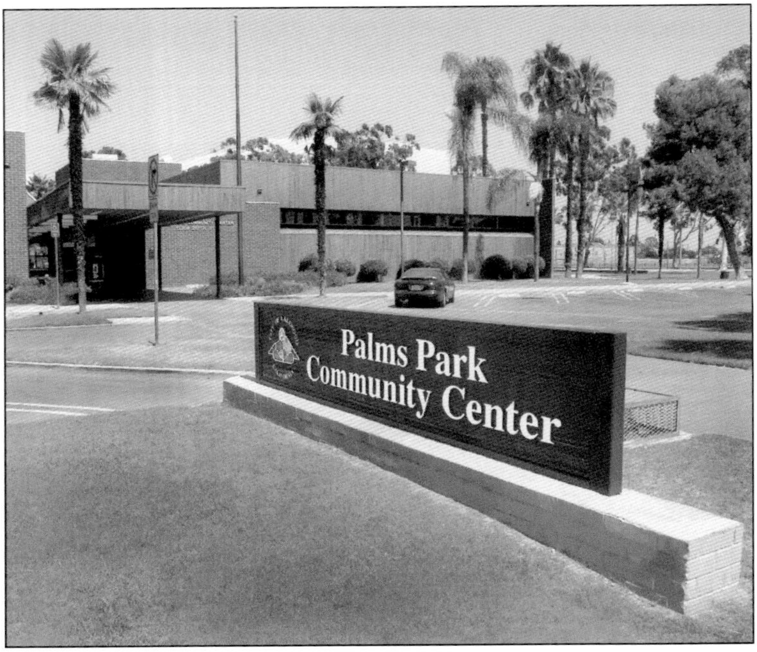

Palms Park and Community Center. Eastern Lakewood gained another park in 1969 with the dedication of Palms Park. In 1979, using federal funds and a grant from the Weingart Foundation, the city rededicated the park and built a community center and library. Despite fundraising efforts by neighborhood residents and the city council, the county closed the library in 1993 during a wave of budget cuts.

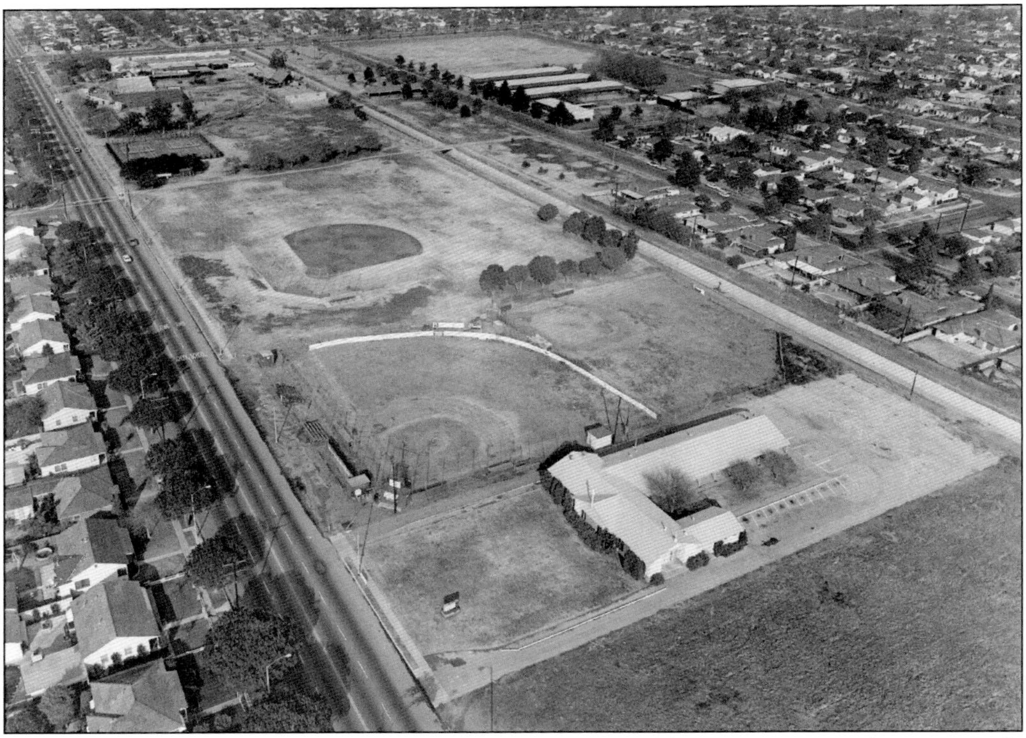

Mayfair Park, 1968. Mayfair Park, the city's oldest—and for many years its largest—park, adjoins neighborhoods in all directions, making it easy in the 1950s for youngsters to walk to the park and pool. East of the park is Stephen Foster School. The flood control channel through the park was covered in the mid-1980s.

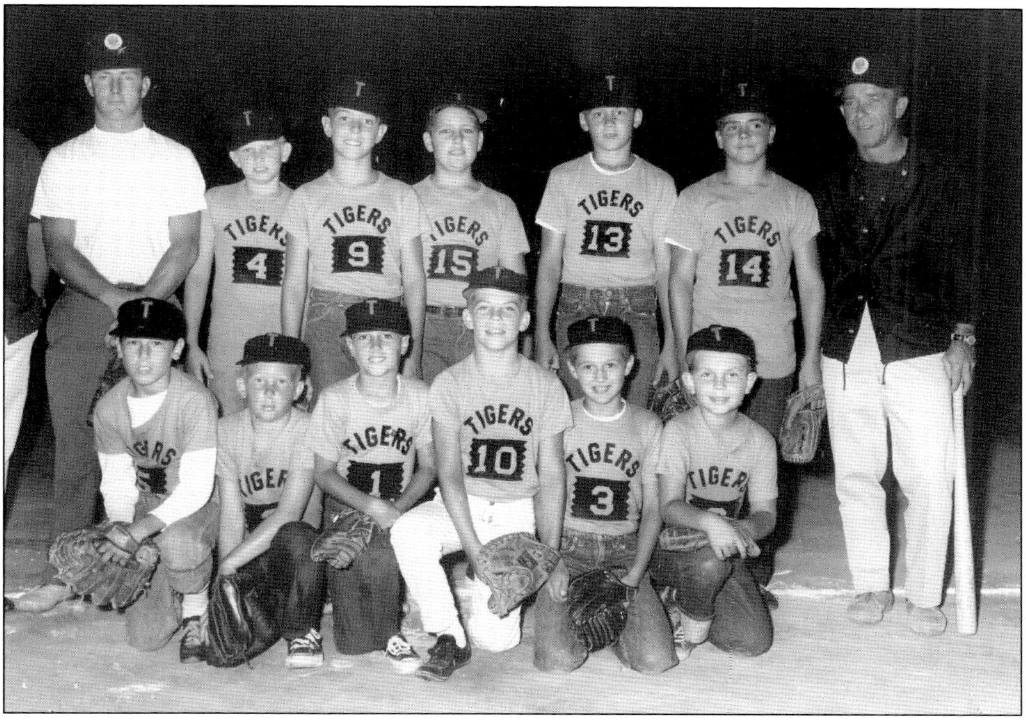

Teams and Volunteer Coaches. By 1960, the sports programs at city parks were recruiting hundreds of parents a year to volunteer as team coaches. Volunteers enabled the city to offer sports programs either free or at very low cost, and every child was given the chance to play in every game. Many parents continued coaching after their kids were grown, a tradition that continues today.

Jim Knaub, Hall of Fame Athlete. Jim Knaub, a record-holding disabled runner, was the first Lakewood Youth Hall of Fame Athlete of the Year. The Youth Hall of Fame, established in 1981 by Mayor Larry Van Nostran, recognizes Lakewood's high school and college athletes, coaches, and sports boosters. The Youth Hall of Fame has a permanent home at the McDonald's restaurant on Woodruff Avenue.

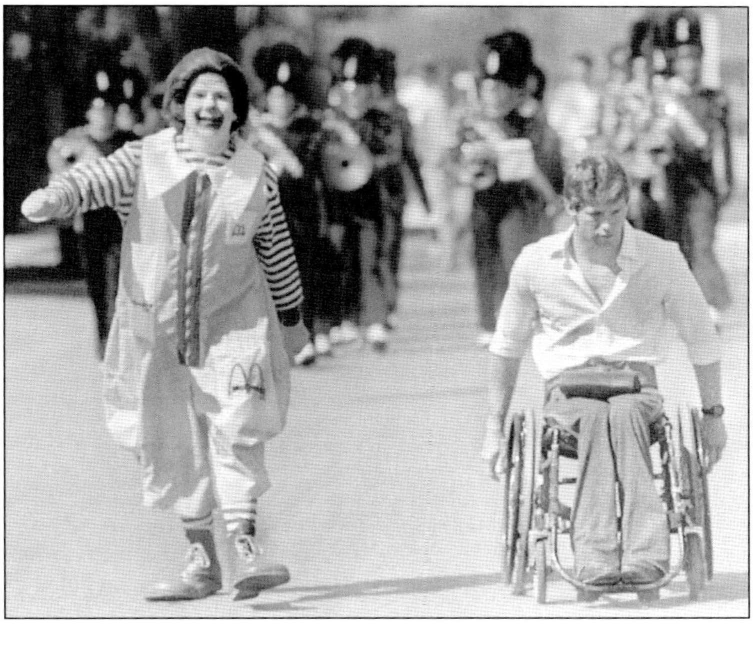

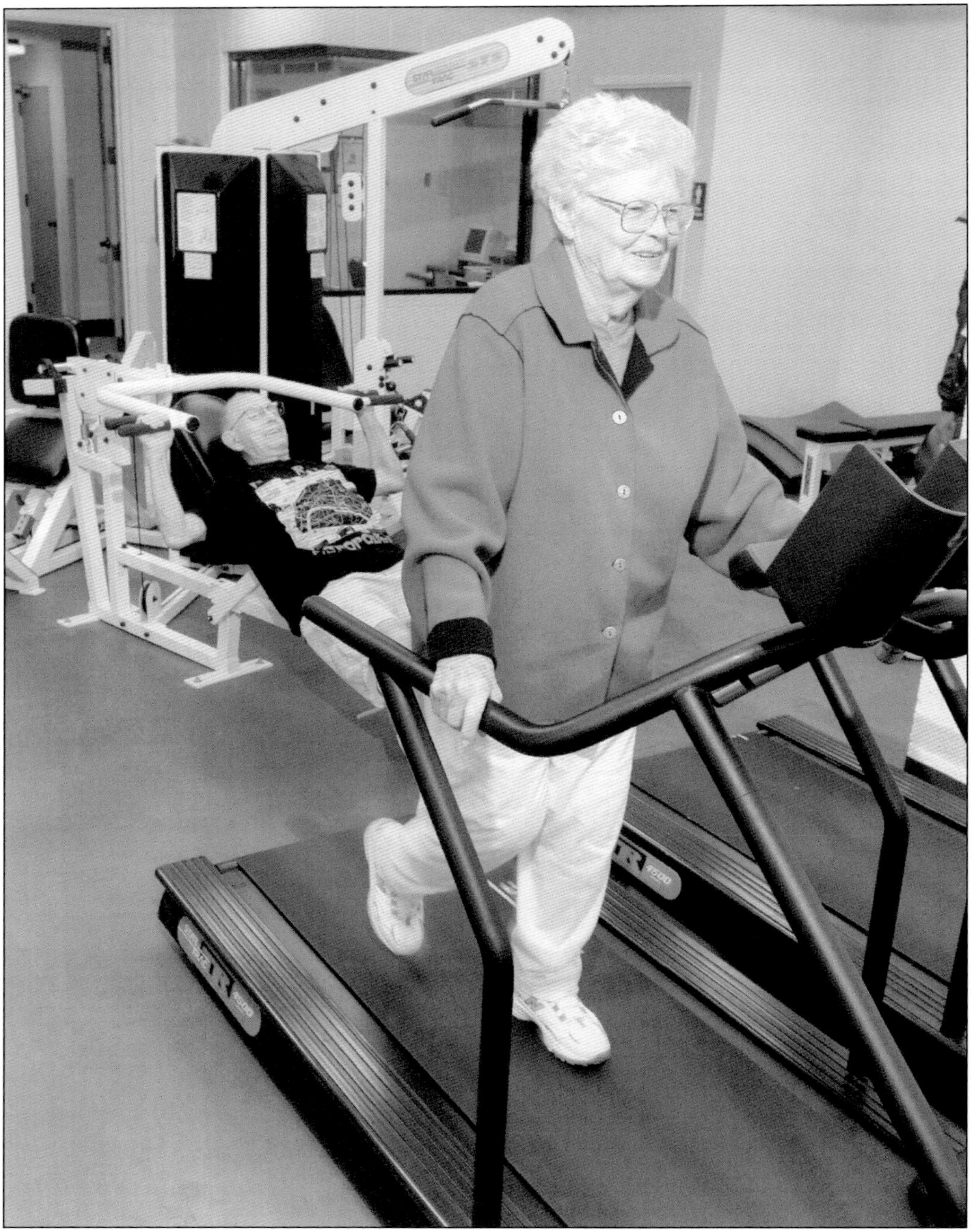

A Place for Active Seniors. Lakewood's opportunities for a lifetime of fitness and fun grew in 1981 with the opening of the Weingart Senior Center on Oliva Avenue. Built with the aid of the Weingart Foundation, the senior center offered fitness programs, social service assistance, friendly noon meals, activities, and excursions. To meet the needs of a growing senior population, the senior center began a series of expansions and renovations in the 1980s. One of the center's most popular facilities is a fitness room that features treadmills, recumbent bicycles, and resistance exercise equipment.

Seven

Picturing Lakewood

Lakewood's achievements can be measured in many ways: in miles of roadways repaved, in the number of young players on park sports teams, in the pleasant atmosphere of its family-oriented neighborhoods, in the strength of Lakewood's public safety programs, and in the spirit that motivates the volunteers of Meals on Wheels, Project Shepherd, Pathways Volunteer Hospice, and Lakewood's many civic and social service clubs.

Lakewood's achievements also can be remembered in the images that were collected by many anonymous photographers during the city's early years.

In 1954, Lakewood voters defied conventional thinking at every turn by building strong neighborhoods and creating a stable political culture, despite criticisms that neither of these achievements would be possible. By the 1980s, the city and its residents had even managed to quietly and calmly become as culturally, ethnically, and racially diverse as any community in Southern California.

In the midst of change, Lakewood's character as a community of homes has not changed very much. As citizens reflect on where they have been and reach out to the new generations of Lakewood residents to come, perhaps these images will kindle a memory and prompt a story to be shared with children or grandchildren.

It is in these stories—in the handing down of Lakewood's traditions and values—that the sources of our bright future can be found.

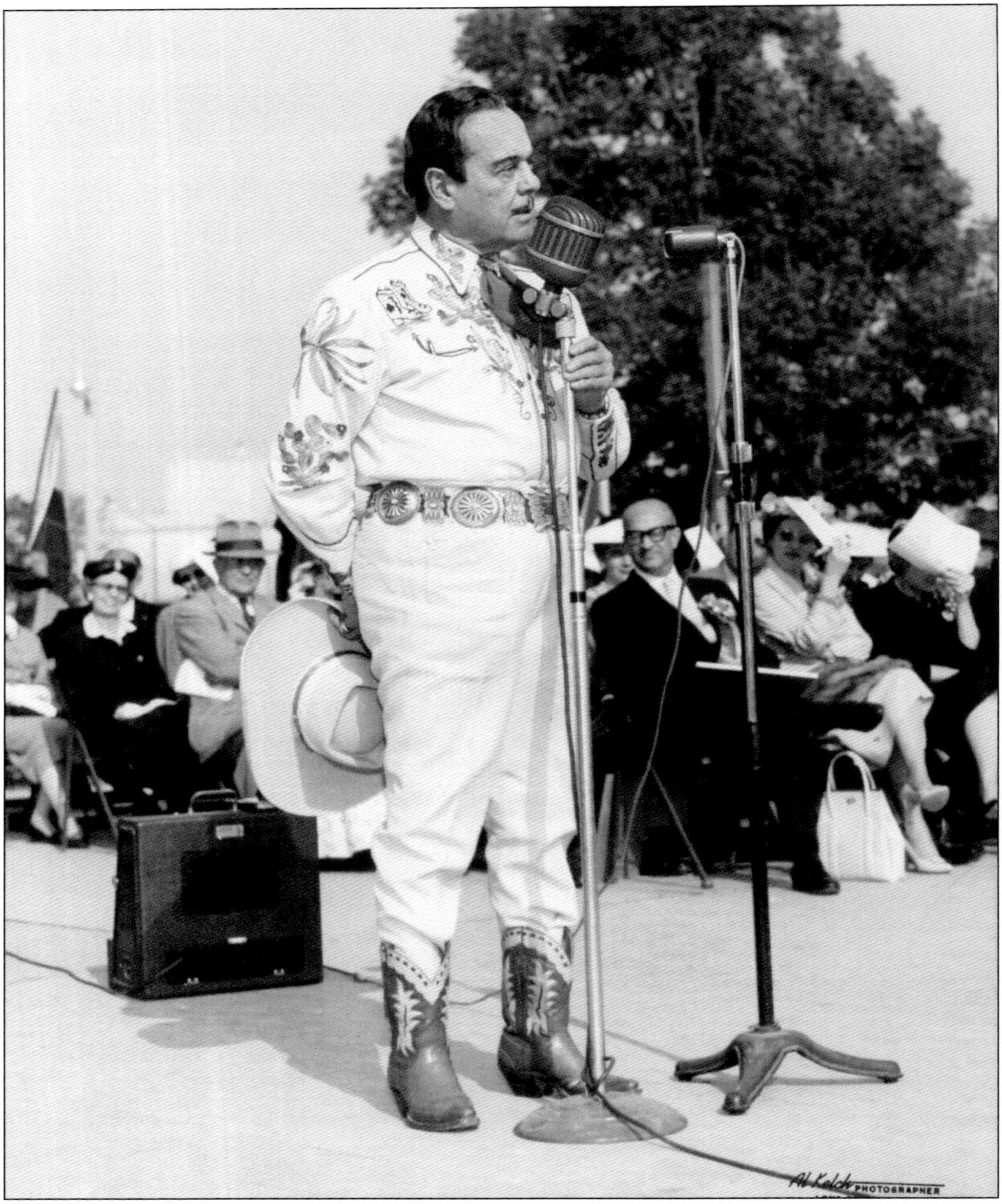

LATINO FILM AND TV STAR. Famed film and television actor Leo Carrillo—a descendent of Spanish and Mexican-era Los Angeles rancheros—addresses the crowd at an early Pan-American Festival celebration. The original festival took place at Pan-American Park in Lakewood Village, now part of Long Beach. When Lakewood became a city, the celebration was moved to Mayfair Park. The Pan-American Parade, a feature of the festival in its later years, brought floats and bands past the Lakewood Civic Center on Clark Avenue. The Pan-American Festival Association continues to sponsor an annual fiesta with three days of events and activities.

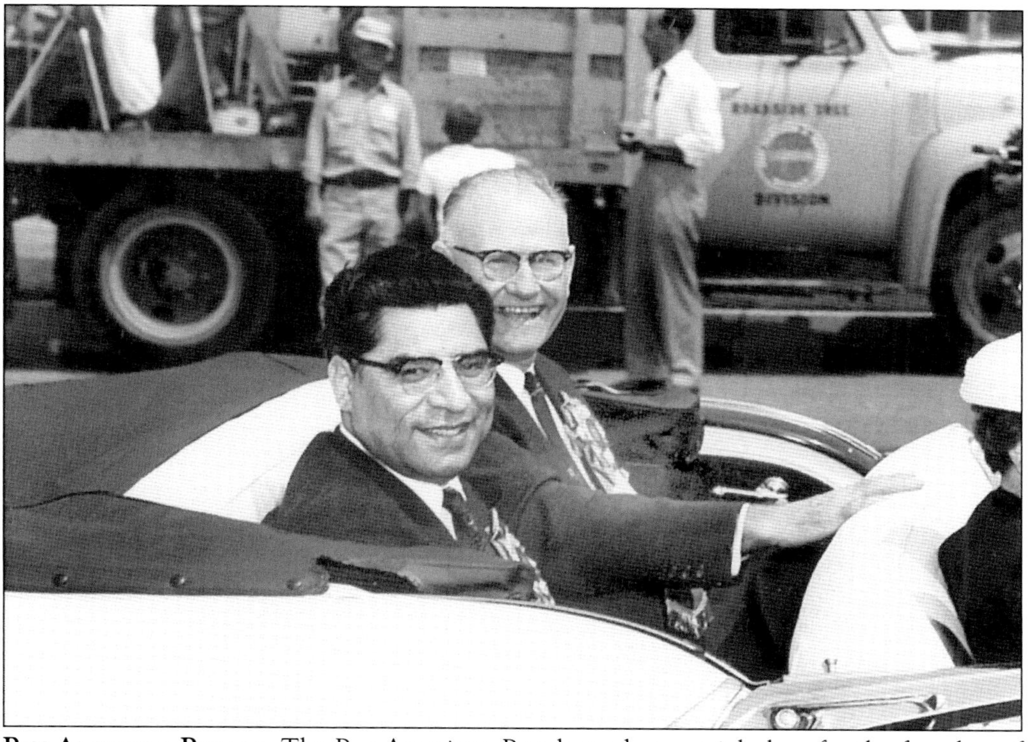

Pan-American Parade. The Pan-American Parade made a special place for the founders of Lakewood's oldest community celebration. Dr. Walter Montano (in front) and Jess Solter (behind), two residents of Lakewood Village, decided to perpetuate the ideals of pan-American friendship with the creation of Lakewood's Pan-American Festival in 1946.

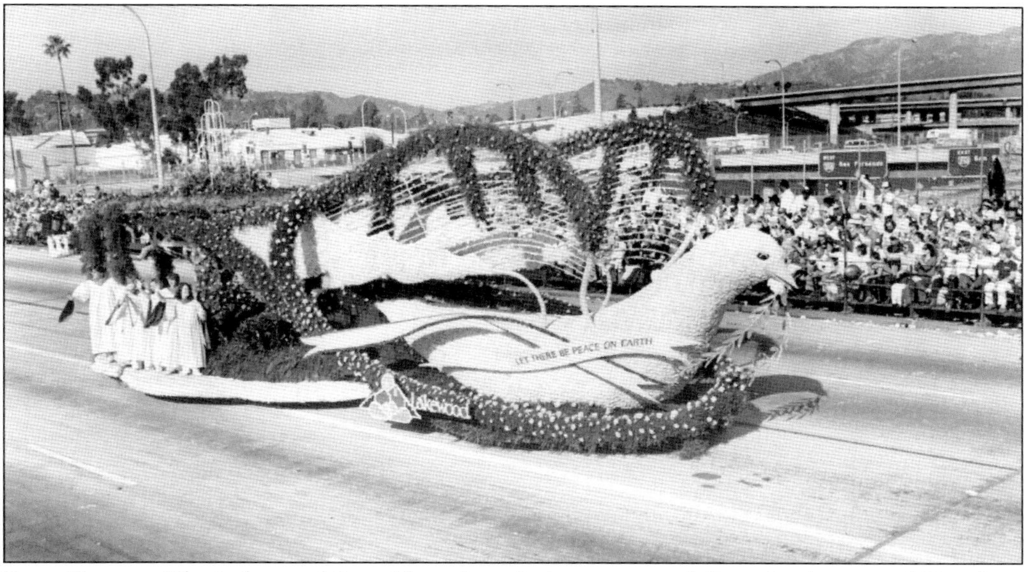

Rose Parade. The Lakewood Rose Float Association sponsored floats in the annual Pasadena Rose Parade for several years. The float in this parade—"Let There Be Peace on Earth"—celebrates the familiar song of the same title, written in 1955 by Jill Jackson Miller and Sy Miller.

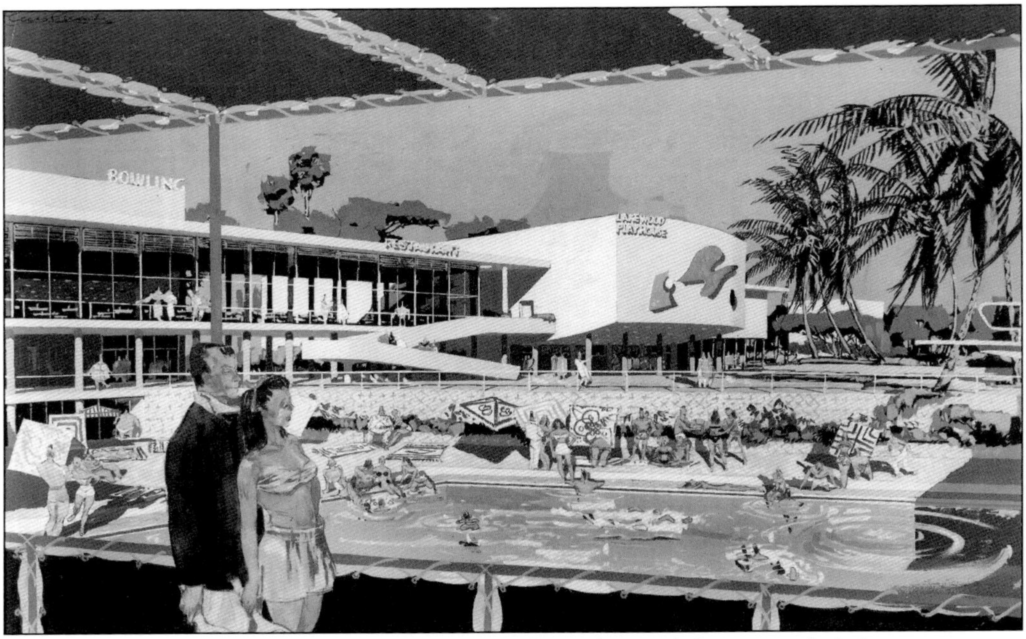

Imagining Lakewood Center. The concepts for Lakewood Center included a community recreation center that would have rivaled a five-star hotel. Along with an Olympic-size pool and dining terraces, Lakewood Center might have had a community playhouse where roadshow productions of plays and musicals would have been staged.

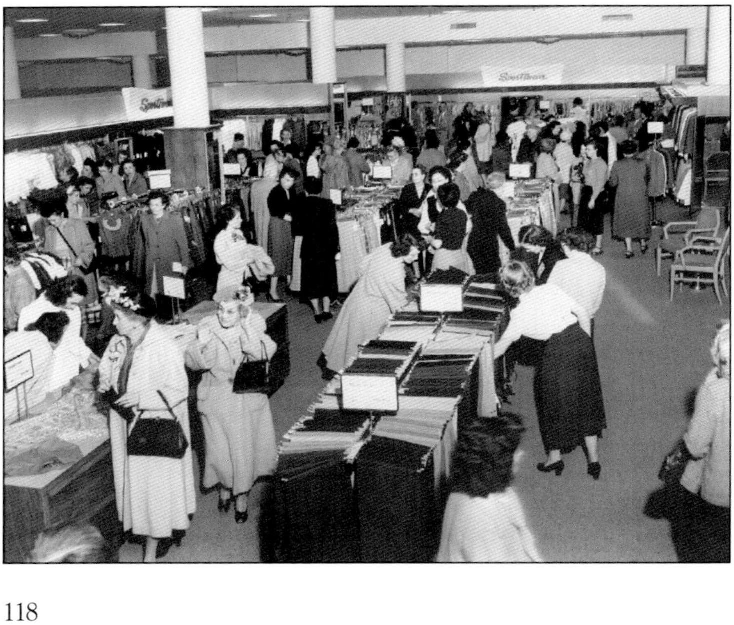

May Company Shoppers. Shoppers could find almost anything in the vast May Company department store in 1953. There were departments for women and men, boys and girls, and infants, and also evening dresses and furs. The May Company sold furniture, musical instruments, china, and silverware. A spacious tearoom in the basement gave weary shoppers a place to rest.

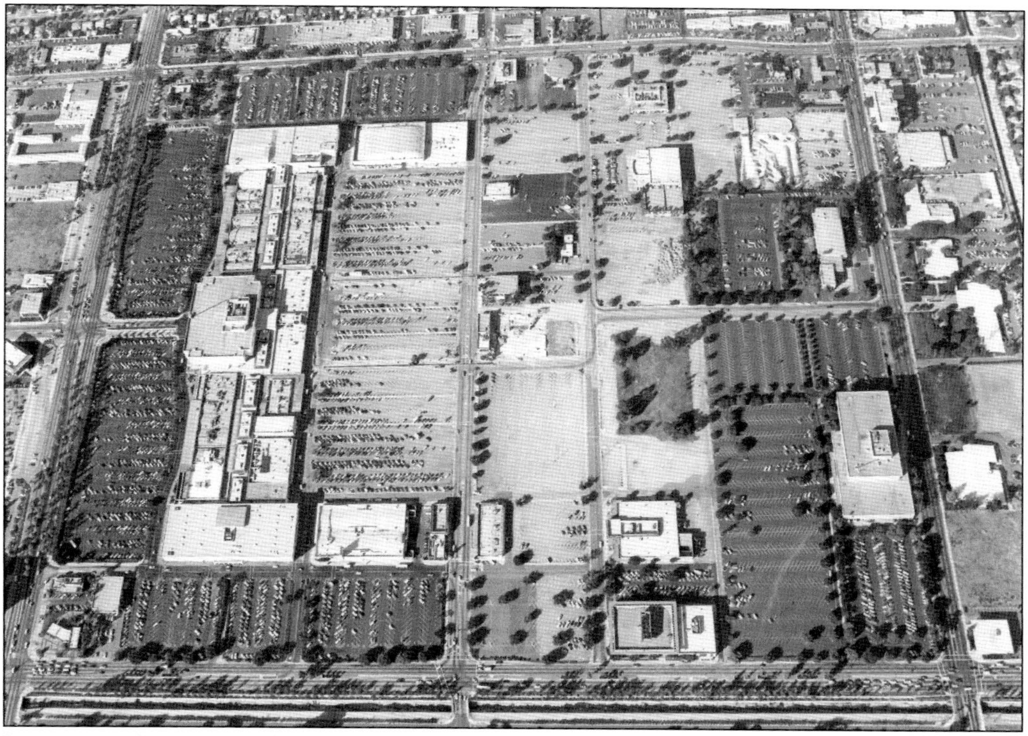

Lakewood Center. Enclosure added new stores to the north and south wings of the mall and brought new retailers to the mall's periphery. In the bottom right of this photograph are Bullock's, Desmond's, and Buffums. Just above is the Akron Store. The Lakewood Center Theatre is farther north.

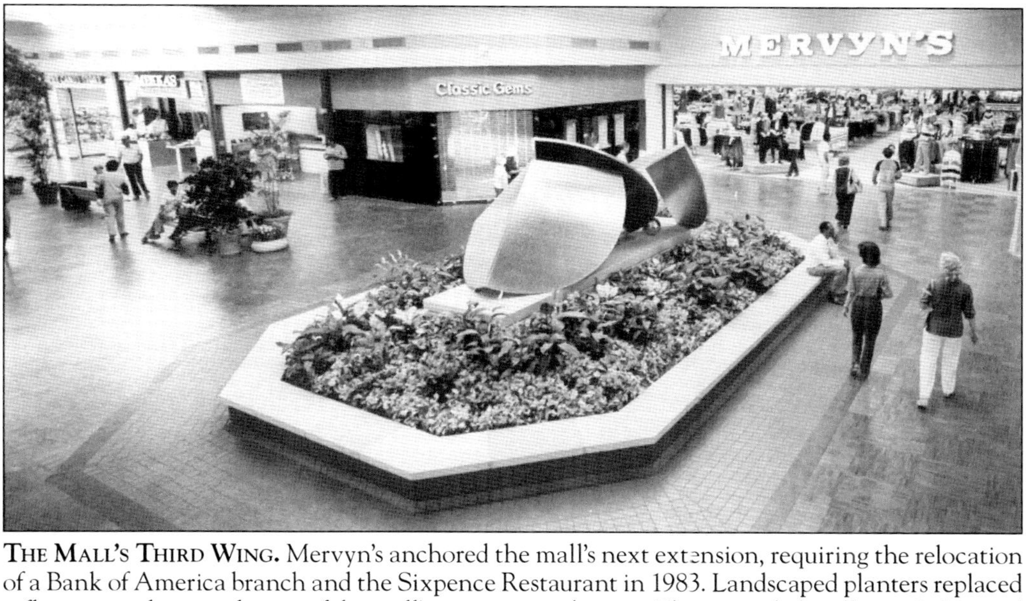

The Mall's Third Wing. Mervyn's anchored the mall's next extension, requiring the relocation of a Bank of America branch and the Sixpence Restaurant in 1983. Landscaped planters replaced reflecting pools around some of the mall's signature sculptures. The expanded mall grew Lakewood Center by hundreds of thousands of square feet of new retail space.

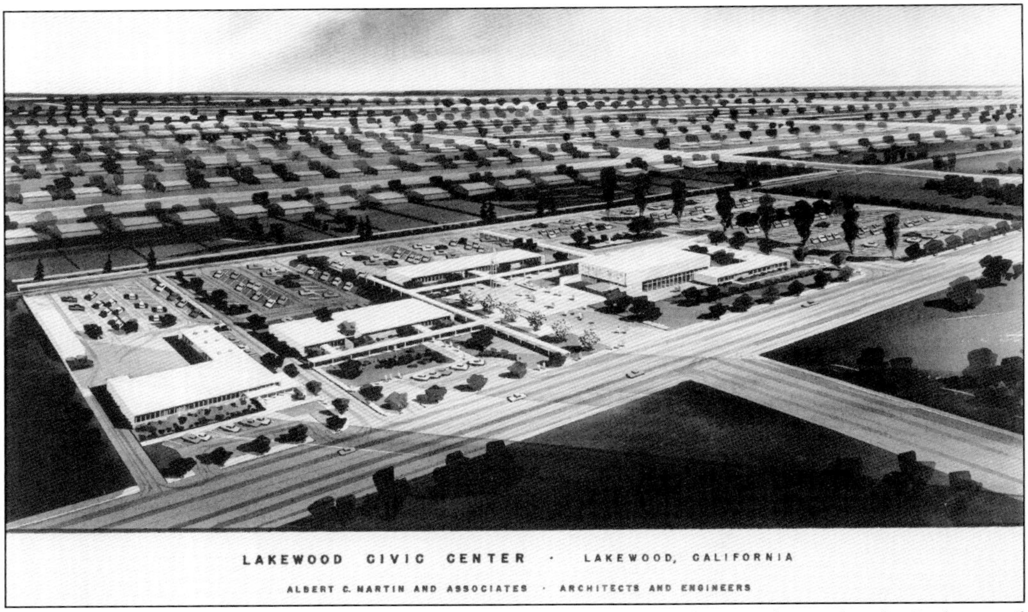

Imagining the Lakewood Civic Center. The original plan, shown above, for the Lakewood Civic Center included city administrative offices, a large community meeting center, a library, sheriff's station, and post office. All of these buildings were to be built with the clean lines of mid-century modernism. A more modest design was built between 1957 and 1964. The Pan-American conference room at city hall, seen below, was paneled in woods from South American countries and a tile mural displaying the flags of the Organization of American States. The outline under them shows the boundaries of Lakewood when city hall opened.

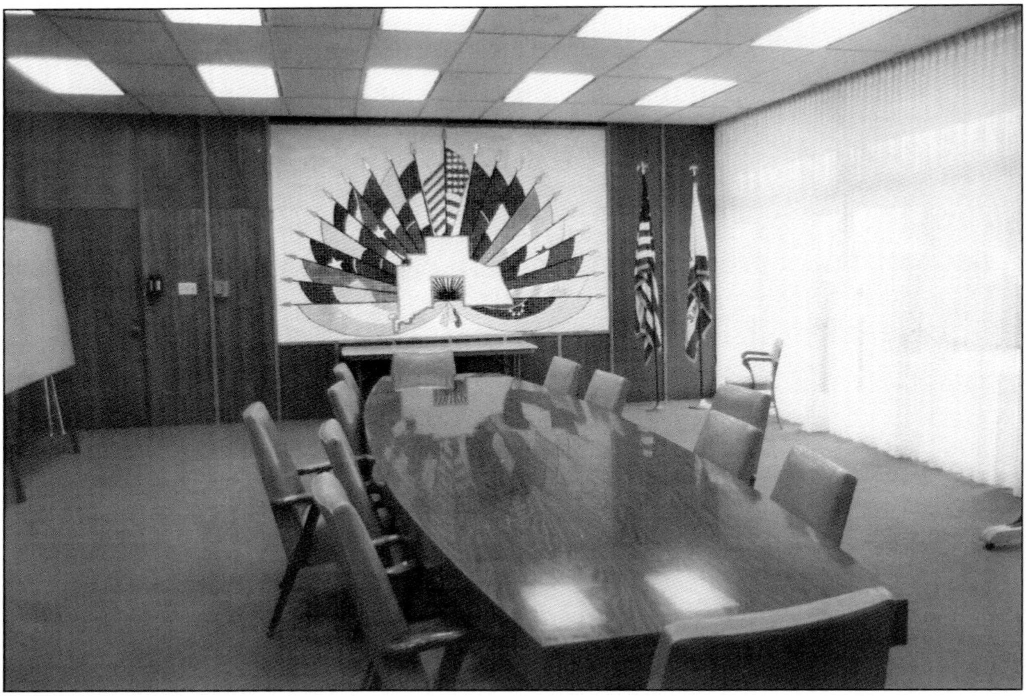

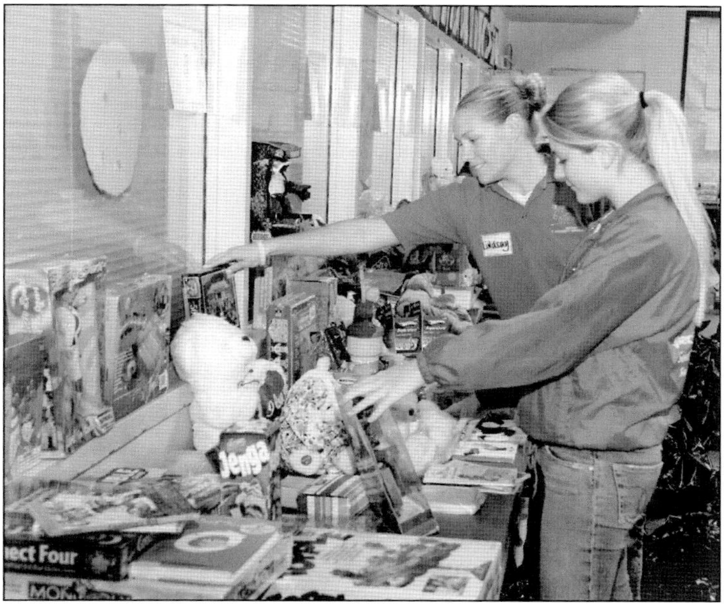

Project Shepherd Shows a Caring Community. Young volunteers and members of the Rotary Club of Lakewood have aided families in need since Project Shepherd began in 1972. Each Project Shepherd box contains staple food items, the makings of a traditional holiday dinner, and gifts for family members. The recipients are Lakewood residents who are unemployed, on public assistance, or who have no way to pay for gifts for their children.

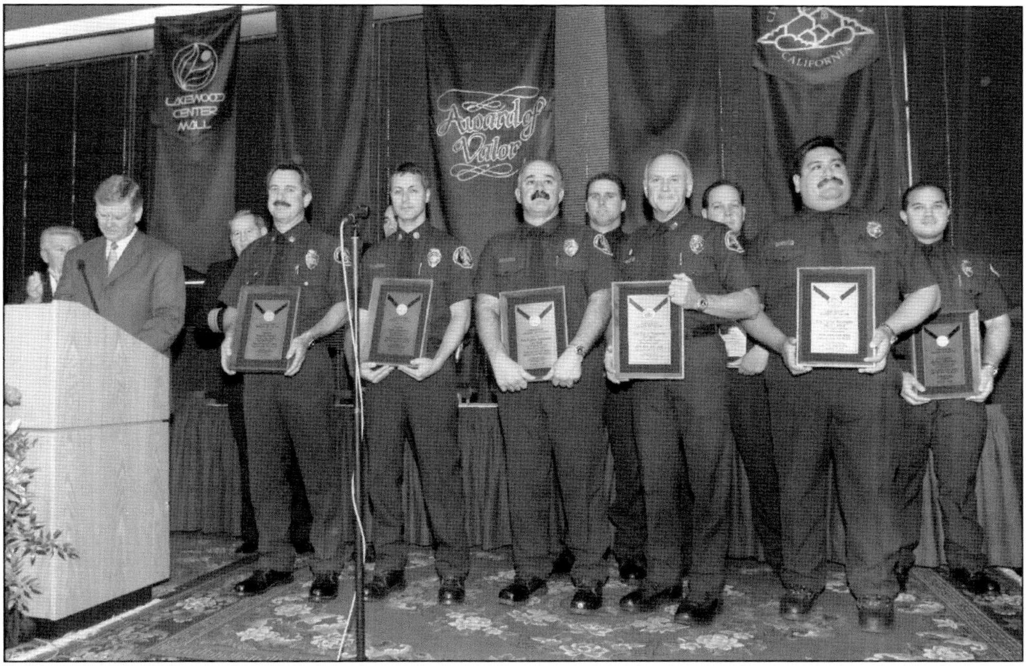

Award of Valor Honors Heroes. In 1980, the first Lakewood Award of Valor program honored three deputies and three firefighters. In the years that followed, the city's award for heroism has recognized hundreds of deputies, firefighters, citizens who earned a Mayor's Award for their courage, volunteers of Neighborhood Watch, members of Volunteers On Patrol, and members of the sheriff's civilian volunteer program.

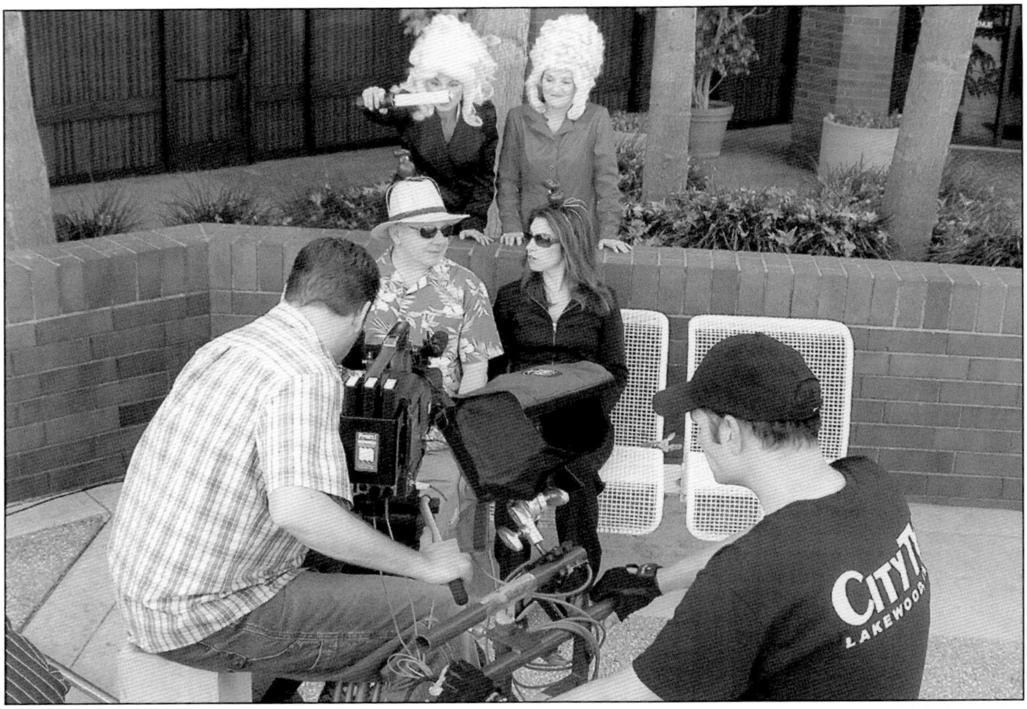

CityTV Tells Lakewood's Story. Cable television came to Lakewood in 1984 and quickly became part of the city's active public information program. CityTV productions like *Crime Stoppers*, *Game of the Week*, *Lakewood Annual Report*, *Ticket to Ride*, and *Café 5050* joined cablecasts of city council meetings and community events to inform, entertain, and delight local cable subscribers.

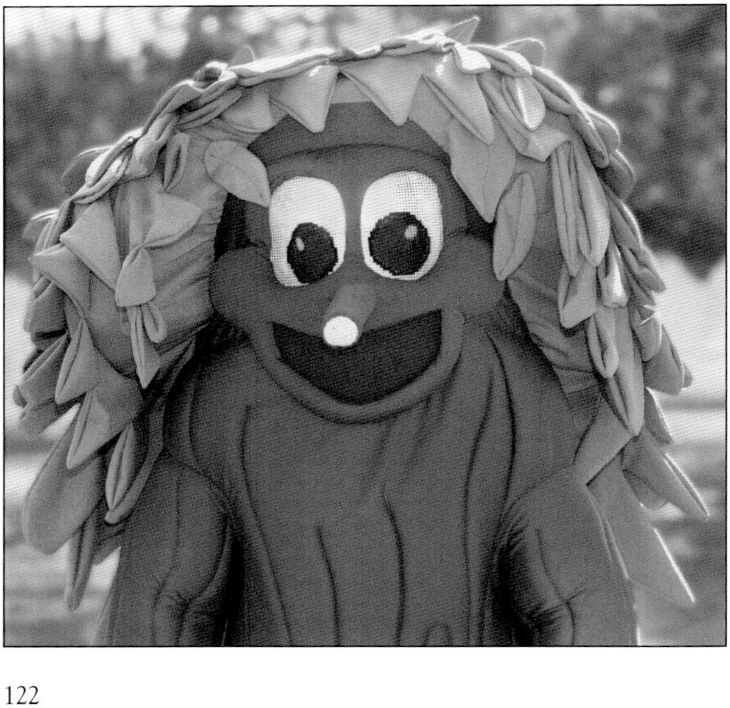

Learning About the Environment. Woody the Tree attends every Arbor Week event in Lakewood, teaching youngsters about the value of Lakewood's "urban forest" and its place in the ecology. Lakewood's natural beauty is homegrown, arising from its 36,000-park and street trees. For its efforts at urban forestry, the city has been a repeated recipient since the mid-1980s of the Tree City USA award given by the National Arbor Day Foundation.

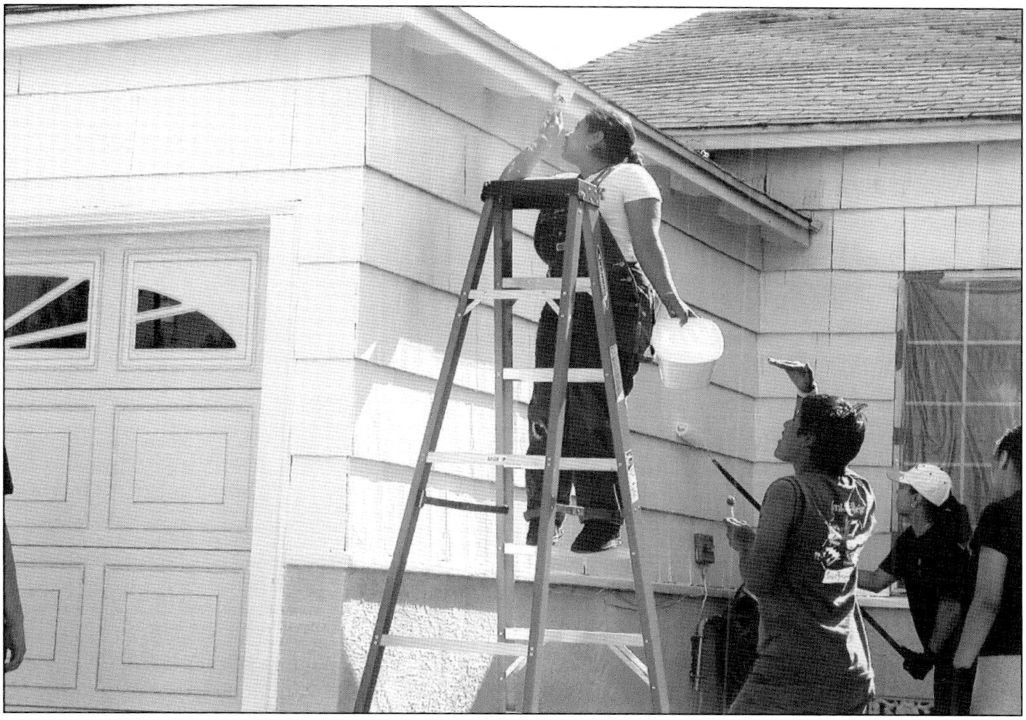

Volunteers for a Caring Community. Lakewood's volunteers have aided their community as participants in the annual Volunteer Day, shown above, by fixing up the homes of neighbors in need, as members of the Volunteers On Patrol program, shown below, by assisting sheriff's deputies with traffic control and security patrols, as well as participants in Meals on Wheels, Pathways Volunteer Hospice, Project Shepherd, Lakewood Tot Lots, Lakewood Neighborhood Watch, Teens in Lakewood Care, and Special Olympics, and as Lakewood's specially trained disaster response workers, and a great many more. Volunteers can be found in every kind of community-building activity in Lakewood schools, clubs, and places of worship.

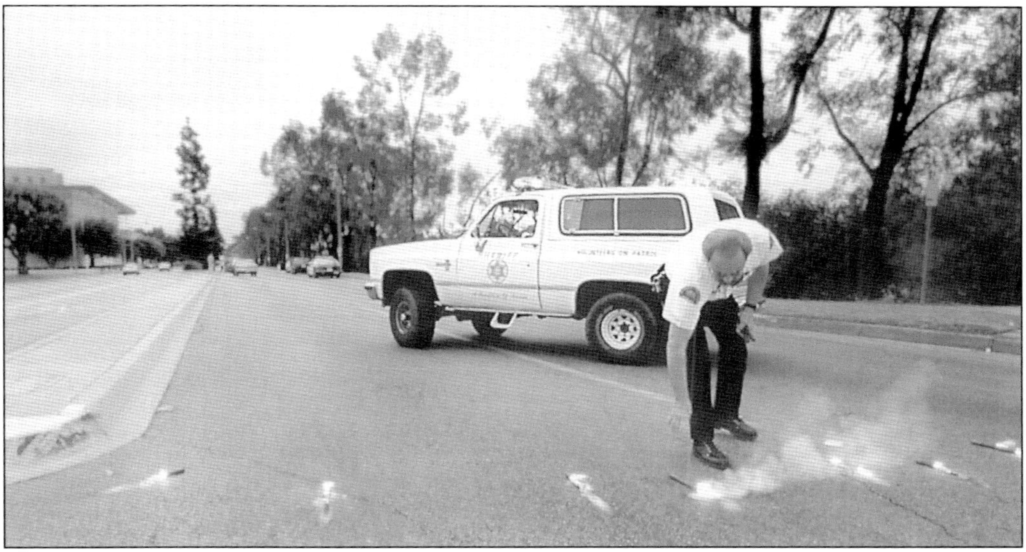

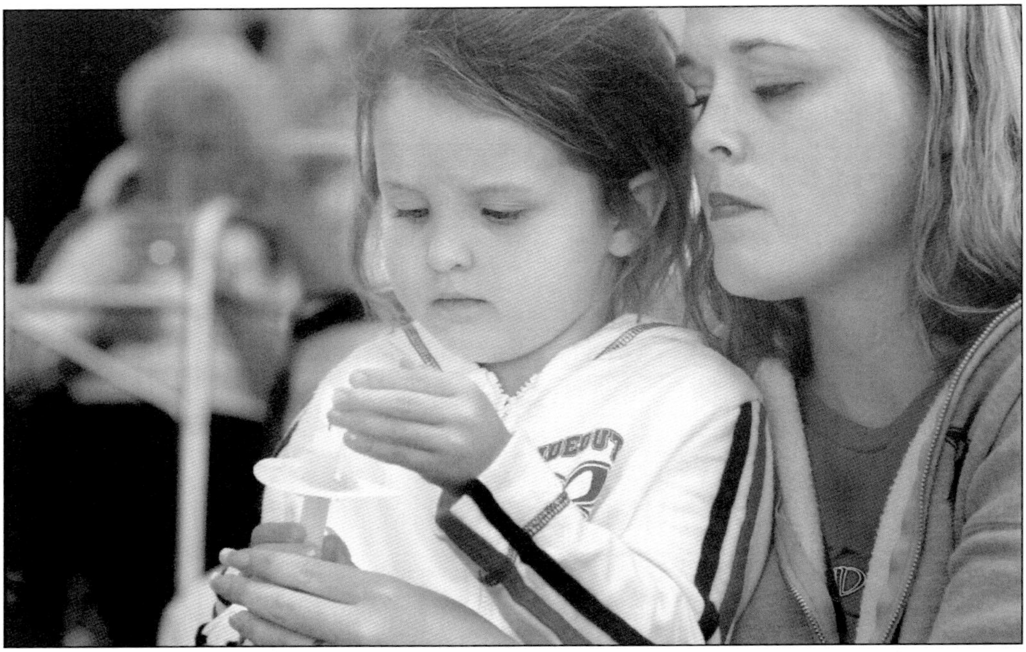

Remembrances and Celebrations. Lakewood has remembered the events of September 11, 2001, with annual Patriot Day programs at Del Valle Park. The commemoration includes a candle lighting, shown above, in silent recognition of lives lost on that tragic day. The annual Lakewood Block Party in the Lakewood Civic Center, shown below, gives a rousing start to summer with music, kids' activities, and a Taste of Lakewood dining experience. Lakewood also pauses to reflect at the Mayor's Prayer Breakfast and celebrate at the Lakewood Award of Valor, the Lakewood Youth Hall of Fame, the Lakewood Beautiful Home Awards, and Lakewood Celebrates receptions.

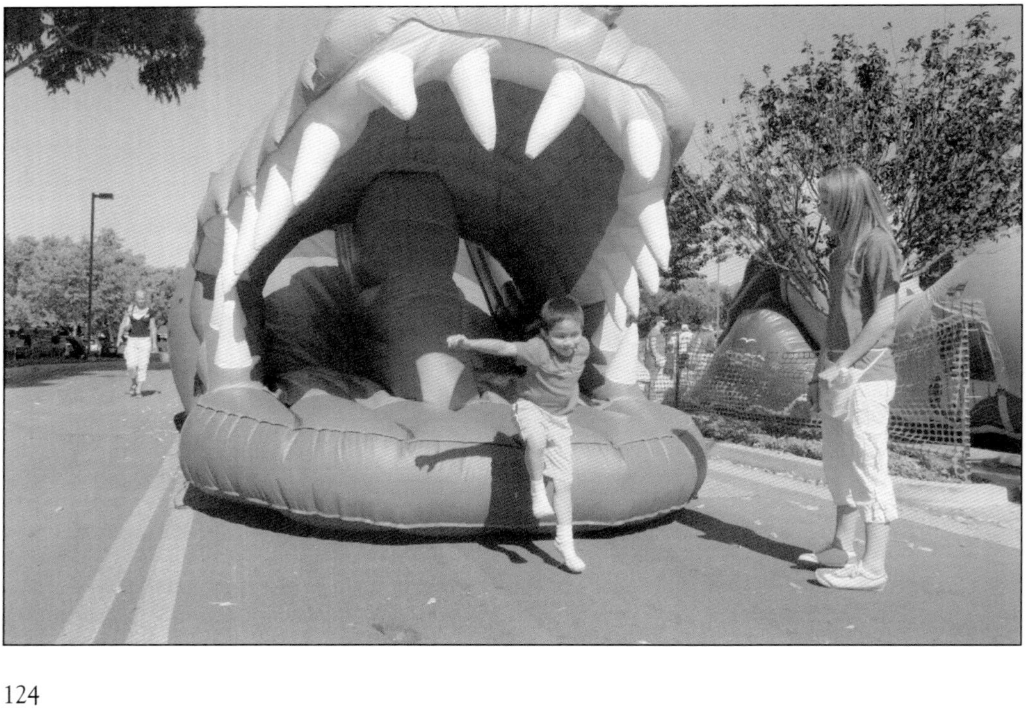

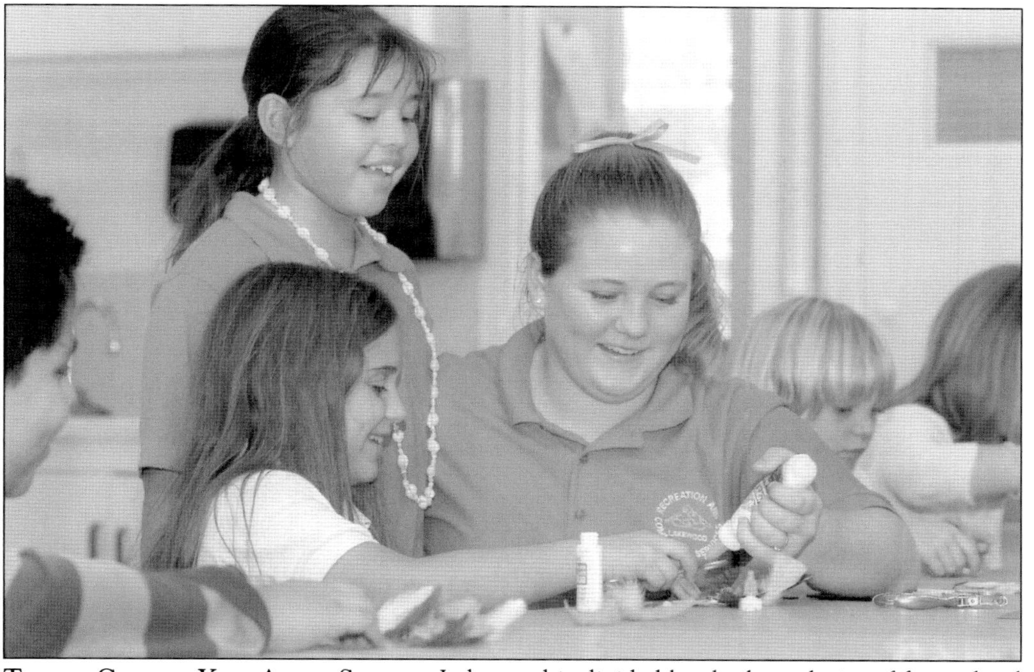

Taking Care of Kids After School. Lakewood is divided by the boundaries of four school districts, making it imperative that the city provide safe after-school activities that reach every neighborhood. After-school programs bring supervised play, fun craft activities, and homework-free time to Lakewood's parks.

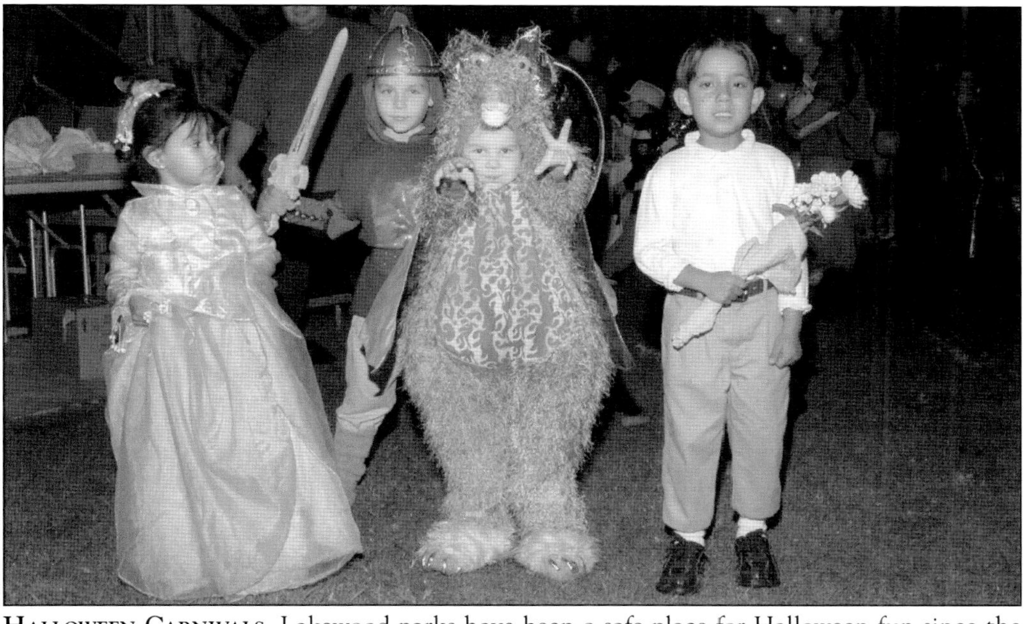

Halloween Carnivals. Lakewood parks have been a safe place for Halloween fun since the 1970s. Today, parent volunteers assist city recreation staff members in assembling a carnival where youngsters can dress up, compete for prizes, and, if they dare, make their way through a not-so-scary haunted house.

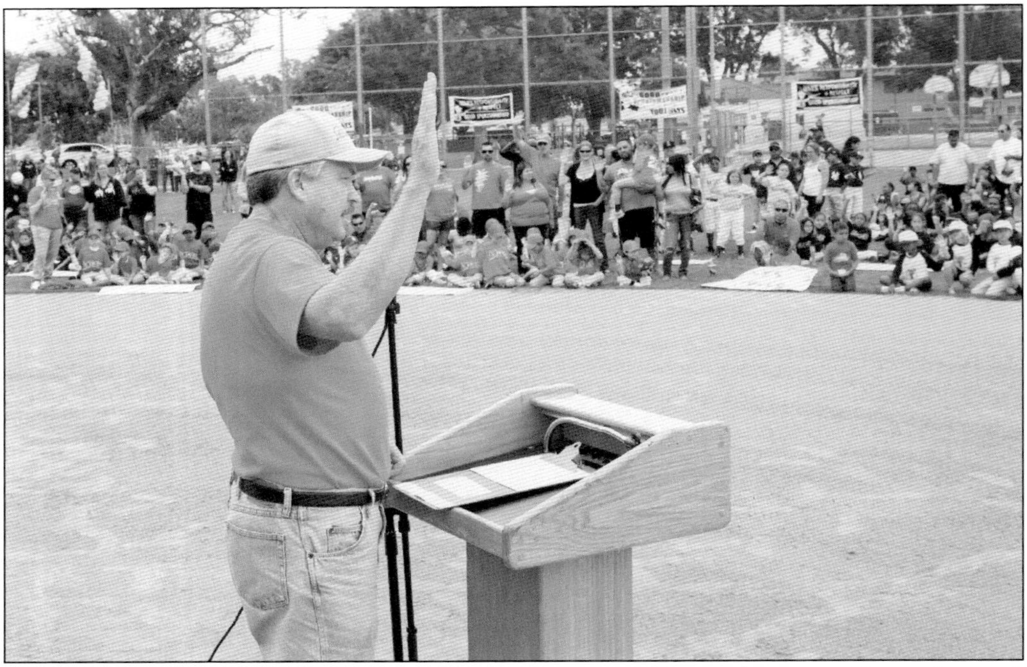

Teaching Team Values. The Lakewood Youth Sports program is almost as old as Lakewood. The mission of the program since 1957 is to give every young athlete the opportunity to play and learn the values of teamwork and fair play. Administering the sportsmanship pledge is part of every LYS Opening Day program.

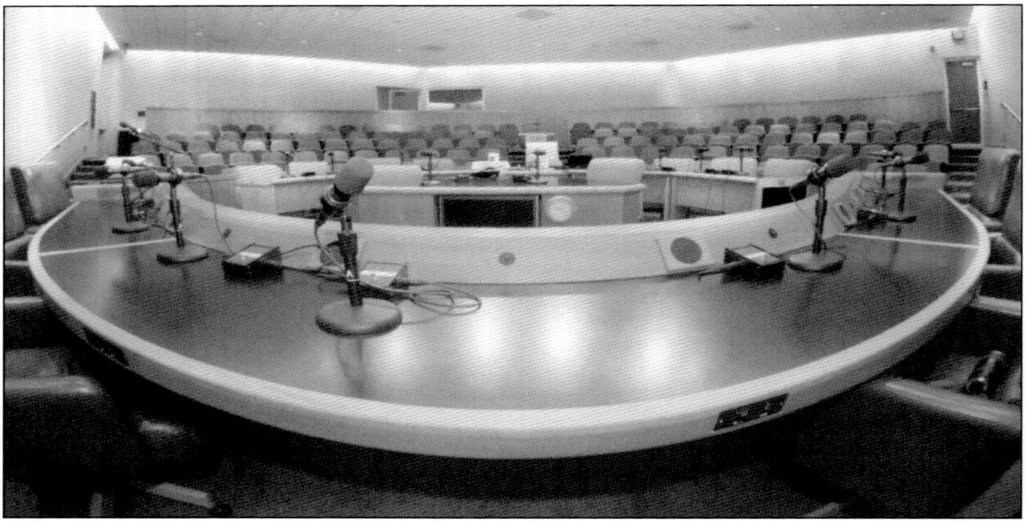

Civic Values. Lakewood City Hall was redesigned in 1984, when these new city council chambers were dedicated. The city council continues to meet on the second and fourth Tuesdays of each month, as it has since the first council meeting in 1954. The public is always invited to see its government at work.

TOMORROW'S LAKEWOOD. Lakewood still has the energy of its youthful origins, as these young gymnasts at the Palms Park Community Center exuberantly portray. A community where families might live dignified, safe, and productive lives was the promise when Lakewood's first homes were sold. Lakewood strives to still be that kind of community.

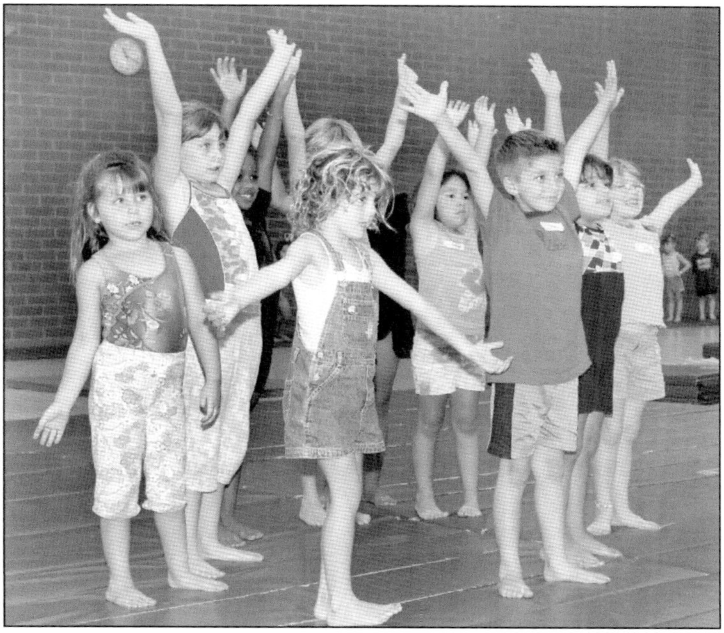

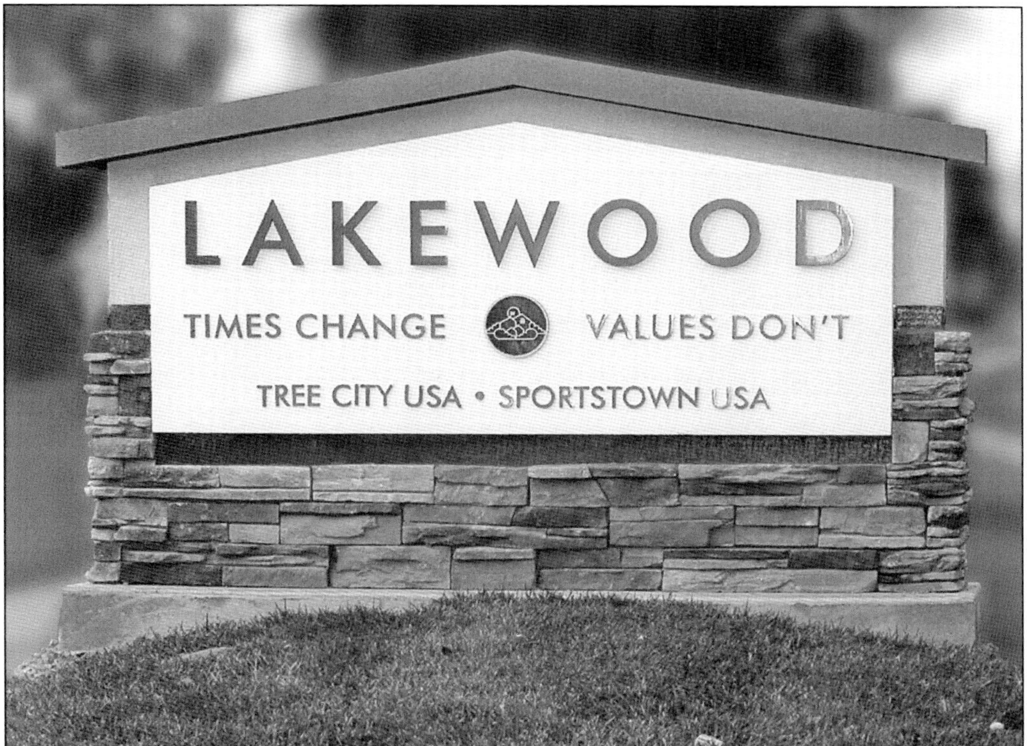

A REMINDER OF VALUES. Lakewood has identified itself in many ways over the decades. The theme of enduring community values has been uppermost. On city monument signs, that theme is expressed by the 50th anniversary motto, "Times Change. Values Don't."

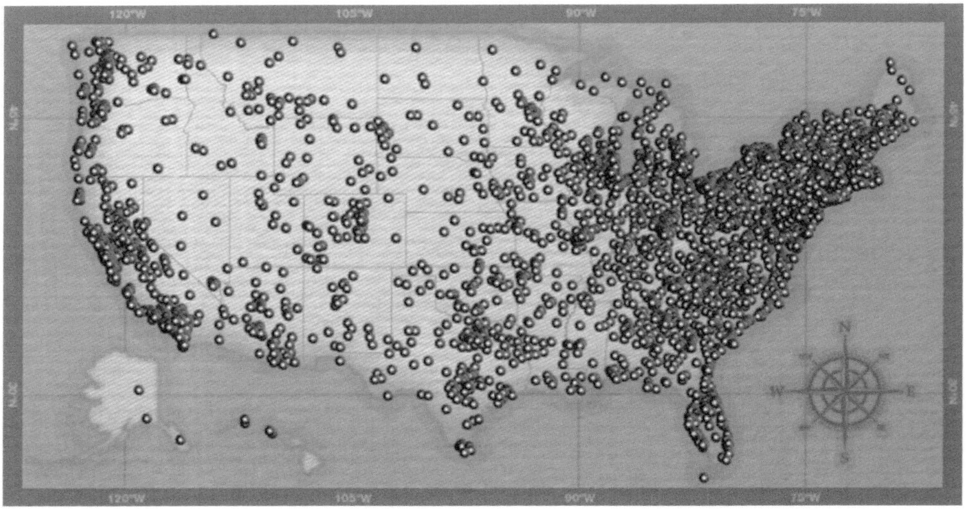